Women Writers and the City

Women Writers and the City

Essays in Feminist Literary Criticism

SUSAN MERRILL SQUIER, editor

The University of Tennessee Press / Knoxville

The paper in this book meets the guidelines for permanence and durability of the Committee on Production Guidelines for Book Longevity of the Council on Library Resources. Binding materials have been chosen for durability.

Library of Congress Cataloging in Publication Data

Main entry under title:

Women writers and the city.

Bibliography: p.
Includes index.
1. English fiction—Women authors—History and criticism—Addresses, essays, lectures.　2. City and town life in literature—Addresses, essays, lectures.
3. American literature— Women authors—History and criticism—Addresses, essays, lectures.　4. French literature—Women authors—History and criticism—Addresses, essays, lectures.　5. Feminism and literature—Addresses, essays, lectures.　I. Squier, Susan Merrill.
PR830.C53W66　　　1984　　　　　809'.93321732　　　　　83–17109
ISBN 0–87049–415–5
ISBN 0–87049–416–3 (pbk.)

London itself perpetually attracts, stimulates, gives me a play & a story & a poem, without any trouble, save that of moving my legs through the streets. —Virginia Woolf

Acknowledgments

The editor has enjoyed the assistance and support of many people during the compilation of this volume of essays, and wishes to extend her sincere thanks to them all. For their patience and enduring enthusiasm for this book through the years of memos and delays which attended its evolution, she would like to thank all of its contributors. For encouragement, advice, or careful readings at different stages of this project, she wishes to thank in particular Sue Bialostosky, Helen Cooper, Louise A. DeSalvo, David E. Laurence, Jane Marcus, Maureen F. Monck, Gowen Roper, Karen Rowe, and Brenda R. Silver. For her candor and steady support from the very beginning of the project, she would like to thank Carol Orr, director of the University of Tennessee Press. And for arriving in the midst of work on this collection, making that work both more difficult and more meaningful, the editor wishes to give special thanks to Caitlin Merrill Squier-Roper.

The editor wishes to dedicate her part in
this collection of essays to Connie and John.

Contents

Women Writers and the City

Introduction

The passion of my life, that is the City of London—to see London all Blasted, that too raked my heart. Have you that feeling for certain alleys and little courts, between Chancery Lane and the City? I walked to the Tower the other day by way of caressing my love of all that.[1]

So WROTE VIRGINIA WOOLF to her friend Ethel Smyth, after a visit to wartime London in the last months of her life. It was September 1940, and German bombers were slowly destroying that well-loved, familiar setting. "London looked merry and hopeful, wearing her wounds like stars," Woolf remembered, and then wondered, "Why do I dramatise London perpetually?"[2] Why indeed? Woolf's interest in the city in part reflects a literary tradition; poets and novelists have written about the city for as long as it has echoed their dreams and fears. From the town-country debates in Virgil's *Eclogues* to T. S. Eliot's urban wasteland, the city has provided a moving metaphor for the human condition. And ambivalence has always been a vital part of this literary response. Good or bad, sacred or secular, virtuous or a pit of vice, the city has even appeared in more modern times as "beyond good and evil," as Raymond Williams and Carl Schorske have shown in their surveys of the city's fluctuating literary image.[3] Yet in 1940, Virginia Woolf wondered, "Why do I dramatise London perpetually?" and this question by the author of *A Room of*

[3]

One's Own, the first serious study of the experience of women writers, prompts consideration of the specifically female aspects of urban experience.

The city has a special significance in the works of women writers because—as women—they have a unique relationship to the urban environment, whether it is considered as an actual place, as a symbol of culture, or as the nexus of concepts and values determining woman's place in history and society. For women, as for men, the city may be either hostile or nurturant to their selves, desires, and goals. But whichever quality it demonstrates, it does so in a different way where women are concerned. Whether we think of Katherine Mansfield complaining to her father shortly before her death, "London . . . is an awful place to live in. Not only is the climate abominable but it's a continual chase after distraction. There's no peace of mind—no harvest to be reaped out of it," or of Virginia Woolf writing passionately at twenty-two, "People say how lucky I am, and how glad I ought to be to be out of London. They dont [sic] realise that London means my own home, and books, and pictures, and music . . . the only place I can be quiet and free," what emerges in examining women writers' vision of the city is that whether city experience is pleasurable or painful depends, in large part, on whether it allows them access to creativity and autonomy.[4]

One reason for the particular significance the city holds for women writers is that, like the novels and poems in which its image appears, the city is a cultural artifact, and women have always had a problematic relationship to culture itself. Traditionally, women have been excluded from cultural realms, by both biologically based and socially enforced stereotypes. Because their physical experiences, culturally transmitted psychic structures, and social roles have combined everywhere, throughout history, to ensure that they are perceived as closer to nature (and to "natural" domestic space) than men, women have traditionally been relegated to pastoral or interior settings, both in life and in literature.[5] So George Sand found it a fierce struggle to escape her country life as Amantine Aurore Lucie Dupin to live merely part of each year in Paris as a free woman and a writer. Woman's "appropriate" social habitat has become so narrow that she is often judged "less fit" for the wider demands of public life, particularly the urban marketplace. Consequently, women's experience of the city has generally been mediated by men, whether husbands, fathers, brothers, or the male columnists over whose columns in *The Rambler* Charlotte Brontë pored, as she sat in her Haworth parlor, looking for news of London, "the great city which is to me as apocryphal as Babylon, or Nineveh, or ancient Rome."[6]

Yet if the city can exclude women, as a cultural community in which men alone transact business, govern the nation, and enforce laws, it can also free women for the first time from their isolation in the private home, as recent work on feminist urban design reveals.[7] The city can provide women with space and cultural tools with which to transcend enforced domestic servitude: with "a room of one's own," an education, a job. Moreover, cities at least hold out the possibility of sisterhood, as women who have escaped from the private home gather in public spaces to work, to play, and to discover that—like Virginia Woolf's Chloe and Olivia—they like each other. Although such nurturant cities are most familiar from utopian fiction, history has recorded a number of times when the urban environment served women as a gate of escape from bondage to the natural, rural past.[8]

There is, then, a special reason why the city has shifting values to women writers. In its literary image, women confront and challenge the culturally enshrined opposition between domestic, natural, female labor and public, cultural, male labor. Needless to say, this challenge is central to their very survival as writers. Furthermore, in writing about cities, women reveal their response to culture itself: they consider the difficulties they face working in that cultural realm from which their gender has traditionally barred them, and they celebrate the immense pleasures of that new frontier.

A critical study of the city's role in the lives and works of women writers will yield valuable insights to scholars and common readers concerned with gender and class relations, artistic production, and the exercise of power by individuals or groups. As Carl Schorske has pointed out, "No man thinks of the city in hermetic isolation. . . . He forms his image of it through a perceptual screen derived from inherited culture and transformed by personal experience. Hence the investigation of the intellectual's idea of the city inevitably carries us outside its own frame into a myriad of concepts and values about the nature of man, society, and culture."[9] Although this assertion reveals another sort of perceptual screen in its assumption that the city dweller is male, and that the culture from which he draws *his* perceptual screen is (like the implied reader's) also male, the observation is equally true for the female literary tradition and the women writers it omits to mention. Any analysis of the city's treatment by women writers requires a foray into questions not merely literary, but psychological, philosophical, political, and social. In its many guises—as symbol, theme, setting, even character—the city speaks fluently of woman's public and private life, of her literal and literary confinement in patriarchal models for experience, and of her struggle to win freedom from such constraints in life and art.

This collection of critical essays is the first to explore women writers' literary treatment of the city. While not intended to be comprehensive, it includes essays documenting the urban environment's shifting values in the works of a wide range of important women writers of the past two centuries. Some essays explore women writers' reasons for valuing the city: as an arena of stimulation; a place which promises anonymity and freedom from familial demands and imposed gender roles; an environment which continually challenges complacency, schooling people in "the uses of disorder," or, as Virginia Woolf saw it, bombarding them in its streets with question after question.[10] Other essays consider the reasons for which women writers have reviled the city: its identification with male models for experience (the family, politics, religion, economics, language, even culture itself) which not only caused it to renege on its promise for women, but turned it into an oppressive environment of concrete yards where nothing can grow, and dimly lit streets where women are sexual prey.

The essays in this volume are united by their common interest in the city's role as symbol system and vehicle for the exploration of feminist concerns in the works of women writers, yet they differ in both methodology and geographical-historical milieu.[11] Ranging from literary history and criticism to critical and feminist theory, they exemplify diverse approaches to the text as well, from thematic and mythic, to structuralist and socialist-feminist. Furthermore, in order to avoid the blurred cultural distinctions resulting from treating the city as one generalized ideal, or mythic, entity, the essays have been classed as Continental, British, or North American based either on the city in question or on the writer's origin. Of course, neither the writers nor their characters always honor such national boundaries. George Eliot's *Romola* is set in Florence rather than London, while both Virginia Woolf and Vita Sackville-West readily left England behind for fictional sojourns in foreign countries, which appealed to them not for the weight of history which fascinated Eliot, but for the licensed exoticism which so many British visitors found in the East and which, in their cases, took on unmistakably feminist and erotic overtones.[12]

It is intriguing to distinguish between Continental, British, and North American women writers' treatments of the city in literature. Perhaps because French women have had to struggle against an obdurate gender division, with the accompanying stereotyped sex roles, built into their language, Flora Tristan and Marguerite Duras emphasize the city's hostility to women and women's concerns. Sandra Dijkstra's essay surveys Tristan's experience of the city from a socialist-feminist perspective, while Susan Rava studies Duras from a perspective closer to French feminism, yet both essays reveal cities in which the means of production (on material and cultural levels) are controlled by men. In their cities, women are shadowy figures existing on the margins: of mind, of work, of speech, of culture.

The response of British women writers like Katherine Mansfield, Virginia Woolf, and even Doris Lessing appears less explicitly negative to the city than their French counterparts. However, the British writers reveal an ambivalence perhaps best described by Virginia Woolf in *A Room of One's Own*. Writing about the troubled heritage of women writers, Woolf characteristically used a city image to capture the ambivalence they feel, faced with an urban culture which excludes them: "If one is a woman one is often surprised by a sudden splitting off of consciousness, say in walking down Whitehall, when from being the natural inheritor of that civilisation, she becomes, on the contrary, outside of it, alien and critical."[13] While they are drawn to the city's opportunities for literary experimentation, anonymous wandering, and sexual freedom, British women writers are also oppressed, intimidated, even disgusted by the patriarchal tradition which they often see as its informing characteristic. Nancy L. Paxton's essay documents the anxious soul-searching of George Eliot when confronted with Florence; Sydney Janet Kaplan studies a freer attempt to revise the city's meaning in the works of

Katherine Mansfield; Louise A. DeSalvo and Susan Merrill Squier explore the feminist vision of the city in the works of Vita Sackville-West and Virginia Woolf; while Christine W. Sizemore demonstrates the palimpsestic nature of urban experience in Doris Lessing's *The Four-Gated City*. Even the most enthusiastic praise of the urban environment is still tempered by an acknowledgment of its other side, however, where the sense of belonging gives way to an icy exclusion. This sense of isolation from the centers of urban power led writers of the feminist fantasy novels of the twenties to imagine a retreat to a wilderness of their own, as Jane Marcus demonstrates.

Perhaps resentment of colonial oppression joins the heritage of the French language to breed hostility to the city in Canadian writers, for, as Sherrill E. Grace shows, their vision of the urban environment is far less sanguine than their other North American counterparts. Ultimately, the Canadian women writers' antipathy to the city expands to transform the significance of categories themselves: city and country, culture and nature, male and female. In contrast to the negative or ambivalent urban visions of the Continental, British, and Canadian women writers, the treatment of American women writers reveals optimism. In their works, the city at least holds out the possibility of intellectual and social growth to those who inhabit it, although, as Carolyn Mitchell demonstrates, that possibility may only become reality through an aggressive appropriation of the city's spiritual meaning.

Whether they praise the city or blame it, women writers respond to the urban environment in a significantly different way from men. In their revisionary approaches to the image of the city in the works of women writers, the essays in this volume offer an exciting new look at the complex interactions between women, culture, and nature in the urban environment. Considering not only *what* women writers have written about the city, but also *how* they have used the city to express both personal concerns and cultural critiques, they suggest the rich array of symbolic structures and narrative techniques with which women writers have addressed these issues.

Notes

My thanks to Helen Cooper and Karen Rowe for their helpful comments on an earlier draft of this introduction.

1. *The Letters of Virginia Woolf, Volume Six: 1936–1941*, ed. Nigel Nicolson and Joanne Trautmann (New York: Harcourt Brace Jovanovich, 1980), 431.
2. Ibid., 434. For a further glimpse of Woolf's fascination with London, see her reading notebooks, particularly those compiled while she was preparing to write *Three Guineas*. Brenda R. Silver, ed. *Virginia Woolf's Reading Notebooks* (Princeton: Princeton Univ. Press, 1983).
3. Carl E. Schorske, "The Idea of the City in European Thought: Voltaire to Spengler," *The Historian and the City*, ed. Oscar Handlin and John Burchard (Cambridge, Mass.: MIT Press, 1963), 95–114, 96. Raymond Williams examines the social background for the images of country and city in English literature in *The Country and the City* (New York: Oxford Univ. Press, 1973), while Irving Howe offers a more general survey of "The City in Literature," *Commentary* 51, no. 5, (May 1971), 61–68. For a discussion of the image of the city in eighteenth-century British literature, see Max Byrd, *London Transformed: Images of the City in the Eighteenth Century* (New Haven: Yale Univ. Press, 1978). Alexander Welsh brilliantly analyzes *The City of Dickens* (Oxford: Clarendon Press, 1971), and Donald Fanger considers the city's significance in Russian literature in *Dostoevsky and Romantic Realism* (Cambridge, Mass.: Harvard Univ. Press, 1967). Richard Sennett's writings on the city are justly celebrated, although he has yet to devote the same careful attention to woman's experience of the urban environment which he has shown to man's. Sennett's works are *The Fall of Public Man* (New York: Knopf, 1977), *The Uses of Disorder: Personal Identity and City Life* (New York: Knopf, 1970), and *Classic Essays on the Culture of Cities*, ed. Richard Sennett (Englewood Cliffs, N.J.: Prentice-Hall, 1969). Malcolm Bradbury has surveyed "The Cities of Modernism," *Modernism*, ed. Malcolm Bradbury and James McFarlane (Harmondsworth: Penguin, 1976), and Monroe K. Spears has explored the meaning of the urban image in literary modernism in *Dionysus and the City: Modernism in Twentieth-Century Poetry* (Oxford: Oxford Univ. Press, 1972). The relationship of modern writers to the city is studied by a number of critics and writers in *Literature and the Urban Experience: Essays on the City and Literature*, ed. Michael C. Jaye and Ann Chalmers Watts (New Brunswick, N.J.: Rutgers Univ. Press, 1981), and the nonliterary side of woman's urban experience is surveyed from a number of perspectives in *Signs Special Issue: Women and the American City*, ed. Catharine R. Stimpson, 5, no. 3 (Spring 1980). Marshall Berman interprets the complex relationship between literary and artistic modernism, technological modernization, and the urban environment in *All That Is Solid Melts Into Air* (New York: Simon & Schuster, 1982) and Burton Pike surveys *The Image of the City in Modern Literature* (Princeton: Princeton Univ. Press, 1982).
4. Sydney Janet Kaplan, "'A Gigantic Mother': Katherine Mansfield's London," in this volume; *The Letters of Virginia Woolf, Volume*

One: 1888–1912, ed. Nigel Nicolson and Joanne Trautmann (New York: Harcourt Brace Jovanovich, 1975), 147.

5. For a further discussion of the relationship between women, nature, and culture, see Sherry Ortner, "Is Female to Male as Nature Is to Culture?" *Women, Culture, & Society*, ed. Michelle Z. Rosaldo and Louise Lamphere (Stanford: Stanford Univ. Press, 1974), and M. Z. Rosaldo, "The Use and Abuse of Anthropology: Reflections on Feminism and Cross-cultural Understanding," *Signs* 5, no. 3 (Spring 1980), 389–417.

6. Elizabeth Gaskell, *The Life of Charlotte Brontë* (Harmondsworth: Penguin, 1970), 149–50.

7. Julia Kristeva explores the political nature of the suprafamilial community which the urban environment embodies in *About Chinese Women* (New York: Urizen, 1974). See also Dolores Hayden, *The Grand Domestic Revolution: American Visions of Household Liberation* (Cambridge, Mass.: MIT Press, 1981).

8. Virginia Woolf, *A Room of One's Own* (New York: Harcourt, Brace & World, 1957), 86–88; Barbara Berg, *The Remembered Gate: Origins of American Feminism* (Oxford: Oxford Univ. Press, 1978).

9. Schorske, 95.

10. Sennett, *The Uses of Disorder*; Virginia Woolf, "Why?," *The Death of the Moth and Other Essays* (New York: Harcourt Brace Jovanovich, 1970), 227.

11. That common interest was the focal point of my Modern Language Association special session, "Cities of Sisterhood," December 1979, at the San Francisco MLA Convention, in which this collection of essays had its origin.

12. For further discussion of the exotic and erotic overtones of the East for western visitors, see Edward Said, *Orientalism* (New York: Vintage, 1978); Louise A. DeSalvo, "Every Woman Is an Island: Vita Sackville-West, the Image of the City, and the Pastoral Idyll," in this volume.

13. *A Room of One's Own*, 101.

Part I

Continental Writers

SANDRA DIJKSTRA

The City as Catalyst for
Flora Tristan's Vision of Social Change

Introduction

WHO WAS FLORA TRISTAN? A female intellectual with strong political conviction based on her experiences as a woman alone in Paris, in mid-nineteenth-century France, her popular image has been the object of distortion and attack during her lifetime and after. In a society which accorded women status only through marriage and which rendered her a legal inferior by that very act, in which motherhood and domesticity were declared to be female virtues, Tristan scandalized her contemporaries. She refused to trade upon her widely admired beauty. Although she allowed her portrait to appear in "Les belles femmes de Paris . . ." for the year 1840, she regarded her physical attributes in the main as a handicap, complaining, "Since the age of 21, I have lived *alone* and I have had the enormous misfortune to be a *pretty Woman.*"[1] She rejected a life restricted to motherhood because of her disgust for the egotism involved: "This family life seems atrocious to me and how immoral! To forget humanity in order to take care of one's daughter, of one's son."[2] Thus her more illustrious contemporary George Sand attacked her for lacking a proper maternal urge. Tristan's defects as a wife were brought to public attention in 1838, just after the appearance of her first book, *Pérégrinations d'une paria, 1833–1835*, describing her visit to her father's family in Peru and including a detailed account of her unhappy marriage. As Tristan's enraged husband stood trial for his unsuccessful attempt to murder her, he sought clemency based on her poor performance in the domestic sphere.[3]

Tristan shocked good French society and sought to live as an independent woman by means of her pen. The more progressive men and women had to take her seriously, even when they disagreed with her, as her writing and activity became increasingly political. And even in the intellectual sphere, her efforts were overshadowed by her gender. Her more famous grandson, Gauguin, whom she never saw, left a disparaging description of her as a "bas bleu socialiste" which has stood until recently as one of the common descriptions of her. Yet, in her own age, despite her lapses from proper feminine behavior, she was recognized as one of the more incisive commentators on the problems of the day.

Given these perceptions of her intellectual activity, Tristan determinedly maintained her own self-image, constructing it in such a way to permit her to break all taboos. Thus she was able to withstand the attacks of her contemporaries. Her self-image underwent change in the decade for which she left a written record, 1835–44, but true to romantic fashion, it can be characterized as "exalted" throughout. In her early writings, she presented herself as the "pariah," the outcast, because of her illegitimate birth, her loss of family name, prestige, wealth, and, because, having left her husband, she was an outsider to good French society. By the end of a decade of literary and political activity, she had come to see herself and convinced others to see her as a "femme forte," a "femme guide," a superior, strong woman, called to lead the people, particularly women, out of their present state of subjection.

Self-educated, living precariously in a social, economic, and legal sense, Flora Tristan came to her vision of social change through her own experience of life in one of the nineteenth century's largest cities at a particularly fertile historical moment. This period witnessed the development of feminist consciousness, and working-class consciousness, including some of the first strikes.[4] By 1835, the two movements arising from this new consciousness suffered repression. The law against the organization of workers and the law establishing censorship of the press were instituted in 1834, and these measures led to a period of relative calm.[5] Her feelings of isolation and sometimes of discouragement were warranted: by 1835, when she began her writing career, the Saint-Simonian movement was dispersed, its leaders in jail, its true believers on a mission to the Middle East in search of the Mother. The most active apostles of feminism within that movement had ceased publishing their journals.[6] Fourier, with whom Tristan had made contact, was dead, and his followers, led by Victor Considérant, were busy deradicalizing the master's thought, especially its feminist dimension, perhaps influenced by the fate of the Saint-Simonians. Only one feminist journal persisted, the *Gazette des femmes*, but it preached a kind of bourgeois feminism, focused only on political and legal equality for women.[7]

In this atmosphere, Tristan began to develop her perspective of the city, viewing it alternatively as the *lieu* and the agent of modernization. As she came to understand the phenomenon of industrial capitalism and to perceive its inhuman face, her writing took a variety of forms—travel memoir, novel, and political tract. The significance of her contribution is only now beginning to be recognized more widely by feminists and socialists alike.[8]

II

Why connect Flora Tristan to the question of the city and its effect on women? Not only did she nearly always live in cities, and travel to cities, but she constantly wrote about them and they had an important influence on the shape of her esthetic and political theories. After a childhood on the rural edges of Paris she was taken to live in one of the worst districts of the metropolis at the age of fifteen. She guarded a memory of the countryside which would color her utopian thought.[9] Her contemporary Balzac described the area in which she grew up, the district of the rue du Fouarre, accurately according to historians:

Today it is one of the dirtiest streets in the XIIth arrondissement, the poorest district in Paris, in which two-thirds of the inhabitants lack firewood in winter, the district which sends the most bastards to the Foundling Hospital, the most sick to the Hotel-Dieu, the most beggars onto the streets, the most ragpickers to the garbage dumps at the corner, the most sick old men to lean against the walls in the sun, the most unemployed workers to the squares, the most indictments to the police courts.[10]

Approaching adulthood in such an atmosphere left an indelible impression on Tristan, who preferred to identify with her paternal noble Peruvian ancestors, but whose profound identification with the people of the slums shaped her life's work. It was not just poverty which came to impress her, but the ever-increasing evidence of the contrast between the rich and the poor. Hobsbawm's juxtaposition of two pieces of social history illuminate the contradictions of the period:

The time when the Baroness Rothschild wore one and half million francs worth of jewellery at the Duke of Orleans masked ball (1842) was the time when John Bright described the women of Rochdale: '2000 women and girls passed through the streets singing hymns—it was a very singular and striking spectacle—approaching the sublime—they are dreadfully hungry—a loaf is devoured with greediness indescribable and if the bread is nearly covered with mud it is eagerly devoured.'[11]

These painful social facts were becoming more evident every day: as the cities grew, the misery did also.

Flora Tristan was a precise observer of the urban malaise at a propitious moment. Within Tristan's lifetime, in the first half of the nineteenth century, Paris doubled its size. Since "the increase occurred in an old city which had not changed at the same rate; which indeed, had been unable to do so,"[12] the effects were startling. "In these years, Paris looked around and was unable to recognize itself. Another larger city had overflowed into the unaltered framework of streets, mansions, houses and passageways, piling man on man and trade on trade."[13] Officially and unofficially, Paris began to study itself, to gather statistics on such a wide variety of social problems that one historian refers to the first half of the nineteenth century as "the prime age of statistics."[14] Essentially these researchers examined Paris's "pathological state" viewing the city as if it were a diseased entity.[15] In much the same way as eighteenth-century explorers were drawn to study the exotic in far-off places, now Tristan's generation turned to examine the new industrial world surrounding them, finding not only disease and suffering but also a criminality so rampant that it seemed a part of urban life.[16] Most of these studies of such subjects as sewers and hygiene, cholera and prostitution, exposed the economic bases of these problems and proposed remedies.[17]

Tristan was a part of this generation, although she was one of the rare women to participate in the effort to assess the impact of the new metropolis. She was influenced by its scientific pretensions, its faith in statistics; these were propagated not only by the "enquêtes" but also by the new and booming mass media. The *Gazette des Tribunaux*, which first appeared in 1825, became an important source of information for novelists: one sociologist of literature, Louis Chevalier, believes that it (and the phenomenon of "enquêtes") account for the development of description in the novel.[18] It is difficult to gauge the effect of this constant mediation of her vision of social reality by the press: Tristan was fascinated with its power, as is clear from her novel *Méphis* where her central character recognized the importance of journalism, and from the last pages of her final publication, *Union ouvrière*, where she announced her own project for a workers' newspaper.[19] It is clear also that she was interested in the subject of this mediation, the city itself: it was Méphis's goal in life to draw up precisely such a tableau of Paris. In her next book, *Promenades dans Londres*, Tristan herself undertook the same project for London; in her last work, a journal, she drew a tableau of the provinces of France. She bolstered her observations with statistics when necessary. For example, she referred her reader to the *Gazette des Tribunaux* for a true picture of "the state of women's exasperation" with her enslavement in marriage (*UO*, 65).

Tristan treated the social evils recognized by male researchers, such as the effects of size, of disparity in income, but she had a special sensitivity to the woman question and to the effects of the new sexual division of labor which relegated women to the domestic sphere, as public and private domains drew apart in the reorganization of work brought on by industrialism.[20]

Unlike other researchers, Tristan did not content herself with description and prescription[21]; she wanted to help implement her remedy, she wanted *action*, not just statistics or theory. Therefore, she chose to work in a succession of genres moving from political pamphlet, to travel memoir, to novel, back to travel memoir, and then to political pamphlet. Her last work, a journal, *Tour de France, état actuel de la classe ouvrière sous l'aspect moral, intellectuel, matériel*, published in 1973, is an impressionistic account of the subject which came to preoccupy her most, the plight of workers (of both sexes) in the cities of France.[22]

It seems accurate then to view the city and the problems it came to pose in the nineteenth century as the stimulus which set her pen in motion. Her vision of it coalesced slowly, but her preoccupation with it was constant. As she diagnosed its diseases, and located the causes of them, the cure became more apparent to her. Especially after her fourth visit to London, the true monstrosity of the new metropolis became apparent to her. "London, far more than Paris, was the monstrous city, the city of poverty and crime,"[23] historians now say, and so Tristan was on the mark: she entitled the opening chapter of *Promenades dans Londres, La Ville monstre*.[24] And, she introduced the second edition (of 1842) with a "dédicace aux classes ouvrières." By then Tristan realized that "we are not living in ordinary times; people are no longer content with their partial liberation . . . the privileged are frightened . . ." (*PR*, 53). She came to the conclusion that she was witnessing a tremendous change in what Marx would later call the "mode of production," that human beings were being enslaved in a new and perhaps more dehumanizing manner, more devastating than earlier forms of slavery.

In my view, slavery is no longer the greatest of human misfortunes now that I've seen the English proletariat: the slave is sure of his bread for all his life, and of care when he falls ill, but there exists no link between the worker and his English master (*PR*, 115).

Ah! These capitalists, these big landowners, who the proletarians make so rich by the exchange of a piece of bread for fourteen hours of work; they have no idea of the evils and disorders that result from their accumulation of riches (*PR*, 126).

But it was especially the workers she wanted to reach and to educate. As she came to grasp the enormity of social, economic, and political damage wrought by the new industrial capitalist system centered in the metropolis, Tristan decided she must abandon literature.

We must leave to happier days the songs of the poet, because it isn't the time to amuse ourselves by reading novels, poems, fables or dramas. The *useful*, first of all, the useful. And what is urgent is that workers understand *the causes of their suffering and the means to remedy them* (*PR*, 54).

This passage, from the second edition of *Promenades dans Londres*, is to be found in Tristan's most significant addition to that volume, a "Dedication to the working classes." We recognize how far her vision had evolved if we contrast its radical statement warning workers that they must concern themselves with "the social order, the base of the edifice . . . and not with politics which is only an artificial power . . ." (*PR*, 52) with the reformist stance she took in her first published work, a little pamphlet entitled, *Nécessité de faire bon accueil aux femmes étrangères*. Also, her concerns widened from a focus on women's plight to a focus on the plight of *both sexes*.

III

Tristan's first work dealt with the problems foreign women faced in the metropolis. (In the term "foreign" she included women from the French provinces, who in increasing numbers were strangers in the city.) While she recognized that all migrants to Paris faced "a cold and empty city"[25] she knew from her experience that women traveling alone met even worse, scandal and contempt. Not only did they lack the traditional support systems best exemplified by the extended family, but also they were entering a space barricaded by taboos. Often fleeing from the shame of an illegitimate pregnancy or an abandoned husband in their village, on reaching the city (Paris), these singular exiles would have a difficult time, their social and economic options limited. Tristan's solution seems minimal in contrast to her later thinking: she hoped to establish a kind of urban haven, not unlike the modern YMCA, to counteract the isolation and fear and to provide shelter. She recognized here that urban civilization posed particularly difficult problems for women. To confront these successfully, they must recognize their common plight and unite, transcending class differences. Then the city would not seem nearly so formidable.

IV

Tristan's concern for women, whom she regarded as "an entire class, forming one-half of humanity,"[26] only increased during her sojourn in Peru, where she sought unsuccessfully to recoup her lost heritage. While there, she wrote a travel journal, published in 1838, under the title, *Pérégrinations d'une paria, 1833–1834*. In this, her first book, she studied the various institutions which incarcerated women, particularly marriage and the convent. Looking for signs of autonomy and independence, she found these characteristics manifested in two groups of women: rural women, exemplified by the Ravanas; and women of the city, epitomized by the Lima women. The first group, a kind of all-female militia, seemed to represent to Tristan "proof of the superiority of women."[27]

However, in her view, the Ravanas were the antithesis of the modern woman and could not provide a model for her existence within an urban setting. If they symbolized the past strength of women, the Lima women incarnated the present form of power based on feminine wiles. They succeeded because of certain legal and economic advantages (the male dowry system, which gave them access to an independent income), and because, aided by the urban setting and fashion (their dress, the *saya* and *manto*), they could travel about the city with their identity concealed. This possibility was naturally attractive to Tristan, whose husband was constantly tracking her down in Paris, and she admired the freedom thus achieved by the Lima women, but she warned that until they strengthened their intelligence through education, they had better hold onto these protective customs, or they would fall to the status of European women.[28] But until then, until equality between the two sexes existed, Tristan felt that women would have to make use of feminine wiles and feminine dress. The strongest woman she met in Peru, la Présidente Gamarra, lost her power for attempting to do without them, in Flora Tristan's view.[29]

Clearly, the problem of women's independence in the modern world obsessed Tristan. She desired it not only for herself, but for all women. Ironically, the publication of this book closed off one avenue to its achievement: her uncle's offer of a minimum stipend was withdrawn because he objected to her depiction of what she termed "the corruption of the highest classes in Peru."[30] But, by its success, the book opened up another possibility: Tristan might be able to support herself as a woman of letters. Her exposure of the details of her married life in the preface to *Pérégrinations . . .* had been held against her in court, where her husband was on trial for having kidnapped and raped his daughter. But, under the cover of fiction, she might explore with less constraint the social questions which haunted her. Paris became the center of her next book, a novel.

We cannot separate Tristan's horrific view of the city, presented in her novel, *Méphis*, from her experience there. On the one hand, the city seemed to represent hope for the future: all the great thinkers and artists were clustered there. It promised—or seemed to promise—the accumulation of wealth or power or both. But Tristan lived at the level of genteel poverty, and though she had correspondence and contact with intellectuals, social reformers, and artists, as a woman she was treated differently. For example, the leader of the Fourierists, Victor Considérant, asked her to "understand" the social rules which prevented his group from including women at their political and social "banquets."[31] Indeed, Tristan's bold independence of thought, the forthrightness with which she distinguished herself from existing groups, and with which she criticized the limitations of contemporary ideologies, did not endear her to members of the various progressive sects.

Moreover, within the city itself, Tristan found she was constantly being harrassed by her husband, who had the law and the city's police on his side, his brutality sanctioned by the Napoleonic Code. Released from jail after only one month for lack of evidence that he had raped his daughter (Aline's testimony, and that of her brother, was apparently insufficient), he was back on the streets, trailing Tristan. She finally sought and obtained a legal separation, but that did not protect her from her husband's rage at her independence. He attempted to murder her on September 10, 1838: luckily he was unsuccessful, although it is likely that the bullet which remained lodged within her chest weakened her considerably, and contributed to her premature death (at age forty, of typhoid).[32] Thus, for Tristan, the city, Paris, represented both freedom/life and entrapment/death, and she strove to engrave its two contradictory faces on her novel.

V

In *Méphis*, Tristan's only novel, Paris is not merely the neuter setting: it represents the male domain par excellence. Determined not to write a simple love story, Tristan chose instead to focus on the sexual division of labor coming into being as France edged slowly toward industrial capitalism. Paris is seen mainly through male eyes: it is the scene of predominantly male activity. But Tristan also wanted to present Paris as the locus of the class struggle, though her understanding of this phenomenon had not yet fully developed (partially because the class struggle in France was, like capitalism, still in its early stages). Thus, she presented Paris through the experience of a male member of the proletariat,

Méphis, who traversed the various strata of society, seeking not only survival, but also to understand the city about him, to draw up a tableau of its social and economic organization, and to attempt to transform society, beginning with women, whom he viewed as a necessary part of the vanguard for social change. A male protagonist was essential because he would have access to the various strata of society: the city was his native habitat. Besides, under the cover of a male character, Tristan could more convincingly present her own progressive views, and indict the traditional role for women so idealized by her own society. But a female companion was needed for Méphis's experiment, his attempt to transform woman from a self-sacrificing, passive creature to a strong individual. Therefore, Tristan placed a couple at the center of her novel.

Their names, Méphis and Maréquita, betray the allegorical purposes of this didactic novel, as well as Tristan's dialectical mode of thought. Both names begin with the first person singular pronoun: the syllables "mé" and "ma" seem to refer back to Tristan's own desires, and to the profound autobiographical basis for the novel. At one level, the characters certainly represent alternative sides of Tristan's own character, her hopes, her fears. The last syllable of both names, "phis" and "quita" resemble in sound and stress the two cities which played a major role in Tristan's life, Paris and Aréquipa (where her father's family lived in Peru), the one evoking the present, the other the past, on a symbolic level. And finally Méphis's name is a shortened version of Mephistopheles, the archetypal tempter and transformer, and Maré clearly evokes the Virgin Mary: thus, one character, the male, represents change; the other, female, tradition.

In one sense, the opposition in the novel between Méphis and Maréquita is based on sexual lines, male versus female, but it also reproduces the dichotomies city/country, present-future/past. Méphis incarnates the city as a force for modernization and change, a force to which women respond very slowly.

Women represent the countryside. There we find Maréquita's abode, a place of tranquility, seclusion, stasis. For an idyllic moment, love can flourish within the confines of her rural retreat, but it is thwarted by Maréquita's fear for her reputation, and by the invasion of legal authorities from the city, who disrupt their adulterous tryst.

Women appear in the city only rarely in this novel, and on each occasion they are depicted in relation to the male protagonist, Méphis. Maréquita surfaces briefly at an aristocratic *soirée*, and is shown through Méphis's admiring eyes as she sings romantic and revolutionary songs. She seems to represent an ideal of womanhood: the fusion of beauty, truth and strength. His first love, an Englishwoman whose family rejected his suit on the basis of his lowly birth, turns up at a masked ball disguised as a prostitute: when he unmasks her, revealing her identity, she freezes into insanity and has to be carried off. This woman incarnates debased womanhood: ugliness, falsehood, and weakness. Her inordinate sexual desire and her madness seem to be linked. The third woman, a duchess with whom Méphis has a liaison in the city and who repents for her adultery, dies while giving birth to his child. The duchess represents more traditional womanhood, and it is not surprising that her most significant act is to transform Méphis's painting of his idealized image of woman, the *Femme Guide*, into a Virgin Mary. In fact, only the *Femme Guide*, Méphis's visionary painting of the ideal woman, travels with him through the various segments of Parisian society. Therefore, not woman herself, but an image of ideal womanhood offers the most constant presence of the potential of woman in the city, perhaps implying that progressive feminist ideas would have to be launched in the city even if urban women at each level of society might resist them. Méphis's social esthetic, as represented by the *Femme Guide*, is also rejected by his fellow students at the studio where sensual and materialistic depictions of women (à la Delacroix and Ìngres) are in vogue, and finally by Maréquita herself, who is not ready to move beyond her traditional view of womanhood. The violence with which this idealized image of womanhood is received (by the art students and by women themselves) is clearly overdetermined. At one level, it indicates the enormous resistance from both sexes which greeted Tristan's ideal of womanhood in her day. At another level, it represents women's complicity in maintaining their lowly status.

To the very end of her life, Tristan continued to have faith in an ideal of womanhood admittedly taken from the Saint-Simonians; the notion of "the superiority of woman" (*UO*, 68) gave her strength even if it was shared only by those others regarded as fools.[33] She recognized that the "emancipation of workers is impossible as long as women remain in this state of degradation. They will stop all progress" (*UO*, 68). In the novel, that is clearly the case. Maréquita is too much a prisoner of the countryside, of the past, of tradition, to transform herself into a strong, active woman. Although she, like other women of her epoch, exists "outside the *Church*, outside the *law*, outside *society*" (*UO*, 44), exercising no functions within these institutions centered in the city, she has been indoctrinated by their ideologies and is thus their prisoner. Méphis must therefore fail in his attempt to make her his equal in the struggle for change.

The novel closes with the hope that the next generation of women will carry on the struggle. Both protagonists die, and Méphis's tableau of Parisian society is passed on to their daughter: if Tristan had any illusions about her daughter's assuming a similar role, they were destroyed by the time she died. Her journal records her disappointment:

She [Gauguin's mother, Aline] is far from satisfying me. What she lacks is faith, love, enthusiasm, devotion, activity. She understands the greatness of the plan, the beauty of the idea, but she will sacrifice neither herself nor her interests to make it succeed. The lack of faith, of love, places between my poor daughter and myself a wall of iron. The older she gets, the thicker the wall. . . . Count on one's children to make you friends, disciples, successors—what folly! In the grocery and the bakery perhaps, but in the intellectual domain—absurd![34]

If the city is impoverished by its exclusion and degradation of women, and by its socialization of them into traditional roles, its grandeur is diminished also by its lack of community. Neither sisterhood nor brotherhood can flourish within its walls: it is now a vast container rather than a community, collecting numbers of unrelated people. Like so many migrants, Méphis is "without fortune, without relations, without friends, a poor and unknown stranger."[35] The face of the modern city is unfriendly: "The Arab in the middle of the desert is less isolated from help than the stranger lost among the crowd, which elbows him in the streets, without worrying if he is hungry, if he has found shelter, and if, that very day, he is not going to throw himself in the river" (*ME*, I, 161). Human bonds have become distorted, and the individual feels estranged from his coinhabitants in a society "where money has become the measure of all merit" (*ME*, I, 223).

The city presents a paradox: it collects the intellectual and political vanguard as well as the established leaders of society; it assembles masses of people hitherto unseen, yet they remain isolated, individualistic; it represents the future, yet it is set up to repress social progress. Méphis finds that his values are unpopular in this materialistic society. He follows his plan to "know intimately the diverse classes of society in order to draw up a survey" (*ME*, I, 230), the more easily because his views often result in his loss of a job.

The image of the city rendered by Méphis's experience in it is mainly an ideological portrait: Tristan is more adept at transcribing the lessons Méphis learns at each stage than in reproducing the actual texture of his experience. This is probably due in part to Tristan's preference for ideas over reality, but we can also trace it to her own exclusion from the workaday world of Paris; as a woman of the middle class with intellectual interests, she had not yet made contact with it. Méphis's life pattern corresponds more closely to Tristan's psychological, political, and ideological concerns than to his need to survive.

Thus Tristan's concern about the effects of the sexual and class division of labor in the new metropolis emerged in these schematic portraits of Méphis and Maréquita. She also assessed rather accurately the difficulty she and others would have in mobilizing and emancipating French women, even as she foretold the slow but steady rise of the proletariat whose shadow looms over Paris by the novel's end. Predicting revolution unless this "slave of the rich" was either "made happy or deprived of learning" (*ME*, I, 205–6), Tristan allowed only one synthesis in her novel: the constituents of community, true brotherhood and true sisterhood, must be sought in the future. In 1838, the role of the intellectual was to delineate the effects of their absence. The intimate knowledge of the city helped give shape to this social fact.

VI

For those who reflected seriously on the future, London offered an object lesson. When Tristan returned to London for the fourth time in 1839, she seemed to have clarified her task: "Proletarians, my work is the exposition of the great social drama England is playing for the watching world" (*PR*, 52). She chose to situate her book in London, because there, as she surmised correctly, "riches were more unequally distributed than anywhere" (*PR*, 125). Indeed, without knowing urban history, Tristan had come upon one of its most significant foundations: that the city offered

"the best means for visualizing the crystallization of class relations."[36] For Tristan it also offered insight into the situation of
women. The protagonists of this "social drama" were clear: on
the one hand, the devastating poverty of workers, of women, of
children, in contrast to the wealth in the city; on the other, the
clear beginnings of an effective organization for change, the
Chartist movement, and mechanisms for assistance, women's
charitable organizations. Faced with the necessity of assessing
these realities, Tristan decided to abandon art. It no longer suf-
ficed to treat the dehumanization she witnessed. "What is Art
next to Humanity? Nothing, absolutely nothing."[37]

Finally in London the terms of the class struggle were clarified
for Tristan. She defined them in a manner that anticipated the
Communist Manifesto:

The great battle, that which will transform society, is the battle undertaken on the one side, by proprietors and capitalists who have everything, wealth and political power, for whose profit the country is gov-
erned, and on the other, the workers of cities and countryside who have
nothing, neither land, nor capital, nor political power, who pay
nonetheless two-thirds of the taxes, who furnish recruits for the armies
and navy, and who are starved by the rich according to their purpose, in
order to make them work more cheaply. (*PR*, 85)

Before Marx formulated the concept of surplus value, Tristan
understood it without naming it: "These capitalists, these big
landowners who grow so rich by the labor of the proletariat giving only a bit of bread in exchange for fourteen hours labor . . .
they have no idea of the evils and disorders that result from their
accumulation of riches!" (*PR*, 126). It was in the factory that the
law of capital revealed itself most clearly: "So the life of men is
exchanged for money" (*PR*, 120). The reduction of humanity to
the service of profit startled her. Horses were treated better than
humans in England, but she understood why: "Yes, but a horse
costs the manufacturer forty to fifty pounds sterling while the
country furnishes men for nothing!" (*PR*, 121). Dehumanization
occurred in the production process under industrialism where
the division of labor had made intelligence irrelevant and reduced
the human to a minute part of the process. Gone were songs she
remembered hearing in French workshops; here there reigned "a
silence of death," broken only by the din of machines (*PR*, 114).
Faced with this situation of deprivation, it was the workers' duty
to educate themselves, for "the school, the Church, and the press

are accomplices of the oppressors" (*PR*, 50). In her "Dedication to the Working Classes," Tristan added a significant radical note, reminding workers that "resistance to oppression is not only a *natural* human *right* but that even more, when people are oppressed, insurrection becomes a sacred duty" (*PR*, 50).

While Tristan found encouraging signs of brotherhood in London within the Chartist movement, sisterhood seemed to be completely absent, especially in the political domain. Only in the fields of charity and education were women active, but these efforts mitigated without altering women's plight (*PR*, Chap. 16). Capitalism negated the specific humanity of women as well as men. In a society where everything can be bought and sold, women become objects of exchange. If industrialists reduced working men to mere extensions of the machines, man in general treated woman "as his *thing*, like a piece of *furniture*, which can only serve him . . ." (*PR*, 267). Women of the various social strata were each isolated from one another, experiencing a form of degradation specific to their class. The only women who might have composed a comprehensive picture of the process were those with the intellectual tools to do so—writers. But of this numerous group, Tristan lamented, "not one has yet dared to embrace the cause of women's emancipation, that emancipation without which all the others are so short-lived, that emancipation for which it is especially appropriate for women authors to fight" (*PR*, 272). Mary Wollstonecraft, writing a half century earlier, was the only feminist Tristan could find to cite, and she quoted extensively from the *Vindication of the Rights of Women*, a text which still seemed all too appropriate to describing women's condition in mid-nineteenth-century England.

In London, Tristan found women to be in a state of "extreme dependence," reduced by men to a level of "nullity" not seen elsewhere, due to the enormous economic disparities (*PR*, 267, 269, 125). At the bottom of the social scale, prostitutes represented to Tristan "the most hideous of wounds produced by the unequal division of the world's goods," more extensive here than elsewhere (*PR*, 124). Tristan blamed the state, not women: "As long as woman is subjected to man's yoke, or to prejudice, as she receives no professional education, as she is deprived of her civil rights, there can exist no moral law for her!" (*PR*, 125). At the other end of the social scale, middle-class women are victims even though they lead "respectable lives." They are "reduced to machines for making babies"; they are ruled by an English husband whom Tristan views as a "kind of *seigneur* or *master* from feudal times . . . [who] believes he has . . . the right to demand of his wife the passive obedience of a slave, submission, and respect" (*PR*, 270, 267).

The fact that Tristan chose to focus on these roles which were based on the primitive exchange of woman's body indicates the degree to which she found the sexual division of labor to be entrenched in London. Indeed, Tristan was accurate in presenting the increased restriction of women to the private sphere. Generally, labor historians have found that "as industrialism advanced fewer and fewer married women worked."[38] Since industrialism was more advanced in London than in Paris, it is not surprising to discover that "only one-third of London women had an occupation, while in Paris the proportion was one-half."[39] Still the missing term in this book is women who work outside the home, a subject which would receive treatment in Tristan's next book, *Union ouvrière*. (For a more precise and comprehensive survey of the workplace, including women, one must turn to Engels's *The Condition of the Working Class in England*, a book which seems to have based itself on many of the premises enunciated in Tristan's text.)[40]

Promenades was well received in Paris, especially by writers of the more progressive press. Yet, even some of them seemed to share the reaction of a member of the "sisterhood" of women writers, Hortense Allart, who warned Saint-Beuve: "You won't be able to read it, so much does it lack taste and delicatesse."[41] Tristan's visit to the brothel was *shocking*. Here we observe the injunctions against a woman's moving beyond the bounds of propriety. Tristan, obviously anticipating this kind of reaction, wrote elsewhere:

If you don't feel all this, Women, abstain from making a judgment on the works of a woman who feels with all her heart the chains which lie so heavily on *half* the human race. Stay comfortably curled up on your sofa *praying* and *making Gods*, and allow her to fight for you.[42]

"Promenades," the activity implied in the title, was a word rarely used by Tristan in the first edition of her book. Normally, the word evokes an image of an activity related to leisure, one which only the rich have time to enjoy. But even for them, as Tristan showed in the first chapter, walking is unpleasant: the city is too large and labyrinthine; the fog too impenetrable, the crowds too imposing. Unpurposeful walking is exhausting in London. Only those inhabitants of the city who have deciphered its new and strange face, who have learned its law—that all activity must be purposeful and profitable—engage in walking, the streetwalkers. And, Tristan actually employed the term "promenades" mainly in reference to their activity. Tristan must have chosen the title in order to sell her book, by passing it off as a travel book. Its contents refused that category; the picturesque elements are minimal. With the appearance of the second edition, Tristan renamed the book *La Ville monstre*, a much more appropriate title for what she had found in London.

VII

To deal with the monstrosity of modern urban life, Tristan had found literature insufficient. *Promenades* allowed her to explore the city without the aesthetic constraint of fiction, but the travel tale format had its own exigencies, designed as it was for an upper-class, leisure-oriented audience. She wanted to direct her efforts at the working class, the group within the city whose plight most concerned her. Abandoning all pretense at "literary" efforts, Tristan in her next book did not appeal to a commercial publisher—but solicited support from those who believed in her cause. Based on all she had learned about the "drama" unfolding in the city, Tristan, in *Union ouvrière*, now sought to explain to the workers their rights, and outlined a plan for their attainment. Before Marx, she described the foundation of the workers' wealth and rights: "The worker without land, without houses, without capital, has nothing but his *arms*. . . . The only property, the only property that the working class can ever possess is their *arms* . . . their only riches!" (*UO*, 22, 23). These arms which constitute their "instrument of work" allow the working class to produce, to be useful only if the worker has the *right to work*. In order to achieve this, the working class must unite, because otherwise, as in 1789, and in 1830, this basic right will not be recognized, and without it "the rights of man, the rights of citizenship are of no value" (*UO*, 22). To this most radical and innovative call, Tristan added her appeal that women be included in this action. Men at least all benefited from the Revolution, but women's "social individual" must still be recognized, and "absolute equality between male and female established" (*UO*, 69). Only then can the workers' movement move forward to the establishment of "an INTERNATIONAL UNION OF MALE AND FEMALE WORKERS" (*UO*, 69). Only then will the inequities women suffer in the home and at the workplace be eradicated.

Union ouvrière represented Tristan's partial solution to the problem of the city. Unionization would undoubtedly improve the lot of the worker. But she had another, more immediate prospect, one which indicates her profound attraction to the theories of Fourier (and Owen) and to the countryside. As we have seen, Tristan's view of the city had evolved from a recognition of its multiple promises (of culture, of independence, of modernization—all of which were drawing provincials to the city and transforming them), to a horrific view of the city as a destructive force. While it seemed to contain liberating forces (progressive people, new technology), it also embodied the repressive mechanisms to restrain them, to exploit the most productive members of society. Therefore she chose what Carl Schorske describes as "an archaistic solution" based on the premise that "the good life simply could not be lived in the modern city."[43] Her proposal to the working class was that the most concrete resolution of the urban crisis was to be found *outside* city walls; not closer than eight kilometers or further than twenty-four from the nearest city where the union's central committee would sit, Tristan hoped to erect "workers' palaces" built with their own funds. These centers of "industrial work, agricultural labor, moral and professional instruction" would be a combination "dwelling place, factory, farm" (*UO*, 94). Located in a pretty place, with good air, fertile soil, and running water, the palace would hold approximately two to three hundred people. Apparently her idea held tremendous appeal to the working class. "On this point, I found everyone in agreement. . . . The idea of having for themselves a beautiful place to live, where they can raise their children well, where wounded workers can be received, where they themselves can retire when old, this prospect thrills them" (*UO*, ix, xi).

Clearly, in many respects, Tristan intended these workers' palaces to be the antithesis of the evils she had found in the modern city: in them, communitarian spirit rather than individualism will preside; respect for human dignity will be primary;

work will be distributed according to skill and interest; cleanliness and care for health will prevail; dress will be comfortable, practical and pleasing to the eye (no corsets or ties); work will be respected, not disdained; ignorance and poverty will be banished. Here true equality will be established. Clearly a utopian solution, one which marked the idealistic end of a painful dialectic for Tristan, it was of course a solution which she never lived to realize, for which the working class was unprepared.[44] She came to understand their unpreparedness as she toured France, in order to distribute her little book and to begin the organization of the workers' union.

VIII

One could argue that Flora Tristan's most complete study of women in the city, and of the city itself, is to be found in her notes for an uncompleted book, which were recently published posthumously under Tristan's title, *Le Tour de France, état actuel de la classe ouvrière sous l'aspect moral, intellectuel, matériel*, based on the comments in her journal, written the year before she died, 1843–44. Here we find the foundation for a comparative study of the state of the working classes, of their consciousness as well as their material situation, in the major cities of France. In its journal-like form, an unedited version of Tristan's major preoccupation emerges.

We have seen how, throughout her work, the city was essential to her thinking, both as the subject and as the shaping force of her writing, and later, political activity. By the end of her short life, Tristan realized that, given the state of consciousness of the people, sisterhood and brotherhood, which for her were mutually inclusive, were far in the future. The only means of attaining them was through organization and unionization.

Utopian though she may seem to us, Flora Tristan testified to the socioeconomic changes she witnessed in the city, and her testimony had repercussions. As she toured the provinces lecturing and gathering adherents to her plan, distributing and gaining subscribers to her *Union ouvriére*, she laid the groundwork, for the experiments and aspirations of 1848 and for the theories of Marx and Engels.[45]

NOTES

I would like to thank the libraries and librarians of the city of Paris for their assistance, in particular: La Bibliothèque Marguerite Durand, La Bibliothèque de L'Arsenale and La Bibliothèque Nationale.

1. "Lettre à Charles Fillieu" (July 30, 1843), in Stéphane Michaud's "Flora Tristan: Trente-Cinq Lettres," *International Review of Social History* 24 (1979), 122. See also his *Flora Tristan: Lettres* (Paris: Editions du Seuil, 1980).
2. Flora Tristan, *Le Tour de France, Journal inédit, 1843–1844*, preface by Michel Collinet, notes by Jules-L. Puech (Paris: Editions Tête de Feuilles, 1973), 123.
3. "Mémoire à consulter pour Chazal contre Madame Chazal," *Recueil des Factums de la Bibliothèque Nationale*, 4° F 3, Pièce 6318. Sand's recorded critique is preserved in a "letter to Edouard de Pompéry," no. 3082 (Jan. 1845), in *Correspondance*, VI, ed. Georges Lubin (Paris: Garnier Frères, 1964–75), 789.
4. E. J. Hobsbawm, *The Age of Revolution, 1789–1848* (New York: New American Library, 1962), 249.
5. Jean-Pierre Aguet, *Les Grèves sous la Monarchie de Juillet* (Geneva: Droz, 1954), 126.
6. Marguerite Thibert, *Le Féminisme dans le socialisme francais de 1830 à 1850* (Paris: Marcel Giard, 1926), 253ff.
7. *La Gazette des femmes* (July, 1836), 1. See Evelyne Sullerot's *Histoire de la presse féminine en France, des origines á 1848* (Paris: Armand Colin, 1966), 191–209, for the peculiar history of this journal.
8. See, for example: S. Joan Moon, "Feminism and Socialism: The Utopian Synthesis of Flora Tristan," in *Socialist Women and European Socialist Feminism in the Nineteenth and Early Twentieth Century*, ed. Marilyn J. Boxer and Jean H. Quataert (New York: Elsevier, 1978); Dominique Desanti, *A Woman in Revolt: A Biography of Flora Tristan*, trans. Elizabeth Zelvin (New York: Crown, 1976).
9. Jules-L. Puech, *La Vie et l'oeuvre de Flora Tristan, 1803–1844* (Paris: Marcel Rivière, 1925), 5–9.
10. Louis Chevalier, *Laboring Classes and Dangerous Classes in Paris during the First Half of the Nineteenth Century*, trans. Frank Jellinek (New York: Fertig, 1973), 409. See also Lynn Lees, "Metropolitan Types: London and Paris Compared," in *The Victorian City: Images and Realities*, v. I, ed. H. J. Dyos and Michael Wolff (London: Routledge & Kegan Paul, 1973), 414.
11. Hobsbawm, 215.
12. Chevalier, 201.
13. Ibid., 51.
14. Ibid., 54.
15. Ibid., 14.
16. Michelle Perrot, *Enquêtes sur la condition ouvrière en France au 19e siècle* (Paris: Microeditions Hachette, 1972), 38; Chevalier, 13; Friedrich Engels, *The Condition of the Working Class in England*, trans. W. O.

Henderson and W. H. Chaloner (Stanford: Stanford Univ. Press, 1968), 29.

17. See, for example: A. J. B. Parent-Duchâtelet, *De la prostitution dans la ville de Paris*, 2d ed., 2 vols. (Paris: Bailliére, 1837).

18. Chevalier, 47.

19. Flora Tristan, *Union ouvrière*, 3d ed. (Paris: Editions d'Histoire Sociale, 1844), 150. All subsequent references will appear in text as (*UO*). This work has been described as "the first published project of a world-wide Workers' International," by G. D. H. Cole, in his *Socialist Thought: The Forerunners* (London: Macmillan, 1962), 187.

20. See *Women, Work, & Family*, by Louise A. Tilly and Joan W. Scott (New York: Holt, Rinehart & Winston, 1978), for full discussion of this phenomenon.

21. Perrot remarks that most of these diagnosticians were "both descriptive and prescriptive," 9.

22. In *Tour de France . . . .*, Tristan left behind an outline of projected chapters (285–86), having announced the book's appearance for Jan. 1845 on the back cover of *Union ouvrière*.

23. Chevalier, 146.

24. Flora Tristan, *Promenades dans Londres, ou l'aristocratie & les prolétaires anglais* (1842), ed. François Bédarida (Paris: François Maspero, 1978). All subsequent references will appear in text as (*PR*).

25. Flora Tristan, *Nécessité de faire un bon accueil aux femmes étrangères* (Paris: Delauney, 1835), 9.

26. Ibid., 3.

27. Flora Tristan, *Pérégrinations d'une paria, (1833–1834)*, II (Paris: Arthus Bertrand, 1838), 123. Reprinted by Maspero, Paris: 1979.

28. *Pérégrinations*, II, 375. "Nowhere else on earth are women freer . . . than in Lima. There they reign. . . . One must observe to what extent the dress of these women favors and enhances their intelligence, allowing them to acquire the great liberty and dominating influence which they enjoy."

29. The example of la Présidente Gamarra was instructive. Her total rejection of the "feminine" was seen by Tristan to be the one major cause of her political demise. *Pérégrinations*, II, 454–56.

30. Ibid., preface, vii.

31. "Lettre de Victor Considérant à Flora Tristan," in Stéphane Michaud, 98.

32. Cf. Puech, 71–83; 88–94.

33. *Tour de France*, 82.

34. Ibid., 20.

35. Flora Tristan, *Méphis*, I (Paris: Ladvocat, 1838), 161. All subsequent references in the text will appear as (ME).

36. Norman Birnbaum, "Crisis of Industrial Society," in *Nineteenth-Century Cities: Essays in New Urban History*, ed. Stephen Thernstrom and Richard Sennett (New Haven: Yale Univ. Press, 1969), 422.

37. *Tour de France*, 153.

38. Louise A. Tilly and Joan W. Scott, "Women's Work and the

Family in Nineteenth-Century Europe," *Comparative Studies in Society and History*, 2, no. 1 (Jan. 1975), 5.

39. Lynn Lees, 422.

40. Cf. Engels, 158ff., *UO*, 54, in particular.

41. Puech, 116. A journalist for the *Revue de Progès* (Oct. 1, 1840), criticized "certain boldnesses unexpected from a woman," Puech, 114.

42. Michaud, "Lettre à une dame" (Paris, 1839?), 102.

43. Carl Schorske, "The Idea of the City in European Thought: Voltaire to Spengler," in *The Historian and the City*, ed. Oscar Handlin and John Burchard (Cambridge, Mass.: MIT Press, 1963), 104.

44. In contrast, as Schorske points out, neither Marx nor Engels "suggested that the clock be turned back; nor did either support the 'model community' solutions so favored by the nineteenth century utopians." Unlike Tristan, Engels "rescued the idea of the city by integrating its very vices into his economy of social salvation" (105, 107). Tristan did not live long enough to recognize the limitations of her plan.

45. See Maurice Agulhon, "Flora Tristan et la grève de l'Arsenal à Toulon," *Provence historique* (April-June 1957), 131–54. See also his *Une Ville ouvrière au temps du socialisme utopique: Toulon de 1815 à 1851* (Paris: Mouton, 1971); also Maximilien Rubel, "Flora Tristan et Karl Marx," *La Nef* (Jan. 1946), 68–76.

SUSAN RAVA

Marguerite Duras: Women's Language in Men's Cities

In the works of Marguerite Duras, the city inaugurates a conflict between the female search for authentic speech and the male linguistic domination. While Duras's work covers many genres, themes, and forms, her settings have frequently been cities: Duras uses those specific locations as starting points for an exploration of human relationships which concentrates on intensely charged dialogues between a limited number of characters. In Duras's earlier novels, using urban backdrops, she explores the particular difficulties a woman faces in adapting herself to the language men have created.[1] The city becomes a symbol of that language. Traversing great distances, from the mute solitude of the private home to the noisy public life of the city, women in Duras's works are typically not liberated—as they had hoped—but rather trapped by the linguistic and social constraints embodied by male language and culture. Duras's works repeatedly pose one problem: how do women participate in the activity of the city, exemplified by verbal power in the public realm, and still preserve the individual identity nurtured in the silent isolation of the home? This dilemma is the focus of my study, which will demonstrate that in cities—particularly cafés, parks, bars and hotel rooms—Duras's women struggle to seize male language, to use it, even to re-create it.

Born in Indochina in 1914 to a family of French colonials, Marguerite Duras came to France for her university studies and has remained there ever since. Her works draw on the great tradition

[35]

established by nineteenth- and twentieth-century French novels which has viewed the city as embodiment of male linguistic and political power. Activists, Balzacian *arrivistes*, revolutionaries, and seducers—all have derived some of their charm from the typically urban, masculine attribute of linguistic virtuosity. For such heroes the city has served as battlefield, apprenticeship, and proving ground. Yet while men have found in the city an arena for the exercise of linguistic and cultural dominance, women have been excluded from the challenges and traits of the urban environment, because they have been excluded from the masculine language the city enshrines.

Anne Desbaresdes in *Moderato cantabile*,[2] the young maid in *The Square*,[3] and Claire Lannes in *L'Amante anglaise*[4]—focal points of my study—have all been accustomed to silent isolation from the masculine mainstream of city life. While one critic has described that typically feminine silence as a deliberate protest against the language imposed by men, the three characters reveal not a conscious refusal of language but rather a difficulty making authentic use of it.[5] Although they begin in traditionally female domestic circumstances, the characters seek a change; the core of all three novels is the moment of speech, when the women break into urban life. Claire Lannes is accused of a murder which sets public bureaucracy in motion, offering her a chance for self-expression; the maid, in contrast, finds in an afternoon outing to the public square the occasion—and audience—for storytelling; in *Moderato*, finally, an anonymous city scream breaks into Anne's private world to free her for her first verbal—and public—adventure.[6]

The city's appeal lies fundamentally in the public expression it makes possible.[7] Yet paradoxically, that very freedom is difficult for women to attain precisely because of its linguistic character. Claire's "confession," in *L'Amante*, illustrates this paradox. Puzzled detectives and citizens gather in a café to try to solve a murder; their task is impossible because the head of the dismembered body has not been found. The body, and by extension the victim, has no identity because it lacks its rational center; the crime cannot be solved. In the context of *L'Amante*, the only way to solve the crime is to find the head, whose hiding place can be revealed only by Claire.

Claire's "confession" exemplifies the tension of the female experience in the city, the tension between the masculine demand for order (in language as well as in society) and the female resistance to ordering principles. Thus, male authority says that Claire's "confession" must be clear and concise; one word would close the matter, and Claire's extraneous rumination, which seems folly to the men interrogating her, would be forgotten. Society's only concern is the coherent reconstruction of the crime so that all of its parts fit together into a decipherable, identifiable whole. Yet Claire refuses to participate in this masculine ordering activity of "confession"; she wishes, instead, for her voluminous outpouring of words to stand. Although the reporters and detectives, like the city they symbolize, have no use for Claire's incoherent ramblings, her "confession" stands as both a social statement and a personal act. Transgressing linguistic order, she flaunts masculine teleology as well. She manipulates the interrogation to her own ends, producing not the result vital to the communal interest (in the masculine system of social order), but rather creative self-expression.

Anne Desbaresdes in *Moderato* and the maid in *The Square* encounter similarly paradoxical conflicts between verbal liberty and social restrictions in the city. For Anne, the small port city of *Moderato* first seems to represent a seductive freedom from the rigid, bourgeois life she has known as the wife of a factory executive. And for the maid, the city offers the answer to a vague malaise, her desire to be free in a way as yet undefined: " 'I know that women, even those who appear to be happy, often start wondering towards evening why they are leading the lives they do . . .' " (*Square*, 44). To both Anne and the maid, the unfamiliar urban world first seems to offer freedom for passion, anonymity, productive activity, even violence—all qualities outside traditional bourgeois roles for women. Ultimately, however, instead of finding social or economic freedom, purposeful physical work or emotional involvement, Anne, Claire Lannes, and the maid all discover their potential as linguistic creators. Thus, all three novels function as allegories "of the nature of language and the creative process itself."[8]

Yet while the city offers those three women the power of language use and creation, the terms of that power are dictated by men, and embodied in their world: the city. Although Anne initiates the conversation with Chauvin in *Moderato*, the bar in which they meet is an exclusively male domain, where Chauvin quickly takes control. He orders the wine, guides Anne to an isolated table, and—most important—directs their conversation. In his control of the dialogue, he even goes so far as to contradict himself, urging her at one moment to " 'Keep talking to me. Soon I won't ask you anything more,'" only to intervene soon after (*Moderato*, 105). Similarly, a detective attempts to direct Claire's "confession" in *L'Amante*, while the salesman in *The Square* makes conversational overtures to the maid.

Language belongs to the masculine world, where openings and guidance are male-generated; silence and nonverbal communication are, in contrast, woman's province. Duras prizes such self-expression as a special bond between women which men often misunderstand. For instance, Anne identifies her own birthing cries with the scream of a female murder victim, leading to an implicit connection between the women; her conversation is also punctuated with nonverbal utterances, moans, and murmurs. Such primordial, nonordered expression is incomprehensible, even frightening, to men, Duras implies in *Hiroshima, Mon Amour*. There, Duras creates the tale of a Frenchwoman who is punished for crying out.[9] Punishment means banishment to the cellar until the heroine promises not to cry out anymore. The episode emphasizes woman's need to curb her sounds in order to participate in a communal life of established words.

In spite of Duras's belief in the force of nonverbal sounds, she urges women to launch themselves in the public verbal arena. She articulates this sentiment in her conversations with Xaviere Gauthier:

If I am a professional, I take pen and paper . . . I try to translate the illegible [from within me] by using the vehicle of an egalitarian, undifferentiated language. So I deprive myself of the integrity of the inner darkness which, in me, balances my lived life. I rise from the interior mass, I project outside what I ought to do inside. . . . Woman must project out, be turned toward the outside like man.[10]

However, projecting out and talking freely do not seem to come naturally to the women in Duras's novels; for Anne, Claire, and the maid, primordial noises and maternal gestures come more easily. Furthermore, the vehicle for expression, at least within the novels, is not egalitarian. The conditions for dialogue are prescribed by men; in *Moderato*, for example, Chauvin controls who speaks, when, and how. In spite of obstacles, however, the three women produce unique verbal "works" distinct from those of their mentors. Their "works"—storytelling, dialogues, confessions, and commentaries—all reflect a rupture with customary linear or sequential constructions. Images and sensibilities welling up from the female unconscious manifest themselves in deformations of "normal" grammar and syntax.

In Claire's "confession," a sensitive intelligence (which men have construed as madness) is revealed as words pour forth unconstrained by convention:

> I had thoughts about happiness, and plants in winter, certain plants, certain things, food, politics, water, thoughts about water, cold lakes, the beds of lakes, lakes on the beds of lakes, about water, thirsty water that opens and swallows up and closes again, lots of thoughts about water. (*L'Amante*, 101)

Anthropomorphic and nonhierarchical, this sentence continues for almost a page, with fragments which—in French—are woven together by assonance or onomatopoeia. Duras also uses double-entendre, as in the passage above, and puns; for example, the title of the book, *L'Amante*, is juxtaposed to *la menthe* later in the text.

While Anne adapts externally to the routine of linear time—embodied in the city by the regular movement of the workers and by the siren—and to the masculine mode of exchange, language, she molds language to her own ends. She breaks, for example, with linear narrative chronology as she recounts the history of her house and its inhabitants simultaneously with her own past and with that of the murder victim. This she does by occasionally inserting the present verb tense into a survey of the past. Furthermore, she confounds conventional narration, where one voice concerns itself with a single narrative focus, in her multilayered recitation. Anne, thus, gives her language an individuality reflective of her inner self. In the public sphere she finds the possibility of verbal creation and of an audience as stimulus and sounding board.[11] While the city—as represented by the workers' routine—might seem to recede into the background of *Moderato*, it both goads and structures Anne's narration.

Anne's rupture with usual narrative techniques mirrors Duras's frequent transgression of novelistic conventions. Duras maximizes the evocative power of language by drawing both reader and characters into the creative moment. She does this by leaving both the sense and the structures of her texts open-ended; her audiences, both within and beyond the text, must help to create the work in progress. The detective in *L'Amante* clearly enunciates the shared nature of this text: " 'A book is starting to come into existence about the crime at Viorne. . . . It's up to you to set the book in motion. . . . We can let the tape recite what it remembers and the reader can take your place' " (L'Amante, 3).

Although the verbal creations of Duras's female characters at first glance seem private undertakings stimulated by the urban environment, Duras often emphasizes the communal, even fraternal, nature of verbal enterprise. The structure and linguistic organization of several of her texts elucidate this notion of collective, city-based effort, and Duras forces her public to participate in several ways. First, she avoids the traditional propensity to delineate people or situations by names. By downplaying the individuality which a proper name bestows on a character, Duras emphasizes urban anonymity and renders dialogue in its purest form, as in The Square.[12] Many characters have no given name at all, are identified only once or twice, or are merely referred to by pronouns. Conversations seesaw back and forth for pages without precise demarcation of the speaker—a procedure which compels the reader to retrace his or her steps or, more important, to create a character's individuality repeatedly during the act of reading. Consequently, individuality arises not from a given name, but rather from the complicity of audience and character alike in the creative moment.

An unusual modulation of French verb tenses in Moderato further heightens the reader's participation. During the dramatic conclusion of the dinner scene, when Anne flees her own party, Duras suddenly switches from the past tenses of previous chapters to the present and then to the future tense to describe Anne's vomiting. The shift implies a collective public which will decide the reality of the event, and colors Anne's physical rejection of her milieu with a paradoxical tint of the inevitable, yet unrealized act of refusal: "Anne Desbaresdes [note the use of her full, married name] will go upstairs. . . . She will go into the child's room. . . . And to the inviolable rhythm of her child's breathing she will vomit forth the strange nourishment that had been forced upon her" (Moderato, 133).

Duras frequently blurs the antecedents of her pronouns—an equivocation rare in the rationally constructed syntax of French—giving the impression of a text-in-the-making, where meaning is not an a priori given, but must be produced by a collaboration of reader and characters. For example, in the last paragraph of the French text of *Moderato*, the *patronne* turns up the radio as Anne leaves the bar: "La patronne augmenta le volume de la radio. Quelques hommes se plaignirent qu'*elle* fût trop forte à leur gré" (*Moderato*, 115, French text, emphasis added). Even though the English translates *elle* as *it*, apparently referring to the volume of the radio, the final sentence in French is ambiguous. *Elle* may well refer to Anne, who has just passed the group of men. Understood in this way, the passage presents a final condemnation by the group of workers who have already watched, commented upon, and judged the "adulterous" wife of one of the town's prominent industrialists. The comment reinforces the distance between Anne as an individual woman and the collective group of men—as unified, urban spokesmen. Furthermore, if taken as a collective assessment of Anne herself, the passage offers little hope that Anne can penetrate the closed and formal masculine world of the bar or—by extension—the city. *Forte* has several meanings—strong, loud, heavy in weight, for instance—as does the expression *à leur gré*, which may indicate personal taste or opinion: taken as a whole, the phrase may reflect a masculine view of Anne as object, just as the rigid finality of the formal literary past tense and imperfect subjunctive may emphasize Anne's lack of options.

In the province of prescribed language patterns no room exists for Anne's deformations; yet, paradoxically, her tools must be those of the men around her, and her audience must include that urban public. Women must, then, relate to the public when they move into the urban settings of *Moderato*, *The Square*, and *L'Amante*; they must measure its capacity for comprehension and extrapolation. Sometimes in Duras's texts, those urban audiences are explicit—characters like Chauvin with major catalytic roles, or like the working men in the bar in *Moderato* who function as a chorus, with a rigid moral code as basis for judgment. Sometimes, in contrast, the audience is only implicit: Duras reaches out of the text to the actual reader, urging her not only to witness but also to participate in the creative moment. So reader, intratextual listener, and character alike join in the generation of a story, spawned in the public world of the city. Not only does the city offer freedom of expression in Duras's works, then; it also holds out the possibility of communal verbal creation.

The very nature of such city-based freedom makes the city both a challenging and a problematic environment for the women in

Duras's texts. Drawn initially to the city because it promises them liberation from domestic routine and the freedom to explore themselves in companionship, passion, and work, Duras's women often find self-realization difficult in a world whose routine and values are male-controlled. Urban life offers neither the private, even silent, primeval security nor the ordered confinement of the home. In contrast, in the city women must relinquish the consolations and limitations of domestic life for the urban adventures of self-discovery, creativity, and interaction with an audience. Even though the "voyage" may lead to feelings of isolation, alienation, and anonymity, its positive culmination is the use of language—or of a chosen silence. Verbal production is the end result of urban activity, producing self-discovery for the maid (and the salesman) in *The Square*, self-revelation in *L'Amante*, and self-liberation in *Moderato*. Through verbal production, Duras's woman engages in the metaphorical "search for a word which would liberate her and which might be *identity* or that feminine version of the masculine *pouvoir* (power) which is *puissance* [potential and ability]."[13] Constrained to use the given tools of collective language, Duras's women struggle courageously, even painfully, to bring their own linguistic and narrative identities into the urban, public world.

NOTES

1. The theoretical base for this essay is my own, and represents an attempt to integrate theory and Duras's writings. The approach was generated in a group of women French professors which has been meeting in St. Louis since the winter of 1980. All members of the group are well grounded in French literature and in contemporary French feminist theory, be it psychoanalytic, linguistic, philosophical, or sociopolitical, according to personal bent. Each woman has brought papers, portions of readings, tapes, and thoughts on French theorists. Thus, the base for this essay developed and was tested during those meetings and was influenced by the support and thoughtful contributions of my friends Anna Amelung, Pierrette Daly, Maryann DeJulio, Mia DeWeer, Emily Guignon, Hannah Langsam, Marguerite Le Clézio, Lucy Morros, Christine Sharp, and Colette Winn. All of us have been marked by the works of Marie Cardinal, Hélène Cixous, Marguerite Duras, Luce Irigaray, Marcelle Marini, George Sand, and Monique Wittig, to name but a few.

2. Marguerite Duras, *Moderato cantabile*, trans. Richard Seaver in *Four Novels: The Square, Ten-Thirty on a Summer Night; The Afternoon of*

Mr. Andemas; Moderato Cantabile (New York: Grove, 1965). Originally published as *Moderato cantabile* in French (Paris: Editions de Minuit, 1958). Future references to this work will follow the citation in this form: *Moderato*, 15.

Moderato tells the story of a strange love affair between Anne Desbaresdes and Chauvin. Anne walks her son to piano lessons in the small port city where she lives. In the opening chapter, during a lesson, a piercing scream rises from a nearby café where Anne and her son find that a young woman has just been murdered by a lover or husband. The lure of the city, represented by the passion and violence of the crime, draws Anne back to the café where she meets Chauvin. The city as setting determines the length of Anne and Chauvin's meetings and provides commentators—workers who come and go regularly. Anne's story, therefore, is that of love and self-expression within an urban framework.

3. Marguerite Duras, *The Square*, trans. Richard Seaver in *Four Novels*. Future references to this work will follow the citation in this form: *Square*, 33.

The Square (1955), one of Duras's earliest works, is the story of a young governess who spends the afternoon in a public square with her young charge. There, by chance, she meets a traveling salesman. The salesman is just "passing through" while the young woman feels hopelessly anchored to her servile life. The city, portrayed as the square, offers a neutral, anonymous meeting place where all is possible and restraints do not exist. It, thus, can serve as a catalyst for the exploration of human communication.

4. Marguerite Duras, *L'Amante anglaise*, trans. Barbara Bray (New York: Grove, 1968). Future references to this work will follow the citation in this form: *L'Amante*, 97.

Originally published in French in 1967, *L'Amante anglaise* is a novel based on a news item (*un fait-divers*) about the murder and dismembering of a housekeeper—a crime probably committed by her employer. The same news item had generated an earlier play by Duras. In the three sections of the novel version, a detective interviews characters who have some apparent connection with the crime, settling finally on Claire Lannes as prime suspect. The city here is depicted as a bureaucratic, ordering force. Like other women characters cited, Claire is both stimulated and repressed by the city.

5. Marcelle Marini, *Territoires du féminin avec Marguerite Duras* (Paris: Editions de Minuit, 1977), 22.

6. Ibid., 18.

7. The notion that place confers possibility, even virtuality, upon characters marks the presentation of both men and women in French literature. In spite of romantic notions that the individual is supremely valuable and responsible, the collective potential of groups of people in towns, cities, or Paris shapes the desires, searches, and evolution of many literary figures, including some in Duras's works. See, for example, Diana Festa-McCormick, *The City as Catalyst* (Cranbury, N.J.: Associated Univ. Presses, 1979).

8. Evelyn H. Zepp, "Language as Ritual in Marguerite Duras's *Moderato cantabile,*" *Symposium* 30 (1976), 257.

9. Marguerite Duras, *Hiroshima, Mon Amour* (Paris: Gallimard, 1960), 90–91. Future references to this work will follow the citation in this form: *Hiroshima*, 21.

Famous as a film by Alain Resnais, *Hiroshima* recounts a brief love affair between a French woman and a Japanese man. The place is Hiroshima, "le terrain commun" (11), a city where, as Duras explains, universal values are laid bare in the aftermath of disaster.

10. Marguerite Duras, *Les Parleuses (Entretiens avec Xavière Gauthier)* (Paris: Editions de Minuit, 1974), 50, 101 (my translation).

11. For further discussion of women and language, see Luce Irigaray's *Ce Sexe qui n'en est pas un* (Paris: Editions de Minuit, 1977). See discussions of women and language on 28–29, 72–82, 86–87, and 96–101.

12. Furthermore, in Duras's film, *India Song*, characters never converse directly, but instead anonymous voices emerge from the background. The viewer may or may not attach the voices to certain characters, may or may not distinguish individual traits in these disembodied sources of words.

While the city is mere background in this film, the distinction between public life and private is a major theme. When the Vice-Consul says he must make a public act, he chooses to scream as he breaks his private silence.

13. Marguerite LeClézio, "Mother and Motherland: The Daughter's Quest for Origins," National Women's Studies Association, Bloomington, Ind., May 1980.

ELYSE BLANKLEY

Return to Mytilène:
Renée Vivien and the City of Women

————————————◆————————————

Mytilène, à travers les siècles disparates,
Du fond de mon passé, je retourne vers toi.
　　　　Renée Vivien, "En débarquant à Mytilène"

RENÉE VIVIEN HAS FOR DECADES remained a shadowy, exotic figure on the fringe of decadent/aesthete French poetry. Born
Pauline Mary Tarn of Anglo-American parents in London in 1877,
Vivien wrote finely crafted French lyrical verse, although her
native tongue was English. She has variously been described as a
Sapphic poet who was the lover of Natalie Barney; a brilliant
neurotic writer who died of self-inflicted starvation in 1909, when
she was only thirty-two years old; and a tragic emblem of the
femme damnée so cherished by writers like Baudelaire and Swinburne. While all these descriptions ring true, none captures her
as hauntingly as does Colette's portrait: "[She was] veiled in
black or purple, almost invisible in the scented darkness of the
immense rooms barricaded with leaded windows, the air heavy
with curtains and incense."[1] Colette was struck not just by the
spectral unearthly figure of Vivien herself but by her oppressive
surroundings, as well: stagnant air, luridly gleaming Chinese
masks and mute instruments crowding the walls, and windows
literally nailed shut.[2] Although this description could come from
any number of symbolist poems or novels, it is all the more poi-
gnant for being real and not imagined. The vision of the nailed

[45]

window is particularly resonant because literature by women abounds in images of enclosure.[3] Dozens of heroines like Jane Eyre and Catherine Earnshaw have chafed at the homes—and roles—in which patriarchal culture has locked them. Renée Vivien's imprisonment strikes us as odd, however, because it was self-imposed: why did she choose to turn her back on Paris and live, instead, in a tomb nailed shut by her own hand?

One critic maintains that Vivien's self-destructiveness, of which her self-imprisonment was a symptom, was the inevitable product of the nineteenth-century male imagination's "doomed lesbian" image.[4] There are striking parallels, for example, between Renée Vivien and Swinburne's Lesbia Brandon, both of whom drink eau de cologne and both of whom literally poison themselves, one with alcohol and the other with opium. Vivien may have internalized this image and fulfilled its tragic prophecy in her own life; she found "la splendeur de la Mort" a seductive image, as many of her poems attest. But were her imagery restricted to morbid symbolist lovers and their deadly lesbian embraces, one might conclude that Vivien's verse—and life—sadly burlesques an aesthete model.

Vivien, however, did not simply transform herself into a tragic emblem mirrored in her verse. Her walls separated her from Paris, the real city, so that she might imaginatively create—indeed, re-create—a visionary female city. Like an archeologist exhuming a lost civilization, Vivien rediscovered with her pen the splendid ancient city of Mytilene, on the island of Lesbos in the Aegean. While the trams and carriages of Paris rattled outside her closed windows, Vivien, self-designated reincarnation of Sappho in the modern world, bridged twenty-seven centuries of patriarchal culture to recover both a matriarchal community and a glorious female genealogy. Mytilene, Vivien's city of women, would be a recurrent artistic preoccupation throughout her brief life.

"Mytilene, jewel and splendor of the sea," sings Vivien in her 1906 collection, *A l'heure des mains jointes*.[5] Lesbos unfolds in Vivien's imagination as an island of female freedom, the perfumed glory of the Aegean, where women's caresses are like "melodious poems,"[6] and swaying female choruses chant on moonlit shores. Vivien's utopian vision transports her hundreds of miles from her home on the avenue du Bois. Paris of the Belle Epoque, however, showed a similar interest in women loving women—so much so, in fact, that by 1900, Paris, in the eyes of several observers, had become a veritable "Paris-Lesbos."[7] Lesbianism was deliciously *à la mode* among some Parisians at the turn of the century. Madame Henri Germain, through whose fashionable salon passed *Tout-Paris* between 1880 and 1910, recalls the whispered confidences of women who'd begun to prefer their own sex: "All the noteworthy women are doing it."[8]

But for those women whose lesbianism was more than changing fashion, like this year's hats or bustles, *fin de siècle* Paris seemed equally accommodating. The nineteenth century witnessed the emergence of secret urban homosexual communities throughout Europe, and Paris was the city most tolerant of deviance (it was to Paris, one might recall, that Oscar Wilde fled in 1897 after his scandalous trial for homosexuality in England). In the words of Natalie Barney, the lesbian doyenne of a brilliant Parisian literary salon, "Paris has always seemed to me the only city where you can live and express yourself as you please."[9] Women could gather, for example, at lower-class haunts such as the Palmyre restaurant in Montmartre, where lesbians, according to Colette, "felt safe within the low-ceilinged room beneath the eye of a frank proprietress who shared their predilections."[10] Here women's discourse could flourish: "once the slow-thinking male had been banished, every message from woman to woman became clear and overwhelming, restricted to a small but infallible number of signs."[11]

Women's gathering places were not restricted, however, to these friendly dives and basement rooms dim with tobacco smoke; lesbianism had emerged at all levels of the social scale, and many highly visible Parisian women were making known their preference for the same sex. In her novel *Idylle saphique*, Liane de Pougy, the Belle Epoque's famed high-class courtesan, celebrated her lesbian affair with Natalie Barney. Sarah Bernhardt, who was obsessed by cross-dressing and costume, formed a semiofficial couple with Louise Abbéma.[12] And in secluded salons like that of the ex-Marquise de Belboeuf, aristocratic lesbians from all over Europe gathered in discreet elegance: "Baronesses of the Empire, canonesses, lady cousins of Czars, illegitimate daughters of grand-dukes, exquisites of the Parisian bourgeoisie, and also some aged horsewomen of the Austrian aristocracy."[13] Paris was thus the international locus for lesbianism, and Natalie Barney's salon in Neuilly was perhaps the most famous meeting place for women of fortune and talent. In her garden, young heiresses and artists presented plays to an almost exclusively female audience that might include Colette, the ex-Marquise de Belboeuf, poet Lucie Delarue-Mardrus, heiress Eva Palmer, actress Marguerite Moreno, Mata Hari— and, at times, Renée Vivien herself. Although an impartial observer might find these garden spectacles embarrassingly theatrical and self-consciously bohemian, they nonetheless represented Barney's early efforts to re-create Lesbos in Paris, a project that in later years would flower at her rue Jacob salon, where she established the Académie des Femmes to promote contemporary literature by women.

With Lesbos thriving in at least one Parisian garden, Vivien need not have looked any further than her own back yard, so to speak, to discover a supportive female community. But her artistic vision resolutely directed her imagination to Sappho and Mytilene, celebrated in dozens of Vivien's poems as well as in her translations of Sappho. The years of Vivien's poetic power, 1904 to 1909, were also years of mysterious seclusion for Vivien. And here appears a paradox: while distancing herself from the lesbian community that might have nurtured her art, Vivien nonetheless anchored her artistic preoccupation in seas that had been exhaustively explored by almost every major male French writer of the nineteenth century. Love among women graces the pages of Balzac, Zola, Pierre Louÿs, Gautier, and Baudelaire, whose lesbian portraits in *Les Fleurs du Mal* remain the *sine qua non* of decadence, imitated by scores of less talented poets and novelists.[14] The nineteenth-century "vice of lesbianism," however, was fundamentally a fantasy created by the male imagination and perpetuated to shock and to stimulate. Despite the proliferation of lesbian disguises—whether of Zola's Nana, Gautier's bisexual Mademoiselle de Maupin, or Balzac's Marquise de St. Réal— these women are set in motion to cavort in front of the male eye poised at the keyhole. The lesbian in nineteenth-century literature is actually a kind of specialized prostitute, argues French critic Jean-Pierre Jacques.[15] Indeed, writers and artists have long regarded lesbians and prostitutes as twin exfoliations of the same rootstock. It is well known, for example, that Toulouse-Lautrec frequented the Rat Mort restaurant to observe prostitutes dance in lesbian embraces. Larousse refers to Lesbos in his definition of "prostitute" from the 1865–1876 *Grand Dictionnaire universel du*

XIXe siècle.[16] The sapphist/whore connection was so well understood by the turn of the century that Belle Epoque "pleasure guides" to Paris extol the brothels whose vestals guard the secret love practices that were so honored on Lesbos.[17] Subtle varieties of erotic vice differentiated Paris's bordellos from those of any other European capital (as one pleasure guide boasts),[18] and the lesbian couple was the crowning jewel of a Parisian brothel. In the lowest terms of encoded international erotic language, "lesbian" at the turn of the century signified a Parisian erotic refinement.

For Vivien, Paris was thus a double-edged sword offering both free sexual expression and oppressive sexual stereotyping. It might cultivate lesbianism like an exotic vine, but it would never nourish it. In front of Vivien—and, indeed, every lesbian—yawned the immense, unbridgeable chasm separating men's perceptions of lesbian women and lesbian women's perceptions of themselves. Moreover, lesbianism's public image might enjoy a certain vogue in limited circles, but for women actually living the life style, each precious freedom was extracted at a price. Few women were able to live as bravely as Natalie Barney; most, in fact, grew weary of playing the sex-role game according to Paris's rules—rules more painful because masked by many illusory freedoms. The lesbian bars and restaurants, for example, remained largely a secret network easily disrupted by outsiders gawking at the "inverts," whose sexual preference represented more than just a fashion. Female cross-dressing was circumscribed by French law, which prohibited transvestism without a special permit from the prefect of police[19] (and, as Colette comments, "Papa" Lépine, the prefect circa 1907, "never could take lightly the question of women in men's clothes").[20] Some women "gave up the struggle, and the sect's most stubborn proselytes never crossed the street or left their carriage without putting on, heart pounding, a long plain cloak which gave them an excessively respectable look and effectively concealed their masculine attire."[21] Thus Paris's comforting lesbian "islands" were surrounded by treacherous waters indeed.

In 1900 Renée Vivien faced the challenge of redeeming Sappho from male authors who had exploited Lesbos as a form of thinly disguised pornography or as a shocking affront to bourgeois morality. She might not completely purge her verse of its Baudelarian borrowings—serpents, jewelry, night journeys, and such—but she would reject the Parisian Gomorrah in favor of an authentic metaphor for the glorious possibilities of women loving women. Lesbos remained a silent island, unarticulated and hence invalidated by literature. Through the lens of Vivien's verse, the myopic nineteenth century would "see" Mytilene for the first time—not as a Parisian erotic object, but as a source of female power.

Vivien's Mytilene is a fertile landscape, its vines and orchards blazing under profoundly blue skies. In "En débarquant à Mytilène" ("Landing at Mytilene"), Vivien addresses this "melodious isle" so "propitious" to the caresses of women. Its golden shores, "heavy with the asiatic perfume of jasmine," provide an exotic setting for the poet and her lover, whom Sappho receives. Yet the sensuality that Vivien redefines on Lesbos is no lurid outgrowth of its lush vegetation; instead, these lesbian kisses have the softness of velvet, she says in "Psappha revit" ("Sappho Lives Again"). Far from the vulgar, terrifying sexual overtures of men, whom she feared and despised,[22] Vivien discovers a gentle female eroticism characterized more by tenderness than by desire ("Le désir est en nous moins fort que la tendresse"). Its delicate caresses make lesbian love the greatest of all loves ("Notre amour est plus grand que toutes les amours").

When Vivien insists in "Psappha revit" that she has conserved the rites of Lesbos ("Certaines d'entre nous ont conservé les rites / De ce brûlant Lesbos . . ."), she speaks not as a male-imagined sapphist prostitute in a *fin de siècle* Parisian pleasure guide but as a woman who understands the subtleties of love among women. Her male predecessors working in the same genre, however, fail to share that understanding and hence shape the contours of a very different lesbian experience. In his "Songs of Bilitis," for example, Pierre Louÿs's description of Bilitis's "marriage" with Mnasidika, a young maiden, reads like a catalog of sensual delights. Sappho herself, pictured as a sexual predator ready to snag an unwary woman, is priestess of a sensual world composed of so many burning thighs, crushed lips, and breasts fluttering like birds. Baudelaire's "Lesbos" is a similar pageant of concupiscence. His island is a "land of hot and langorous nights" where women "caress the ripe fruits of their nubility" in their "mirrors," an act of "sterile voluptuousness."[23] These women touch one another for the benefit of the male audience that watches, just as it might do in a Parisian brothel. Indeed, the absent male is indisputably the scene's reference point, because "sterile" caresses define these women by what they lack (i.e., men, with whom one might share "fertile" heterosexual caresses). Both these authors rob Lesbos of the tenderness that Vivien finds there. Like men who have paid at the brothel's entrance, both Louÿs and Baudelaire watch sexual performances in a fantasy world where all extraneous details have been eliminated. Not surprisingly, Baudelaire's lesbian lovers exist in a vacuum, removed from other women; Louÿs's Bilitis lives among the women of Lesbos, but her contact with them is limited to the exchange of gossip. Thus the female community and its interaction are either trivialized or ignored.

If Vivien appeared to ignore her own female community surrounding her in Paris, she did so because her feminism and lesbianism guided her toward a vision of complete female isolation on Lesbos. Mytilene protects its female tribe from being censured by a disapproving world or transformed into an emblem of erotic perversion. Vivien can live on Mytilene "without shame, without fear or remorse" ("Nos jours sans impudeur, sans crainte ni remords"). "What do we care about the judgment of men," she asks in "Parole à l'Amie" ("Words to My Friend"). Far from the prying male eye, the lesbian choir will welcome the poet and her lover into a world where one may truly live as one pleases.[24]

By turning her back on Paris, Vivien dismisses patriarchal culture's definition of women. Mytilene, however, is not merely a female refuge but an imaginative attempt to formulate major cultural revisions. Take, for example, the name "Mytilene." Many of the nineteenth-century and *fin de siècle* writers, including Vivien, used the name interchangeably with "Lesbos." But Mytilene is also a city on the island, and the name thus carries both pastoral and urban connotations. This is of particular interest to our understanding of Vivien's vision because the fortuitous onomastic ambiguity echoes a profound truth about the island itself: on Mytilene, the lesbian community can escape its urban hiding places and move openly as well as freely between city and country. Unlike the small lesbian "islands" perched precariously above water in Paris, Mytilene is a firm island that can be as large as a continent or a universe. Lesbos is Vivien's gigantic psychic map: her movement there is limited only by her imagination.

Interior and exterior spatial restrictions placed on Vivien in

Paris are likewise modified on Mytilene. "Intérieur" is a gentle poem in praise of the poet's private space that she shares with her lover. The poem addresses the sensual and sacred dimension of her experience behind closed doors—her soul, like a rose, blooms in her "motionless garden" blessed by domestic objects such as furniture and hearth. More important, the poem underscores the poet's need to keep the world *out*: to defend her happiness against the harsh looks of others and the noises outside ("Contre les regards durs et les bruits du dehors"). She continues:

> Je ne sais plus si l'on médit de nous, ni si
> L'on parle encore. . . . Les mots ne font plus mal ici.
> . . . .
> Loin des pavés houleux où se fanent les roses,
> Où s'éraillent les chants, tenons les portes closes . . .
>
> [I no longer know if people speak ill of us, or if
> They still speak of us. . . . Words no longer hurt us here.
> . . . .
> Far from the turbulent cobblestones where the roses wilt,
> Where voices become hoarse, let us keep the doors closed. . . .]

This is Lesbos in Paris. The flower of shared female sensuality will bloom, however, only if the world is vigilantly excluded. Vivien's delicate rose unfolding within her motionless garden is both a sexual and a political symbol: sexual, because it represents the female genitalia, which must be protected from a violating phallus; political, because it represents secret female power, a miraculous treasure that must be shielded from patriarchal culture's harsh withering rays. The scene is luminous but guarded: one listens uneasily for the tumult outside that might quickly upset the delicate balance within. Contrast this scene with "En débarquant à Mytilène," which blurs the boundaries between interior and exterior. On Mytilene, Vivien can exchange her dark, shuttered Parisian boudoir for shorelines opening out to the sea and sky: "I rediscover your waves, your olive trees, your vines, / And I dissolve and fade into your azure skies. / . . . we lay our bodies along your beds of dried seaweed." Gone is the need for secrecy and fear because interiors and exteriors have equal symbolic weight; there is no reason to hide on the magical island.

Mytilene in fact demands that its female lovers redefine the sexual politics of space that have dominated their lives. In Paris,

Vivien must fearfully guard her private world from discovery and disruption. That fear parallels the lovers' fear of the intruding morning sun, as expressed in "II" of "Sonnets" in *Etudes et préludes*:

> Les doigts [de l'aurore] ont effeuillé les lotos du
>   sommeil,
> Et la virginité farouche de la lune
> A préféré la mort au viol du soleil.[25]

> [(Dawn's) fingers pulled the petals from the lotuses
>   of sleep,
> And the moon's fierce virginity
> Preferred death to the rape of the sun.]

These lines juxtapose the basic symbolic bifurcation undergirding western civilization: the dark lunar female impulse contrasts with the Apollonian sun that stands for male reason. Rape and violation are particularly apt images because Vivien, a fierce virgin locked within her dim Parisian rooms, would rather die than be physically or spiritually compromised by Paris's patriarchal culture basking in the sunlight of its male superiority and power. Vivien's staunch refusal allows her to maintain her integrity, but her barred doors and windows also mark the limits of her power.

Mytilene, though, removes these hateful restrictions. In "Vers Lesbos" ("Toward Lesbos"), the timorous lovers journeying to the island at night fear the coming dawn, and they listen apprehensively to the "troubling unknown voices" that reach them from the shore. They fear Lesbos as might any exiles who view with uncertainty the shorelines that define their new home. Yet their fears are more deeply rooted, for these women so long unaccustomed to the light (after years spent in secrecy and seclusion) can barely imagine a sunlit world that will not wither the delicate petals of the rose—that is, a world in which female sexuality and self-definition may flourish openly and with impunity. They have faith in this new dawn, however, because "Happiness is over there . . . one must risk everything" on the magic isle. Vivien's image echoes a similar dawn heralded in Emily Dickinson's poem "There is a morn by men unseen—." Dickinson describes a "different dawn" that breaks over a distinctly female world where "maids upon remoter green" dance and play, perpetually on holiday. And like Vivien, Dickinson also shut herself inside to avoid the stark gaze of "the man of Noon." In the world's eyes, Vivien's interiors are impenetrably dark. But the poet can hear the ancient musicians returning, and she turns her heart, as in "Sunrise on the Sea," toward the "sun, the songs, and the ideal."[26]

While Mytilene eliminates spatial barriers, it alters temporal boundaries, as well. In "En débarquant à Mytilène," Lesbos is Vivien's key to a glorious female past that holds her "antique soul" and the "echo of lyres and voices." Mytilene emerges from the depths of her past ("du fond de mon passé"), implying that this reality has been lived but now lies forgotten, like so many other Amazon communities lost in culture's amnesia.[27] Vivien, however, remembers Mytilene with the conviction of one who has lived there before. And indeed she has, for the lovers stretched on Mytilene's shore are the same lovers who lay on its beds of seaweed in the seventh century B.C. When Vivien asks Mytilene to be today's altar for the ecstasies of yesterday ("Sois l'autel aujourd'hui des ivresses d'hier"), she connects both spiritual and sensual impulses in an ecstatic timeless communion. Paris 1900 would deny that union, for its literary images of lesbian women so often degrade their sensuality and ignore altogether their spirituality: the lesbian is a valuable commodity on the sexual market, but her soul is damned. By abolishing time, which fixes her in the wretched present, Vivien frees herself to discover her true community in the past.

The mirror that history holds up to Vivien in Belle Epoque Paris reflects a terrifying, distorted image of lesbian women. Mytilene is Vivien's only true reflecting mirror. Here women are not martyred and buried on culture's crossroad, as is Woolf's Judith Shakespeare in *A Room of One's Own*; instead, the poet's body—her mirror-link with the lovers on Lesbos centuries ago—recapitulates the glory of that brilliant community. "Our bodies are sisterly mirrors" of the ancient Lesbian women, says Vivien in "Psappha revit" ("Nos corps sont pour leurs corps un fraternel miroir"). Like Alice tumbling through her looking glass, Vivien is pulled toward Lesbos through the female mirror/body. This redefinition of the body is particularly important, because real mirrors have often betrayed women by reflecting male-created images: the body is coiffed, painted, and clothed like a decorative object to be sold at culture's marketplace— marriage—and enshrined in the home. Indeed, as Hélène Cixous suggests, a woman's traditional fascination with the mirror is not narcissistic but *anti*-narcissistic, for women have fallen in love with patriarchal culture's definition of their flesh.[28] Trapped within the body/object, the woman's soul struggles to close the eerie disjunction between inner and outer selves. On Mytilene, however, souls are not closed in bodies that are ill-fitting garments sewn by the male imagination; the self reflected in Lesbos's mirror/body is not man's image of woman but woman's image of herself.

Mme E. de Gramont, the ex-Duchesse de Clermont-Tonnerre, recalls Vivien with a description that provides an interesting gloss to the mirror image. "My country," wrote Vivien while traveling, is "the Bois de Boulogne." Comments de Gramont: "The lake in the Bois attracted her; between the twin mirrors of sky and water, she glided along in nocturnal boats."[29] Like a Lady of Shalott living in her world of art that mirrors the world around her, Vivien lives in the mirror-world of her lesbian vision, surrounded by female reflections. And just as Vivien's mirror-country lies hidden within a Parisian wood, so she, too, represents a secret lesbian island floating in Paris.

To be sure, Paris was not always an environment from which Vivien wished to escape. She was drawn to Paris by the same freedoms that attracted other lesbian women, such as Natalie Barney. Until the age of thirteen, Vivien had lived with her family in Paris and had attended school there. With her widowed mother and younger sister she returned to England in 1890, where she remained for eight years until after her presentation at court. As soon as she came of age in 1898 and became eligible to receive her inheritance from her paternal grandfather, she left her mother and sister in London and hastened back to Paris, which would be her home until her death in 1909.[30] In some sense, Paris would always be Vivien's "loved and longed-for city," as she says in her novel, *A Woman Appeared to Me (Une femme m'apparut)*. One critic observes that Vivien was drawn to Paris because she could easily lead a semicloistered, semiworldly existence there,[31] which she did when she first arrived. She and Barney, together with an English poet, Olive Custance, even made plans in 1901 to revive in Paris the golden age of Sappho. Vivien's devotion to Paris is further demonstrated by her decision to relinquish both fatherland (England) and mother tongue (English) in favor of Paris and the French language—to approximate, that is, a physical and linguistic exile in order to discover an invigorating space in life and language.

But Paris was not enough. As long as it restricted the freedom of lesbian women and used them as symbols of perversion, Vivien would dream of a radically different world on Mytilene. In *A Woman Appeared to Me*, she challenges patriarchal culture's repressive attitudes, personified in the character of Petrus, the scholar who hints that Sappho's lesbian loves are vulgar. San Giovanni, the androgyne and Vivien's mouthpiece in the novel, responds: "I accuse you . . . of being unable to conceive of a love at once ardent and pure, like a white flame. That was the sort Psappha vowed to her melodious adorers."[32] Petrus, for whom lesbians cannot possibly be more than exciting sexual athletes, shares a familiar point of view with some of his Parisian male peers, in whose voyeuristic eyes female couples writhe like performers. When Petrus leaves the salon, "one feels the need to open the windows and shake the hangings" (7).

If the world around her could not be changed, it could at least be excluded. In "Sur la place publique" ("At the Public Square"), Vivien uses poetry to shut out the city. Taking her harp to "the city with blue roofs," she sings in the public square, and her own music so intoxicates her that she doesn't at all hear the noise of the market ("dans l'enivrement de ma propre musique, / Je ne percevais point la rumeur du marché"). Shutting out the greedy haggling and jeering, Vivien listens to the wise trees who have spoken to her from silent forests ("Car je me souvenais que les arbres très sages / M'avaient parlé, parmi le silence des bois"). She sings until the market is empty; she sings "for the joy of singing." Poetry is thus a healing strength, a shield between Vivien and a hostile world. In the midst of the city she listens to a wise voice within her, giving her strength and guiding her toward a world of joy—that world, of course, is her Mytilene.

Even when the sacred woods have lost their power to heal wounds created by the world's censure, poetry will still be Vivien's refuge, as she declares in "Nous irons vers les Poètes" ("We Will Go to the Poets"). "The world has always been cruel to women" ("le monde a toujours été cruel aux femmes"); but the poet and her lover can forget this world by escaping to the realm of the poets ("Nous entrerons dans le royaume des poètes, / Le merveilleux royaume où chantent les poètes"). Poetry thus represents a kind of salvation and refuge for Vivien. And yet poetry has always been a troublesome medium for women, as recent feminist critics have discovered, because it raises questions about female poetic authorship.[33] If verse demands that women poets be assertive and authoritative (qualities that are traditionally *male*), what woman will risk baring herself to a jeering audience that insists, as it does to Woolf's Lily Briscoe, women "can't paint; can't write"? Mytilene is Vivien's answer, for it is a symbolic space in the female imagination that frees the poet from culture's gender judgments. Her audience is female, the "beautiful young women" whom she addresses in "Vous pour qui j'écrivis" ("You for Whom I Wrote"). Her voice is radiant with all the power of Lesbos's glorious past because Sappho herself inspires Vivien with her "harmonious breath" ("De ton harmonieuse haleine / Inspire-nous, Psappha!")[34] Sustained and validated by antiquity, Vivien's verse builds "emerald palaces" in which one may breathe and "dream and finally be free" ("l'on rêve et l'on est libre enfin").

Lesbos remained a great unknown imaginary territory for Paris 1900, despite its many appearances in literature of the period. In becoming Mytilene's first true modern apologist, Vivien did more than reappropriate the pen of Baudelaire, Zola, or Gautier; she rediscovered female poetic tools long hidden in history. When San Giovanni in *A Woman Appeared to Me* protests the legend of Sappho's supposed husband, her humorous rejoinder centers on art: "The man's name, Kerkolas—he who wields the pen— . . . [is] sufficient evidence of the kind of low humor that invented the tale" (7). No man need introduce Lesbos to the Word; indeed, no man can, for Lesbos has emerged from male pens as a sinful Parisian pleasure palace. Vivien, finding her own female voice, retraces the Mytilene that stirs in her memory. Her sister poet-prophets fashion Lesbos's emerald palaces:

> . . . Nous entrerons, grâce aux poètes fraternels,
> Dans le pays créé par leurs vers éternels.
> Dan l'harmonie et le clair de lune éternels.
>
> [We will enter, thanks to our sister poets,
> Into the land created by their eternal verse,
> Into the harmony and the eternal moonlight.]

By filling Mytilene's palaces with glorious queens who stretch from antiquity to the present—Lilith, Eve, Cassiopeia, Aphrodite, Bathsheba, Cleopatra, Lady Jane Gray—Vivien speaks through a female genealogy that is reborn in her body. Like Sylvia Plath, Vivien has a "self to recover, a queen," for she must rediscover female power if she too is to be "reine dans mon royaume" ("queen of my realm"). "Renée Vivien" is ultimately more than a French pseudonym created to facilitate her acceptance by the French literary establishment. Pauline Tarn is "reborn" ("renée") in poetry, reborn as her own splendid powerful queen ("reine-née") in "Viviane":

> Son pouvoir féminin s'insinue à la brune:
> Elle devient irrésistible au clair de lune.
> . . . .
> Vous l'avez pressentie et vous l'avez rêvée
> Longuement, et surtout vous l'avez retrouvée.
> . . . .
> [Her female power insinuates itself in the dusk:
> She becomes irresistible in the moonlight.
> . . . .
> You have had presentiments of her, and you have
>   dreamed of her
> For a long time, and above all you have recovered her.]

In 1904, Vivien traveled to Mytilene, the first of a series of visits to the island. She was accompanied on this trip by Natalie Barney, and the two women set up housekeeping in a pair of interconnected villas, where they wrote, swam, walked, and made love while fragrant Mytilene unfolded before them like a dreamy perfumed paradise.[35] It seemed a perfect idyll, and Vivien spent her days translating Sappho. The trip to Lesbos apotheosized Vivien's dream of a female colony, a dream she had nourished since the turn of the century, when she first began studying ancient Greek with Charles-Brun and Eugène Ledrain. Her pilgrimage to Lesbos would render that dream palpable by overlaying the myth with its counterpart in reality. Other feminists, such as Charlotte Perkins Gilman, might give birth to radiant utopian dreams. But Gilman's Herland is located on the topographical map of the imagination only; Lesbos, on the other hand, actually exists.

Real and ideal, however, rarely unite harmoniously. Despite her dreamy interlude with Barney, the first trip was marred by the inevitable clash of vision and reality. When, for example, Vivien and Barney landed on the island, their boat was greeted

by the strains of a popular Parisian song blaring from a phonograph. "Viens poupoule, viens," insisted the refrain (this translates roughly as "come on, baby, come on"). Vivien, expecting
the melodious sounds of a lesbian choir, was understandably
upset by her coarse welcome.[36] While she dreamed, as did T. S.
Eliot in *The Waste Land*, of the inexplicable splendor of Ionian
white and gold, the world thrust the typist's vulgar phonograph
in her face. The refrain, however, is more disturbing still, for the
word "poupoule" echoes both "poupée" (doll) and "poule"
(slang for whore or tart). At the very instant that Vivien, far from
Paris, set foot on her magic isle, Paris's insistent presence addressed her as it might a public woman in a brothel. What irony,
then, crowns Vivien's escape; for on Mytilene she is welcomed by
an innuendo reminding her that "lesbian" and "whore" are inex-
tricably wound together in a degrading sexual stereotype that she
is powerless to change or to prevent, even on Mytilene.[37] Her real
landing, so antithetical to her idealized landing, could not have
seemed a particularly auspicious beginning.

Other disappointments awaited Vivien. The native women, for
example, proved to be unattractive and disappointing descen-
dants of Sappho.[38] Vivien had no desire to cultivate their friendship, and so her proposed community of women went no further
than the garden walls of her villa. Despite Vivien's avowal to stay
forever on the island with Barney, their paradise was interrupted
by the arrival of a letter from the Baroness Hélène van Zuylen, an
immensely wealthy woman who was one of Vivien's lovers and
who wielded a terrifying influence over her. As a result of this
imbroglio, the pilgrimage was cut short and the dream of
Mytilene shattered. Vivien returned to France with the knowledge that Lesbos could not protect her from the phantoms of
Paris, whether they be personal or cultural.

The vision of Lesbos, however, was too deeply embedded in
Vivien's psyche for her simply to abandon it after her disappointing initial visit to Mytilene. She maintained her villa on the island
and returned there almost every year until her death in 1909.
These visits—sometimes several visits in the same year—rarely
lasted more than a week,[39] a surprising fact when one considers
what distances had to be covered and what primitive transporta-
tion had to be endured to reach Lesbos, which was still a remote
island under Turkish rule. Her odd "commuting" to Lesbos inspired the natives to comment that "she arrives with the swal-

lows."[40] She came alone or with other women; but she remained aloof from the village inhabitants, in whose eyes this strange English woman and her wanderings were legendary (she was even rumored to be a secret daughter of the king of England!)[41] Thus Vivien seemed as mysterious a figure on Mytilene as many people judged her to be in Paris. Had she, in fact, simply traded one cloister for another?

What emerges from Vivien's voyages to Mytilene is the ironic similarity between her Parisian apartment and her Lesbian refuge. In Paris, walls and locked doors protect Vivien's "motionless garden." The garden encircling her villa on Lesbos was likewise guarded by walls—*and* a local young man hired specifically to discourage the curious from approaching the villa.[42] Vivien forbade this night watchman from entering the house or even speaking to her, and he was instructed to remain as invisible as possible, retreating whenever he heard her footsteps in the garden. His presence, however, clearly delineated the boundaries limiting her dreamscape that had become an actual landscape. Even in the gardens of Lesbos, Vivien could not avoid the web of patriarchal power surrounding her.

If her hideaway in Lesbos was as circumscribed as her shuttered rooms in Paris, why did Vivien continue her puzzling commute between the two? One of her letters from Mytilene may help explain: "God, I hate Paris so much! And why does one live there when there are such beautiful countries where one is free because one is a stranger, alone?"[43] Paris, bathed in the prosaic light of day, could not be her magic island; it was indifferent to her poetry, contemptuous of lesbian women, and filled with the disturbing memories of her own failed relationships. On Lesbos, however, she could lose herself in a world saturated with the presence of Sappho. In spite of the man in her garden, her villa was as close to the ideal as one might hope (indeed, at her garden gate leading to the sea, she hung a sign with "Paradise" carved in Greek). Mytilene was thus an important fantasy governing her life. She must have felt the need, however, to anchor her dream in reality, because she continued to return to Paris and never made a complete transition to Mytilene, despite the fact that she lavishly furnished her villa and filled the garden with exotic plants and birds. Her inability to choose between Mytilene and Paris reveals her dependence on both. And perhaps, too, she restlessly moved between these cities so that she might keep the dream alive, each city renewing the vision when the other could no longer sustain it. Her ideal was precariously balanced with reality.

Vivien was an indefatigable traveler and spent as much time on boats and in trains as in her Paris apartment.[44] Her restlessness took her even further than Lesbos, to Scandinavia, to China, to Japan, to the Middle East, stringing together the cities of the world: Paris, Jerusalem, Florence, Venice, Athens, Constantinople, Mytilene. These prodigious wanderings may, in fact, have been prompted by her search for an impossible ideal city, whose haunting outlines might emerge and disappear as easily in Toledo or Venice as on Lesbos. She traveled like a woman pursued by furies,[45] but she herself was chasing the phantom of Mytilene that lived in her poetry.

Vivien's struggle with vision and reality recurs in *A Woman Appeared to Me*, a series of evocative dream portraits of four women seen through the eyes of the narrator, Vivien herself. The novel charts some of Vivien's interurban wanderings, as we follow the narrator from Paris to America and Spain; but the characters are moored in Paris, through whose misty wet evenings they literally swim from one lesbian salon-island to another. We watch the unfolding of a very private interior world of love relationships among women. The radiant visions of love on Mytilene, however, are troubled in Paris by human frailty and jealousy and the hostile male world surrounding these women. Vivien's steps, so sure on the shores of Mytilene, falter in Paris as she labors to connect life with her vision.

In the novel's climactic scene, the narrator (Vivien) must choose between two lovers: Loreley, the temptress with whom Vivien has already endured a heartbreaking and tempestuous relationship, and Eva, the gentle redeemer whose "solemn sweetness" represents hope. As Vivien stands poised between Loreley and Eva in her garden, she agonizes over the painful decision that will determine the course of her future. But her choice is purposely veiled by the novel's ending:

An anguished pause held the three of us. What I was going to say would be decisive and fatal. My whole unshaped future depended on that instant's resolve. Upon me weighed the terror of choosing.
When the words finally were uttered, a sigh rose from the shadows.
"Farewell . . . and till we meet again." (63)

We don't know whom the narrator has chosen, and so Vivien's work of art continues to maintain a balance that life, which demands choices, destroys. Moreover, the garden is perfectly emblematic of this ambiguous balance, for it occupies a place midway between pastoral and urban, between Paris and the country: it is shut away from culture, yet man's designing hand separates it from nature. Indeed, the ending is as artfully contrived as is the vision of Mytilene itself, for each balances on the fulcrum of Vivien's imagination.

This balance is reinforced by an earlier image in the novel, the two sister queens facing each other across a fountain in the Sala de las Dos Hermanas (Room of the Two Sisters) of the Alhambra:

On an evening of memory and nightmare I saw the two royal sisters, Zoraÿda and Zorahaÿda. They were seated facing one another on opposite sides of the fountain. The singing water was a mirror in the shadows, and their innocent eyes smiled as they watched it. (44)

The sisters are twin mirror reflections, like the lovers' bodies on Mytilene. Their balanced female figures echo Eva and Loreley in the garden, and Vivien is the reflecting mirror standing between them. Sisters, lovers, mothers—all long to reach through the mirror and touch their fleshly twins, an echo of the infant's first loving bond with the mother/mirror. The royal sisters, however, fail to establish that bond:

But the fountain separated them more effectively than all the doors of the palace. The fountain seemed to them the insuperable obstacle. They smiled at one another dimly through the veil of water . . . They never dared to sit side by side and join hands. Never would they dare to join their lonely and passionate lips. They would die without destroying in their souls the infinite charm of Desire and Regret. (44)

If art is indeed a dream for awakened minds, as Plato suggests, then Mytilene is the product of a waking dream. The vision of the royal sisters, however, is the product of nightmare. The former fills the world with ecstatic love; the latter, a nightmare of unconsummated passion. Life, of course, demands choices that may lead as much to satisfied desire as to regret, and Vivien understands this only too well. Thus she is reluctant to choose between Eva and Loreley, for in choosing, as San Giovanni counsels, "You'll regret forever the thing you didn't choose" (57). Vivien's real-life suspension between the magnetic pull of Paris and

Mytilene reflects a similar imaginative attempt to maintain a balance.

Although Desire and Regret may have "infinite charm," that charm will never match the radiant splendor of the ideal Mytilene. In "La Mauvaise Auberge" ("The Inhospitable Inn"), published posthumously, Vivien acknowledges the enormous distance separating her vision and reality:

> Le monde inhospitalier est pareil à l'auberge
> Où l'on vit mal, où tout est mal, où l'on dort mal . . .
>
> Et, pendant que le cri des femmes se prolonge,
> Je cherche le Palais Impossible du Songe.
>
> Je fais, dans cette auberge, un modeste repas . . .
> Et songeant à ce qui pourrait être . . . et n'est pas . . .[46]

> [The inhospitable world is like an inn
> Where one lives poorly, where everything is bad, where
>   one sleeps poorly . . .
>
> And, while the cry of women continues,
> I search for the Impossible Palace of Dreams.
>
> I dine modestly in this inn . . .
> And dream of what could be . . . and isn't . . .]

Vivien had spent her life trying, in the words of San Giovanni, to "restore some very ancient and profoundly wise cult—the cult of the Mother Goddess who conceived Infinity and gave birth to Eternity" (15). Compelled by the "cry of women," she recovered a female island and filled it with poetic palaces. Mytilene, however, is ultimately an impossible dream.

But Vivien's vision of Mytilene is more complex than the traditional art/life dichotomy suggests. The seeds of Mytilene's inevitable failure are rooted within the vision's imaginary attempt to connect both the body and the spirit, which are neatly separated in the usual struggle between art and reality. Most visionary artistic cities exist as refuges from the body; Byzantium, for example, served Yeats as an artistic retreat where he might shed his body and become an artificial bird of hammered gold, singing outside time in an imaginary space. But Byzantium is dangerous as well, for any poet who would inhabit its unearthly palaces must remove himself from life and enter palaces for the dead. Thus the body tugs Yeats away from his vision, reminding him, as does Crazy Jane, that Byzantium's imaginary palaces must yield to the

flesh in which the poet lives: "Love has pitched his mansion in /
The place of excrement; / For nothing can be sole or whole / That
has not been rent." Mytilene poses enormous problems for Vivien, however, because its ideal is recognized *through* the body
and emerges from the body's needs. It is both artistic refuge and
vindication of Vivien's lesbianism and feminism—perhaps the
only place where she felt she could truly live, surrounded by
sisters and dignified by Lesbos's heritage in ancient literature and
classical mythology. She cannot separate flesh and spirit, as did
Yeats in Byzantium, because both strands are the indispensible
warp and woof of Mytilene.

How long, though, can a poet inhabit an imaginary city that
must meet both artistic and realistic demands? Small wonder that
Vivien spent her final years restlessly searching for an ideal city in
which both body and spirit might comfortably live; and after 1907,
Sappho and Mytilene appear less frequently in her verse, as if she
had begun to grow weary of her search for a reality that conforms
to her ideal. Visionary Mytilene could retain the poet's footprints
in its sand; the Mytilene that lives tucked away in Paris or real
Lesbos, however, is marked by secrecy and caution: it leaves no
clear path for the women of the future to follow. The ideal beck-
ons with its promise of a loving female community sustained by
heroic ancestral queens, but the ideal city, like Yeats's Byzantium, is finally a city for the dead.

Vivien maintained the tenuous balance between art and life for
nine years marked by an extraordinary literary output of twelve
books of verse, a novel, and other shorter prose pieces, a corpus
that would represent for many other artists the work of a long
lifetime. Perhaps she sensed that she could not for long equalize
the demands of body and spirit, and she worked feverishly to
articulate her struggle. Her best poems date from 1905 to 1907;
after that period, her literary output remained constant, but the
quality declined, paralleling an alarming decline in Vivien's
health. Becoming increasingly reclusive and secretive, she kept
herself alive on very little food and too much alcohol. Just as her
body grew thinner, so the quality of her poetry weakened, as
though in response to her failure to "feed" her verse any longer
with the splendid images of Mytilene. Vivien's conversion to
Catholicism shortly before her death suggests a final desperate
effort to replace the failed visions of Paris and Mytilene with a
vision of the City of God. Her anorexic starvation, which had

started long before this conversion, was the last gesture of a woman who has relinquished the body, grown weary of compromise, so that the spirit might in death complete the pilgrimage to perhaps another visionary city.

NOTES

1. Colette, *The Pure and the Impure*, trans. Herma Briffault (London: Penguin, 1971), 71.

2. Ibid., 73.

3. For an exhaustive treatment of this motif in nineteenth-century American and British literature by women, see Sandra M. Gilbert and Susan Gubar, *The Madwoman in the Attic* (New Haven: Yale Univ. Press, 1979).

4. Lillian Faderman, *Surpassing the Love of Men* (New York: Morrow, 1981), 268.

5. Renée Vivien, *A l'heure des mains jointes* (Paris: Lemerre, 1906). Unless otherwise indicated, all subsequent poems cited in this essay are from this 1906 edition [*At the Hour of Joined Hands*]. Several poems (including "Ainsi je parlerai," "Nous irons vers les Poètes," "Sur la place publique," and "Viviane") were revised by Vivien and included in later collections (*Chansons pour mon ombre*, 1907, under the name of Pauline M. Tarn; and *Poèmes*, 1909). I have decided to quote from the earlier versions of these poems. Although they don't all reflect the author's most recent editorial intentions, some of the earlier versions are clearly superior and more relevant to this essay. All translations are mine. An excellent translation of *A l'heure des mains jointes* has been published: Sandia Belgrade, trans., *At the Sweet Hour of Hand in Hand* ([Weatherby Lake, Mo.]: Naiad Press, 1979). I have chosen, however, to follow each French passage with my own literal translations merely to aid the reader unfamiliar with French.

6. Renée Vivien, "Psappha revit," *A l'heure des mains jointes*.

7. Marie-Jo Bonnet, *Un choix sans équivoque* (Paris: Denoël/ Gonthier, 1981), 207.

8. André Germain, *Les Fous de 1900* (Paris-Genève: La Palatine, 1954), 58 (trans. mine).

9. George Wickes, *The Amazon of Letters* (New York: Putnam's, 1976), 44.

10. Colette, 69.

11. Ibid.

12. Paul Lorenz, *Sapho 1900: Renée Vivien* (Paris: Julliard, 1977), 31.

13. Colette, 62.

14. For closer readings of these works from a feminist/lesbian perspective, see Lillian Faderman, *Surpassing the Love of Men*, 254–85.

15. Jean-Pierre Jacques, *Les Malheurs de Sapho* (Paris: Grasset, 1981), 51–55.

16. Ibid., 53.

17. Ibid., 66.

18. Ibid., 65.

19. For a textual excerpt of and interesting commentary on the 1800 ordinance restricting female transvestism, see Bonnet, 195–224.

20. Colette, 61.

21. Ibid., 62.

22. According to Louise Faure-Favier, Vivien's aversion to men centered on their gracelessness and pervasive odor of commerce and the hunt: the "leather" smell of "huntsmen, furniture movers, porters." From Louise Faure-Favier, "The Muse of the Violets," trans. Jeannette H. Foster in Renée Vivien, *The Muse of the Violets*, trans. Margaret Porter and Catharine Kroger ([Bates City, Mo.]: Naiad Press, 1977), p. 11.

23. Charles Baudelaire, *Les Fleurs du Mal* (Paris: Poulet-Malassis et de Broise, 1857), 188 (translation mine).

24. Despite her poetry's strong reputation among an intimate circle during Vivien's lifetime, her verse was banned from many public places as a result of its lesbian bias. Paul Lorenz refers, for example, to its exclusion from the poetry matinees during the 1920s at the Théâtre-Français because of Vivien's "reputation" (11). Vague rumors of scandal permeate virtually all the memoirs about Vivien written between 1908 and 1928, and Milly insists that Vivien was so injured by the shocking indiscretion of critics who dug through her private life in order to explicate her work, that she "retreated into an ivory tower" where she remained for years, sensitive to criticism, curiosity, and indifference (Milly, "Renée Vivien," *Ecrits Nouveaux*, 1 avril, 1918, 17).

25. Renée Vivien, "Sonnets," *Poèmes de Renée Vivien* (Paris, 1923; rpt. N.Y.: Arno, 1975), 37.

26. Renée Vivien, "Aurore sur la mer," *Poèmes de Renée Vivien*, 13–14.

27. In her excellent introduction to the English translation of *A Woman Appeared to Me*, Gayle Rubin refers to the generalized historical "amnesia" that has suppressed Vivien's own reputation, now relegated to virtual obscurity but at one time the recipient of high critical praise: Gayle Rubin, "Introduction," *A Woman Appeared to Me*, trans. Jeannette H. Foster, 2nd ed. [Weatherby Lake, Mo.]: Naiad Press, 1979, iii.

28. Hélène Cixous, quoted in Christiane Olivier, *Les Enfants de Jocaste* (Paris: Denoël/Gonthier, 1980), 8. Olivier quotes Cixous as follows: "Ils lui ont fait un antinarcissisme! un narcissisme qui ne s'aime qu'à se faire aimer pour *ce qu'on n'a pas!*"

29. Elizabeth de Gramont, ex-Duchesse de Clermont-Tonnerre, *Years of Plenty*, trans. Florence and Victor Llona (New York: Jonathan Cape, n.d.), 278.

30. Personal interview with Renée O'Brien, niece of Renée Vivien, 28 March 1983.

31. Yves-Gérard Le Dantec, *Renée Vivien: femme damnée, femme sauvée* (Aix-en-Provence: Editions du Feu, 1930), 174.

32. Renée Vivien, *A Woman Appeared to Me*, trans. Jeannette H. Foster, 6. Foster's translation is based on the 1904 edition of the novel,

which differs significantly from its revised edition of the following year. All further references to this work appear in the text.

33. Sandra M. Gilbert and Susan Gubar, "Introduction," *Shakespeare's Sisters* (Bloomington: Indiana Univ. Press, 1979), xv–xxvi.

34. Renée Vivien, "Invocation," *Cendres et poussières* (Paris: Lemerre, 1902), 3.

35. Lorenz, 68–69.

36. "Viens poupoule," popularized around 1902, became the virtual theme song of the Parisian café-concert (Caf'Conç') scene. The Caf' Conç' provided entertainment and singing (often of a suggestive or licentious nature) for working-class men, artists, shop owners, young shop girls, pimps and their women, and some homosexuals (Georges Coulonges, *La Chanson en son temps* [Paris: Les Editeurs Français Réunis, 1969], 28.) The upper class assiduously shunned these vulgar spectacles as, we can be sure, did Vivien.

37. The refrain of "Viens poupoule" ("Come on, babe, come on, sweetie, come on! / When I hear singing / It makes me feel a little naughty, oh!") is only one example (of which there are many more in French and English) of a seemingly innocuous term of affection ("poupoule") that linguistically diminishes women by addressing them as one might a child or, worse, a woman of slight morals. Interestingly, "poupoule" as a term of endearment is defined at the word "poule" in the current *Dictionnaire Robert* (petit) under the same subheading that describes "poupoule"'s nearest linguistic relative, "poule" as "whore" (*Le Petit Robert: Dictionnaire alphabétique et analogique de la langue française* [Paris: Le Robert, 1981], 1498).

38. Wickes, p. 65.

39. Jean-Paul Goujon, *Renée Vivien à Mytilène* (Reims: A l'Ecart, 1978), n. pag.

40. Ibid. n. pag. (trans. mine).

41. Ibid. n. pag.

42. Ibid. n. pag.

43. André Germain, *Renée Vivien* (Paris: Crès, 1917), 106 (trans. mine).

44. Goujon, n. pag.

45. Germain, *Renée Vivien*, 105–106. Germain quotes a letter from Vivien, wherein she refers to these furies: "Ici [Athens] je suis calme parce que je suis seule. Les mauvais génies m'ont quittée. Ils sont très loins, ils m'attendent peut-être à mon retour."

46. Renée Vivien, "La Mauvaise Auberge," *Poèmes de Renée Vivien*, 230.

Part II

British Writers

NANCY L. PAXTON

George Eliot and the City:
The Imprisonment of Culture

THERE IS A CONSPICUOUS SILENCE in George Eliot's fiction regarding the Victorian woman's relation to the city. Eliot is most celebrated for her presentations of the quiet country life of the English Midlands before they were disturbed by Victorian industrial progress. Her fiction depicts the natural serenity of the rural worlds of Hayslope, St. Ogg's, Raveloe, Treby Magna, and, of course, Middlemarch. Though in *Daniel Deronda* she does describe London in some detail, it is less vividly realized than Gwendolen Harleth's country home at Offendene. Only in *Romola*, Eliot's single attempt to write an historical novel about the distant past, does she depict her heroine's life in a city by surrounding her by quattrocento Florence, that "adorable city" that Eliot's contemporaries were rediscovering because of their interest in the Italian Risorgimento and in the epic poetry of Dante.[1]

Eliot's unwillingness to depict the urban life of a heroine as creative and unconventional as she was herself has seemed a puzzling, provoking, and—for some readers—an unforgivable omission in her fiction, but her silence seems to reflect her feelings that cities in general and London in particular were somehow threatening. In 1863, while she was writing *Romola*, she sent a letter to her beloved friend, Barbara Bodichon, in which she commented about living in London:

I know you are enjoying the country. I have just been having the joy myself. The wide sky, the *not*-London makes a new creature of me in half

[71]

an hour. I wonder then why I am ever depressed, why I am so shaken by agitation. I come back to London and again the air is full of demons.[2]

Though Eliot had long since rejected her initial puritanical reasons for disapproving of London as a "great Babel,"[3] and though she had come to enjoy with deep appreciation the music, art, literature, and intellectual ferment of the vast English city that she adopted as her home, she nonetheless continued to feel vaguely oppressed by it, and complaints like the one she sent to Bodichon reappear with regularity in her letters throughout her career.

Nonetheless, if Marian Evans had not come to London in 1850 after her father's death and begun to work as the silent editor of the *Westminster Review*, George Eliot would, perhaps, never have been born. At thirty-one, Marian Evans's dearest desire was to free herself from the parochial world of her childhood and to somehow escape from what John Cross has called the "slavery" of her domestic life, "shut up in a farmhouse in the remote country."[4] All the yearning of her "full passionate nature and hungry intellect" that he describes is expressed in a letter written a few months before her father's death:

O the bliss of having a very high attic in a romantic continental town, such as Geneva—far away from morning callers, dinners and decencies; and then to pause for a year and think "de omnibus rebus et quibusdam aliis," and then return to life, and work for poor stricken humanity and never think of self again.[5]

Though she traveled to Geneva in the summer following her father's death, she characteristically did not spend that year of perfect intellectual self-indulgence that she longed for, and though she moved to London by November 1850, she did not easily find the fulfillment in life that she desired. Her career as novelist began, as we all know, only after she made her momentous choice to live unmarried with G. H. Lewes, and only after she had signaled that choice publicly by leaving London with him to go to Weimar, Germany. The painful repercussions of both these choices defined Eliot's experience of London ever afterward, and perhaps some of the reasons for her silence about the city life of an emancipated, educated, and artistic woman like herself can be found in these circumstances of her biography.[6]

One of the most dazzling moments in *Middlemarch*, however, suggests a second dimension to Eliot's silence about the city beyond these details of her private life which illuminates her experiences as a woman writer and sheds a retrospective light on her conception and construction of *Romola*, that single novel about a woman's relation to the city. In describing Dorothea Brooke Casaubon standing in the sunlight before the statue of the reclining Cleopatra in the Vatican Museum, Eliot presents a paradigm for woman's experience in the city by disclosing how men in urban culture make women into subjects of art in order to reinforce their social preeminence by this apparent flattery. Dorothea, brooding about her sudden disillusionment with her "bridal life," does not actually see the statue in front of her, but she is viewed by her cousin Will Ladislaw and by the artist Naumann, who tries to transform her into a suitable subject for his art. Finding a "fine bit of antithesis" in the contrast between the image of the sensuous ideal of womanhood and the flesh and blood reality, he tells Will:

There lies antique beauty, not corpse-like even in death, but arrested in the complete contentment of its sensuous perfection: and here stands beauty in its breathing life, with the consciousness of Christian centuries in its bosom. But she should be dressed like a nun; I think she looks almost what you call a Quaker; I would dress her as a nun in my picture.[7]

Though Dorothea is not herself aware that being transformed into an aesthetic object this way contributes to her sense of the oppressiveness of the Eternal City, Eliot goes on in *Middlemarch* to describe her heroine's struggle to compel Will to see her as a woman desiring love and not as a "poem" or a goddess.

Furthermore, Eliot describes the demoralizing effect that viewing the monumental art of Rome—that "Titanic life struggling on walls and ceilings"—has upon Dorothea:

She had been led through the best galleries, had been taken to the best points of view, had been shown the greatest ruins and the most glorious churches, and she had ended oftenest choosing to drive out to the Campagna where she could feel alone with the earth and sky, away from the oppressive masquerade of ages, in which her own life seemed to become a masque with enigmatical costumes. (ch. 20, pp. 224–25)

Dorothea feels distressed both by the "stupendous fragmentariness" and by the painfully "deep impressions" that this art makes on her, but her dismay is amplified because of her experience as a woman. Educated by that "toy-box history of the world adapted to young ladies" (ch. 10, p. 112), and encouraged to find moral order everywhere, Dorothea is especially shaken when she can find no intellectual or moral unity in this vast wreck of "spiritual and sensuous ideals," Measuring her ordinary woman's life against the conflicting images of heroic womanhood that she sees in the city's museums and churches makes Dorothea feel even more keenly the "moral imprisonment" of her chosen life with Casaubon.

Dorothea's feelings of humiliation, pain, and entrapment in her first confrontation with the art of the Eternal City apparently echo some of Eliot's own initial feelings of "humiliating passivity" in regarding the art of Rome and Florence, but Eliot's use of allusions to Charlotte Brontë's *Villette* suggests that she is describing a sense of oppression shared by other women writers and Victorian feminists. [8] By inviting readers familiar with literature of the female tradition to see parallels between Brontë's heroine, Lucy Snowe, who also stands before the image of the Cleopatra, and Dorothea, Eliot discloses a more subversive and feminist analysis of woman's relation to urban culture. Unlike Dorothea, Lucy actually examines and criticizes the reclining figure of the "indolent gypsy giantess," depicted on a vast canvas rather than carved in stone. While Lucy considers the Cleopatra as "on the whole an enormous piece of claptrap," she nonetheless prefers it to the images of women that her mentor, M. Paul, urges her to study instead: the "grim and grey" images, "cold and vapid as ghosts," which present the four stages of a woman's life: the "Jeune Fille," the "Mariée," the "Jeune Mère," and the "Veuve." Brontë directly describes in this scene how men convert art into propaganda to protect their power, and though Eliot is more subtle in her treatment of her heroine's confrontation with the conventionalized and prescriptive aesthetic ideals of feminity, she nonetheless reveals a similar wary cynicism about the female figures that are enshrined in the temples of culture. The depiction of the Cleopatra as only partially clad, in both cases, makes it graphically clear to both heroines that the power to design, utilize, and preserve particular versions of the feminine ideal and ignore others resides with men. Furthermore, Eliot reveals that the statue Dorothea stands before does not really represent Cleopatra but rather Antigone, and thus she indicates how readily the heroic representations of woman's spiritual perfection are misnamed and reinterpreted by succeeding generations who convert them into images of sensuous amorality. This process of renaming and reinterpreting the ideals of womanhood is particularly confusing to women; both Dorothea and Lucy regard such images of women as either utterly "alien" and "enigmatical" or "grim" and, as Eliot shows, it is no wonder.

While the scene from *Middlemarch* contains in miniature all the elements of Eliot's analysis of woman's entrapment by the city and its art, she presents her most comprehensive study not only of woman's moral but also of her physical confinement in *Romola*. This novel, published in installments in the *Cornhill Magazine*, describes the life of an aristocratic young woman living in Florence during Savonarola's ascendancy, fall, and martyrdom, from 1492 to 1498. Though famous historical figures like Niccolò Machiavelli, Luigi Pulci, Piero de' Medici, and Charles VIII of France move in the background, and the artist Piero di Cosimo and the passionate reformer Savonarola intervene more directly in Romola's life, Eliot focuses her novel deliberately on the historical, unrecorded, private life of a heroic woman. She presents two dimensions to Romola's entrapment by urban culture: the legal subordination imposed on her because she is a daughter, a wife, and a citizen of Florence, and the "moral imprisonment" that confines her because she is, by definition, the subject rather than the maker of the art and literature that surround her in this great center of Renaissance culture.

In choosing to set her novel in quattrocento Florence, Eliot made a choice that clarified and simplified her heroine's relation to the law because this city is the single agent of the state and serves the function later assumed by the nation-state. Even Eliot's less sympathetic Victorian readers recognized that Romola's struggle to free herself from the subjection imposed on her by civil and religious law paralleled the struggle of Victorian feminists.[9] A simple review of the plot makes clear Romola's efforts to escape her confinement by law. Eliot begins the novel by dramatizing the greater freedom of movement allowed Tessa, a young peasant woman from the countryside, in contrast to her heroine, who is completely innocent "about the world outside her father's books" (ch. 5, p. 104) and who does not leave her fortresslike home even to worship because her father has raised her to regard Christianity as mere superstition. Romola is therefore particularly susceptible to Tito Melema's charm when the beautiful young stranger comes to her father's library to offer his services to the blind old scholar. Tito courts and marries Romola and exploits his new family's social connections in his climb to power in the city government. After her marriage and after her father dies, Romola begins her slow and complicated disillusionment and tries twice to leave her husband. In describing this conflict, Eliot emphasizes Romola's legal subjection to Tito, for her heroine's first attempt to leave her husband occurs when she realizes that he has betrayed her father's dying request to donate the Bardo library to Florence and has sold it to the French invaders instead. Romola decides to leave Tito, assuming she has the power to break "an outward tie that no longer represented the inward bond of love" (ch. 36, p. 391).

When Romola is safely outside the gates of Florence, she feels "for the first time in her life . . . alone in the presence of earth and sky, with no human presence interposing and making a law for her" (ch. 40, p. 428). Savonarola, however, interrupts her reverie and urges her to submit to God's law which makes unbreakable her bond to Tito and to Florence. Accepting his argument, Romola returns to the city, reassumes her role as wife, and begins her religious "discipleship" as Florence's "Visible Madonna," which prompts her to move outside her home to feed the hungry and care for the sick in the city's streets. When she discovers that Tito has sold his foster father into slavery and has established a "second marriage" with Tessa, the peasant woman who bears him two children, Romola determines again to leave her husband. Romola confronts Tito directly this time, saying, "I too am a human being. I have a soul of my own that abhors your actions. Our union is a pretence—as if a perpetual lie could be a sacred marriage" (ch. 58, p. 567). By thus refusing to accept the definitions of the good woman legislated by the civil and religious laws of the patriarchs of Florence, Romola claims her freedom from falsely restricting laws and successfully asserts her selfhood when she leaves the city a second time. Romola spends many weeks away from Florence in a primitive, mysterious, beautiful village in the countryside, and finally returns to Florence only to discover that Tito and Baldasarre have drowned together in the Arno and that Savonarola is under sentence of death. Eliot ends the novel with her heroine achieving a liberation from the misogynistic civil and religious laws enforced by father, husband, and priest.

Eliot makes it clear that Romola's subjection to civil and religious law is a function of urban society by sketching the parallels between her heroine's experience of marriage and that of the "contadina" who becomes Tito's "second wife." Like Romola, Tessa is also easily influenced by Tito, but Eliot shows how her ignorance and naiveté put her at special disadvantage in the sophisticated urban world of Florence. From the first, Tessa trusts Tito implicitly and responds with spontaneity to all his gestures of love. Coming from the countryside where domestic relations are less legalistically defined, Tessa innocently accepts the "sham" ceremony that Tito arranges for her as a genuine religious rite sanctifying and legitimizing their betrothal. Later, she takes the coral charm Tito offers her as a symbol of their marriage. In both these episodes, Eliot dramatizes Tito's superior power as symbol maker in the city that formally recognizes and protects male preeminence in both civil and religious law.

In the city, Tessa gladly surrenders her freedom when Tito provides her with a home and a duessa to care for her. Unlike Romola, she remains content with her enclosed domestic world; she is willing to honor Tito's request that she stay indoors, always out of sight, although she does not ever understand the real reason for this prohibition—that he does not want his legitimate wife to discover his "second wife" and children. Eventually, Tessa's love, enlarged by her maternity, becomes the only "uncontaminated" spring of kindness in Tito's otherwise corrupted life. [10] Eliot asserts the power of primitive blood bonds that tie Tito to his children and their mother:

No guile was needed towards Tessa: she was too ignorant and too innocent to suspect him of anything. And the little voices calling him "Babbo" were very sweet in his ears for the short while that he heard them. When he thought of leaving Florence, he never thought of leaving Tessa and the little ones behind. He was very fond of these round-cheeked, wide-eyed human things that clung about him and knew no evil of him. And wherever affection can spring, it is like the green leaf and the blossom—pure, and breathing purity, whatever soil it may grow in. (ch. 50, pp. 501–502)

Nonetheless, Tito finally finds it expedient to abandon his second family along with his first when he plans his escape from the city, and without his protection, Tessa and her children are helpless. It is Romola who rescues them when she returns to Florence. Thus, Eliot contrasts Romola's marriage, sanctioned by the laws of the city and legitimized by the financial settlement that gives Tito the right to control the Bardo house and library, with Tessa's union, blessed only by the natural and erotic bonds that tie the lover to the beloved and the parent to the child, to show how marriage is transformed into a sterile economic contract by the city's laws.

Examining Romola's and Tessa's legal subordination this way, though, makes us ask why Romola fails to escape the city the first time, makes us question why Eliot shows her so responsive to Savonarola's appeal. Eliot demonstrates an answer to this question in her presentation of Romola's "moral imprisonment" by the literature and art of her city, and especially by the image of the Madonna in both its secular and religious manifestations. Eliot's treatment of Romola's "moral imprisonment" was especially complicated, because Eliot herself had tremendous difficulty escaping the patriarchal literature and art of Florence. Her own experiences researching and writing *Romola* and her response to and use of *The Divine Comedy* in her novel illustrate why it was so difficult for Eliot to liberate her heroine from the city.

Modern critics often remind us of the painstaking labor that Eliot expended on *Romola* by invoking her remark, "I began it as a young woman—I finished it an old woman," but they do not adequately recognize the monumental challenge she faced in recreating with any degree of accuracy the "things which have not changed"[11] in the private lives of fifteenth-century women. Eliot clearly recognized the dilemma she faced in trying to unearth what is traditionally regarded as the ahistorical, the mundane, the irrelevant, and she articulated this awareness eloquently in a letter she wrote to her illustrator, Frederick Leighton, when she learned that he planned a trip to Florence:

If you are going to see Ghirlandajo's frescoes, I wish you would especially notice if the women in his group have not that plain piece of opaque drapery over the head that haunts my memory. . . . We have in Varchi a sufficiently fit and clear description of the ordinary male costume of dignified Florentines in my period; but, for the corresponding feminine costume, the best authority I have seen is the very incomplete one of a certain Genevra's trousseau. . . . Approximate truth is the only truth available, but at least one must strive for that and not wander off into arbitrary falsehood.[12]

This letter makes us wonder where did Eliot turn to discover all the carefully researched and historically accurate details of Romola's life. What woman's history survives? Where did she discover what Romola would wear, what she could do to amuse herself, what she would think about? Though Eliot mentions

Cassandre Fidele, a woman scholar of fifteenth-century Venice, she could find no counterpart for Romola in fifteenth-century Florence and was forced to rely primarily on the materials of culture that survive: on men's history, literature, and art.[13]

In depicting Romola, Eliot not only had to struggle to maintain historical accuracy consistent with her realistic aesthetic, she also had to work against one of the most powerful symbols of the Italian Renaissance, Dante's vision of the Virgin Mother, which was associated with Florence in the minds of Victorian readers. Dante defines woman's place in the city by presenting his Beloved Beatrice, who lived in the moral center of the earthly city of Florence, in relation to her spiritual counterpart, the Virgin Mother, who reigns enthroned in the Celestial Rose at the center of the Heavenly City of God. A. B. Giamatti describes how the metaphor of the city functions in *The Divine Comedy*:

Finally, the city includes all; it is amphitheater and rose. Here where will and desire are one, where perfect stillness creates perfect motion, the twin images of Garden and City are married in the final, luminous vision.[14]

In the course of the poem, Beatrice is drawn into the center of the Heavenly City to her place beside the Holy Madonna, and thus Virgin and Mother are seen as one. In effect, Dante's Beatrice can only live in the poet's imagination in Florence, and even in Paradise she moves only to lead him on to the center of the City of God. Eliot, however, wished to reverse this paradigm in order to free her heroine from the city and the prescriptive images of selfless, humble womanhood embodied so powerfully in Dante's Virgin Mother. Thus, she found that while Dante's poetry helped her enormously in imagining the inner life of her characters, it also inhibited her imagination especially in the construction of her heroine.

When Eliot was writing the episode of the novel that describes Romola's first attempt to escape from Florence and her oppressive marriage, Eliot—as if in sympathy with her heroine—suffered from a period of paralyzing depression. In December 1862, she wrote:

I am extremely spiritless—dead, and hopeless about my writing. The long state of headache has left me in depression and incapacity. . . . I am inwardly irritable, and unvisited by good thoughts. Reading the 'Purgatorio' again and the 'Compendium Revelationum' of Savonarola.

After this record, I read over what I have written of Part IX to George [Lewes] and he, to my surprise, completely approved of it.[15]

Though G. H. Lewes's praise of this section of the novel apparently surprised the ever-doubting Eliot, it hardly does us, especially when we remember that he frequently called her "Madonna" during this period of their lives together. Some of Eliot's depression may have come from her despair of ever being able to invent a way to allow her heroine to escape from the role of the Divine Mother—when she, herself, nearly four centuries later, had not completely escaped from the confining image of the Madonna and from the oppression of another city that exalted it as an ideal.[16]

Thus, Eliot remained trapped, in part, by the paradox that faces all women writers: she must use what Adrienne Rich has called the "oppressor's language" if she is to communicate at all.[17] Because Eliot wished to lend heroic stature and spiritual authority to her heroine by using a historically accurate idiom like Dante's, *The Divine Comedy* remained a powerful presence in *Romola*. At the outset, Eliot reminds us that Romola's city is Dante's, and leads us to the "severely simple door-place, bearing this description: 'Qu Nacque il Divino Poeta'" (ch. 1, p. 53), as a point of reference for the drama that follows.

Eliot evokes Dante frequently in her presentations of both Tessa and Romola. In her characterization of the former, Eliot uses the parallels between Beatrice and the Divine Madonna ironically to dramatize Tessa's unconscious sexuality and her instinctive apprehension of the fundamental appeal of the Christian symbol of the Virgin Mother. Tessa responds readily and intuitively to the beautiful icons of the Madonna that she sees in the churches of Florence. She feels a religious awe "over something supernatural and heavenly" (ch. 14, p. 200) when she worships before the image of the Virgin Mother, and she acts out her naive understanding of the Madonna's significance in her subsequent relations with Tito, Baldasarre, and Romola.

Eliot planned originally to preface the chapter introducing Tessa with an epigraph from Dante's *Purgatorio* which refers to Beatrice's appearance in the Terrestrial Paradise.[18] The lines she selected, though, refer to Matilda, who acts as Beatrice's handmaiden and leads the poet to the spring that restores memory. Certainly the similarities between Matilda's gentle submissiveness and Tessa's are clear; both act "as a gentle soul that makes no excuse but makes her will the will of another as soon as it is revealed by an outward sign" (*Purgatorio*, 33: 130–32). Yet this allusion to Dante becomes an ironic comment on Tessa's naiveté and intellectual incapacity, so evident in her first appearance, and similarly forecasts her later action when she unwittingly leads Tito away from his appointments in the city and invites him to fall asleep with his head in her lap as they sit outside the gates of Florence (ch. 10, pp. 153–65).

In her description of this second meeting between Tito and Tessa under the plane tree, Eliot lends the contadina a calm serenity that recalls Beatrice sitting under the great tree in the Terrestrial Paradise (*Purgatorio*, 32: 85–108), as she presents Tessa sitting at what seems to be the still point of the universe, watching over Tito as the world wheels slowly by. Again, though, the allusion functions ironically to display the pitiful inadequacy of Tessa's moral judgment, for, ignorant as she is about Tito's real place in the city and his anticipated marriage to Romola, she feels herself near "Paradise" in this moment they have stolen together outside the city's time and culture. While Tessa finds in the Christian Madonna an image that expresses her own spontaneously loving nature and her instinctive respect for the power of female sexuality and fertility associated with this image since before the advent of Christianity, she is incapable of understanding the symbol in Dante's sophisticated metaphysical terms, and perhaps this is one of the reasons why Eliot abandoned her plan to use epigraphs in *Romola*.

When Tessa becomes a mother, Eliot makes more explicit the contadina's solipsistic identification with the figure of the Holy Madonna. She shows that Tessa's naive responsiveness to the symbol, like her dependency upon Tito in their illegitimate marriage, makes her especially vulnerable in the urban world of Florence. Whenever Tessa leaves her home without Tito's permission, she finds herself helpless and powerless. The first time she steps outside her home, she meets Baldasarre, the man who raised Tito and who seeks revenge upon him. Knowing nothing of this man's relation to Tito, Tessa simply observes his need for love, and, to cheer him, she brings her child to him as he sits sheltered in a barn outside her home. Naively calling attention to the parallels between herself and the Madonna, Tessa tells him, "This is my baby. . . . It is like the little Gesù, and I should think the Santa Madonna would be kinder to me now, is it not true?'' (ch. 33, p. 367). Her remarks thus disclose the unconscious egoism which rules even in her religious life, for by her own analogy, she has become the Holy Madonna. Her altruism has precisely the opposite effect from the comfort she intended, however. As he holds the child, Baldasarre mutters, "Poor thing," with "something strangely threatening in his apparent pity." Of him, Eliot concludes, "It did not seem . . . as if this guileless, loving little woman could reconcile him to the world at all, but rather that she was with him against the world, that she was a creature who would need to be avenged" (ch. 33, p. 367). Baldasarre's transformation from a loving parent to a revengeful one, indicated in his response to Tessa, demonstrates how deeply hostile Florence is to the values of spontaneous love and familial affection that she embraces so instinctively, and in such a world, Tessa's naive identification with the Madonna prevents her from recognizing the real limits of her power as mother.

Eliot shows, though, that while Tessa's identification with the figure of the Christian Madonna is essentially ego-gratifying, she is able nonetheless to recognize that she is in the presence of a love greater and stronger than her own when she meets Romola in the streets of Florence the second time she ventures outside the protection of her home. Tessa is conscious of Romola's superior moral power and stature and associates her with the figure of the Madonna, when, thinking back on her encounter, she muses: "In the dream-like combination of small experience which made up Tessa's thoughts, Romola had remained confusedly associated with the pictures in the churches, and when she reappeared, the grateful remembrance of her protection was slightly tinctured with religious awe" (ch. 56, p. 546). When Tessa later asks Tito "who the heavenly lady that had come just when she wanted and vanished so soon was likely to be—whether she could be the Holy Madonna herself," he tries in his capacity as patriarchal authority to correct Tessa's perception of Romola (ch. 56, p. 546). In this exchange between Tessa and Tito, Eliot demonstrates how the symbol of the Holy Mother is aestheticized and disassociated from any earthly referent in Florence. Only an illiterate peasant woman like Tessa and uneducated followers of Savonarola acknowledge the primitive power that the Christian symbol of the Madonna embodies and find it to be an awe-inspiring force in their earthly world. For men at home in civilization, and for women like Romola who are educated by them, the image of the Madonna is emptied of the primitive meaning that Tessa apprehends and worships. All the men that Eliot describes in Florence—even strangers like Tito and Baldasarre—claim the power to interpret, reshape, or redefine not only the symbol of the Madonna but all feminine images of spiritual and sensuous perfection in order to preserve their hegemony in the city.

Eliot's use of Dante in her characterization of Romola is even more complicated because without the defense of irony used in Tessa's portrait, Eliot had difficulty controlling the parallels between her heroine and Dante's Holy Virgin and Divine Madonna. She presents Romola's experiences with her father, husband, and priest, and her eventual escape from Florence by using some of the symbolical elements of Dante's epic vision of the Holy Virgin in the Terrestrial Paradise (*Purgatorio*, 27–33) and the Divine Mother in the Celestial City (*Paradiso*, 30–33). Nonetheless, Eliot adjusts these elements, as we shall see, so that they are consistent with her woman-centered vision and with her feminist sensibilities. While other critics have documented the ways that Eliot violates her realistic aesthetics by overidealizing Romola, especially by comparing her to the Madonna, they have failed to explain the function of Romola's two flights from the city or to acknowledge the imaginative difficulties Eliot faced in describing them. I would like to show how and why Eliot includes Romola's failed and successful attempts to achieve her extraordinary liberation from Florence and the sensuous and spiritual ideals of womanhood that it imposed.[19]

Because Eliot had to struggle so with Dante's influence in her characterization of Romola, she was forced to confront what it means for a woman to be defined by her culture as the Other. Both times Romola steps outside the walls of Florence, she experiences an existential crisis because she confronts a self that has been suppressed by patriarchal culture.[20] The first time she finds herself "free and alone" outside the city, Romola feels triumph: "A certain awe which inevitably accompanied this most momentous act of her life became a more conscious element in Romola's feeling as she found herself in the impalpable golden glory and the long shadow of herself which was not to be escaped" (ch. 37, p. 400). Yet accepting that which has been repressed by her civilization becomes frightening for Romola when she finds herself in the landscape her brother Dino foresaw in a visionary dream as he was dying. He correctly predicted Romola's two attempts to escape from Florence when he envisioned her marriage:

And the priest who married you had the face of death; and the graves opened, and the dead in their shrouds rose and followed the bridal train. And you passed on through the streets and the gates into the valley, and it seemed that he who led you hurried you more than you could bear. . . . And at last you came to a stony place where there was no water, and no trees or herbage; but instead of water, I saw men of bronze and marble springing up and crowding round you. (ch. 15, p. 215)

Dino assumes the patriarch's privilege and interprets the dream for Romola as a warning against marriage, which he imagines in conventional Christian terms, as the temptation of an "angel of darkness." For a daughter of civilization like Romola, guilt overshadows the "golden glory" of the self when memory thus turns traitor; her first return, then, becomes the return of the repressed. Before Romola can successfully confront her own female nature outside the bounds of civilization, she must see through the symbols of her father's and husband's classicism and the images of her brother's and spiritual advisor's Christianity, those figures of bronze and marble and those scholastic parchments. Only then can Romola transcend them and find herself outside the gates of Florence in a world that has not been predetermined by male authority.

To illuminate Romola's struggle toward self-definition, Eliot demonstrates how her heroine's experiences with the secular and religious symbols of Florence parallel Tessa's but move in the opposite direction as she grows more and more skeptical about the sensuous and spiritual ideals by which the patriarchs define womanhood in her culture. Like Tessa, she begins willing to accept instruction as to the meaning of the female symbols inside the city, and thus she is taught to speak the "oppressor's language" in both words and symbols. Without that secure sense of her own sexual identity that makes the primitive meaning of the Christian symbol of the Madonna real to Tessa, Romola is ultimately compelled to resist the patriarchal authorities who indoctrinate her to the meaning of those symbols within the city. Though she fails to find relief and comfort when she escapes to the natural world the first time, Romola develops a critical consciousness about the sensuous and spiritual ideals defining

[84]

womanhood in her city that made these images seem "alien" and "enigmatical'" to both Lucy Snowe in *Villette* and Dorothea Brooke Casaubon in *Middlemarch*. Ironically, Romola develops this understanding of her place as Other in Florentine culture by playing the part of the "Visible Madonna"—that image that Dante used so effectively to unite the classical and Christian traditions in his *Divine Comedy*.

Romola's escape from her "moral imprisonment" is slow and difficult, though, precisely because she loves the men who act as her teachers, reflecting Eliot's parallel struggle to transcend Dante's vision of woman's place in the earthly and heavenly cities. Romola's indoctrination to the images of womanhood repeats Lucy Snowe's in *Villette*, but the schooling Eliot's heroine receives begins not with art but rather with literature and extends beyond both the library and the artist's studio to the city's churches, those original temples of culture which Victorian museums imitated. In dramatizing how Romola is taught to see her life according to the images of the patriarchy, Eliot demonstrates how her motherless heroine is protected from the influence of women because her father regards it as pernicious. In Romola's first appearance in the novel, Eliot reveals her heroine's pain as her father teaches her about the secular ideals of motherhood sanctioned by the classical texts in his library. Like one of Milton's daughters, Romola reads to her blind father a story about the redemptive power of the mother:

There was a certain nymph of Thebes named Chariclo, especially dear to Pallas; and this nymph was the mother of Teiresias. But once . . . it happened that Teiresias coming as a hunter to quench his thirst at the fountain, inadvertently beheld Minerva unveiled, and immediately became blind. . . . When Teiresias had fallen into this calamity, Pallas, moved by the tears of Chariclo, endowed him with prophecy and length of days, and even caused his prudence and wisdom to continue after he had entered among the shades, so then an oracle spoke from his tomb. (ch. 5, p. 94)

Though this myth clearly expresses the sanctity and power of the mother, Bardo interprets it for Romola by reminding her of the "wandering, vagrant propensities of the feminine mind" and the "feeble powers of the feminine body" (ch. 5, p. 97). He recognizes none of the power of reconciliation expressed in Chariclo's story. Instead, he comments on the "debasing influence" of women "with their sparrow-like frivolity and their enslaving superstition," complimenting Romola with, "Thou has never fretted me . . . with thy petty desires as thy mother did" (ch. 5, p. 100). While Bardo does not perceive the irony in his juxtaposition of past and present mother's stories, Romola comprehends it viscerally as well as intellectually as her angry blush reveals, but her duty and love compel her to accept silently her father's definition of the mother and herself.[21] Romola must try twice before she can escape the self-doubt Bardo's misogyny has inspired. Furthermore, to heal the split between the images of the real and ideal mothers that he describes, she must finally leave the city that fosters it.

Romola's introduction to the sensuous ideals defining womanhood in art echoes Lucy Snowe's experience more directly and anticipates Dorothea's, for it is Tito, her beloved, who tries to flatter Romola into seeing herself in the image of Ariadne. On the day of their betrothal, Tito brings Romola a miniature that portrays Bacchus and Ariadne. Dutifully, like her father's daughter, Romola reads the language of the symbols of the painting as Tito instructs her: "Ah it is you—it is perfect. . . . And I am Ariadne and you are crowning me. Yes, it is true, Tito, you have crowned my poor life" (ch. 20, p. 260). Playing the role of symbol maker that he assumes often with Tessa, Tito encourages Romola to forget her sorrow over her brother's death and enjoy the happiness imaged in the painting, saying, "My Ariadne must never look backward now" (ch. 20, p. 263).

Eliot indicates a further complication in Brontë's analysis of the sexual politics of art as male propaganda by describing the process by which Tito commissions this portrait. The image of womanhood that Tito prescribes actually looks like Romola because he has the wealth and authority to command the artist, Piero di Cosimo, to transform the original Ovidian tale of Theseus's abandonment of Ariadne into a more gratifying image of himself as Bacchus saving Ariadne:

> The young Bacchus must be seated in a ship, his head bound with clusters of grapes, and a spear intwined with vine-leaves in his hand. . . . But I want to have the fair-haired Ariadne with him, made immortal with her golden crown—that is not in Ovid's story, but no matter, you will conceive it all. (ch. 18, p. 244)

In this city where "truth is a riddle for the eyes and the wit to discover" (ch. 3, p. 82), Tito can manipulate art so that it falsifies his relation to Romola by granting the artist permission to depict Romola as Antigone with her aging father as Oedipus. Though Cosimo's version is clearly a more accurate representation of Romola, it is nonetheless distorted because it reshapes Romola to fit the classical myth valorizing a virgin's self-sacrifice for her brother and father.

Like Lucy and unlike Dorothea, Romola recognizes the falseness of Tito's idealizing portrait of her just before she tries to leave Florence the first time. Romola's decision to "renounce Ariadne's crown" and dissolve her marriage to Tito is accompanied by her heightened awareness of how the portrait has served Tito's purposes:

Romola looked at the familiar images with new bitterness and repulsion; they seemed a more pitiable mockery than ever on this chill morning, when she had walked up to wander in loneliness. They had been no tomb of sorrow, but a lying screen. Foolish Ariadne! with her gaze of love, as if that bright face, with its hyacinthine curls like tendrils among the vines, held the deep secret of life! (ch. 37, pp. 397–98)

By describing Romola's bitterness over "foolish Ariadne," Eliot suggests how Tito has manipulated this female image of sensuous perfection. Romola experiences the rage of a woman who has seen how images of beatified wifehood and filial self-sacrifice have served to "screen" reality. The beauty of the former seduces women into imagining that their triumphant powerfulness in love is the perfect complement to their actual powerlessness in marriage. The latter image persuades heroic women that rebellion against the laws of the patriarchy can only be legitimized when it is undertaken not for the self but in the name of the father or brother. By leaving Florence this first time, Romola hopes to escape from these false images of the wife, having already been released from the filial relation because both her brother and father have since died.

Romola, like Dorothea, can only imagine her future life by a "pathetic mixture of childish romance with her woman's trials" (ch. 36, pp. 393–94). The failure of her imagination indicates the effects of living in a city and culture where she is always seen as the subject but never the maker of literature and art. Romola is completely unfamiliar with any exercise in self-definition. Before she sets off for Venice she muses: "She did not know that any Florentine woman had ever done exactly what she was going to do; . . . she had invented a lot for herself—to go to the most learned woman in the world—Cassandre Fidele, at Venice, and ask her how an instructed woman could support herself in a lonely life there" (ch. 36, p. 393). To expedite her flight from the city, Romola puts on a disguise; she wears the costume of a nun, for only so dressed can she move freely through the streets of Florence.[22]

Because Romola is only masquerading as a nun, though, Savonarola recognizes her and calls her back to Florence by playing on her guilt for "withdrawing in secrecy and disguise" and by reminding her of the duties she owes to Church and city (ch. 40, p. 430). Before she returns to Florence, Savonarola also instructs Romola about the meaning of Christian symbols just as Bardo and Tito have. The priest directs her to consider the meaning of the cross she wears by reminding her that it is the "image of a Supreme offering, made by Supreme love." He describes how the symbol should apply to her life: "Make your marriage-sorrows an offering, too, my daughter, to the great work by which sin and sorrow are being made to cease. . . . There is the vision which makes all life below it dross forever" (ch. 40, p. 436). But it is Savonarola's appeal to Romola's integrity that draws her back to Florence; it is not her faith in Church doctrine or her desire to martyr herself to earn a life hereafter. Moreover, it is the image of the Madonna that is the compelling ideal of her religious life; it is not the "image of the cross" that Savonarola prescribes.

When Romola returns to the city, she refuses to retire into the domestic seclusion of her earlier life with Tito, and in this way she offers an important contrast to Tessa. Under Savonarola's guidance, Romola takes up the role of the "Visible Madonna" of Florence and moves about the city ministering to the poor and sick,[23] but Eliot makes it clear that this role is not a natural one for her. Unlike Tessa, she must struggle to transform herself into the semblance of the Madonna: "She had no innate taste for tending the sick and clothing the ragged, like some women to whom the details of such work are welcome in themselves. Her early training had kept her aloof from such womanly labors; and if she had not brought to them the inspiration of her deepest feelings, they would have been irksome to her" (ch. 44, p. 463). In assuming the part of the "Visible Madonna" of Florence, Romola actually takes part in the heroic pageant that seems a "masquerade" to Dorothea. Because of her "old contempt for their superstition,"

Romola is unwilling to join a religious order and take on the role of Holy Virgin; so she models herself after the only other female image that the Christians of Florence revere, the role of the Madonna. Thus she assumes a second costume, but one that allows her to maintain her personal integrity while it grants her free access to the ritual spaces inside and outside Florence's great churches.

Though Romola begins to recover a sense of the dignity and power of her own femaleness by acting as the Visible Madonna of the city, she recognizes finally that the Madonna too—in both its aesthetic and religious forms—is also a "screen" for the reality of a woman's life in patriarchal culture. The men in power in Florence regard the figure of the Madonna in a thoroughly egoistic light; one of the city's proverbs asserts that the Florentines had a "Madonna who would do what they pleased," a saying that Romola recalls when she watches a procession accompanying the ancient icon of the Madonna that is brought into the city during a famine (ch. 42, p. 445). Romola begins to see that the freedom and power she claimed in playing the part of the Visible Madonna are illusory; she, like Tessa, is really powerless as soon as she steps outside the female roles her culture sanctions. When she is threatened by a crowd of irreligious, rough, hungry men, she acknowledges the limits of a woman's power in Florence: "You have the power to take this bread if you will. It was saved for sick women and children. You are strong men; but if you do not choose to suffer because you are strong, you have the power to take everything from the weak" (ch. 42, p. 449). Thus, in her treatment of Romola's career as Florence's "Visible Madonna," Eliot displays how her heroine serves a Church and state which exalt the figure of maternal solicitude and supernatural goodness by the worship of the Virgin Mother, but yet deny and subvert the earthly expression of these values in the material world.

Romola's crisis of faith signals more, then, than a religious questioning; for in challenging the priest's vision of moral law, she sees finally the subjective nature of the entire fabric of classical and Christian myth by which the patriarchs of culture define her. She sees that she has been denied the power to interpret visions and symbols according to her own inward light by Savonarola just as she has been suppressed by the secular agents of the state—by her father and husband. As she kneels on the altar at the Badia before the image of Filippino Lippi's serene

Virgin, Romola realizes how this revelation applies particularly to her experience as a woman living inside a city she does not and cannot control. Romola has just seen one of the sisters of a religious order imitate Savonarola by describing a religious vision that visited her. Recognizing the self-serving nature of the nun's vision and realizing at the same time why Savonarola will not denounce this woman or any of her "spirit-seeing sisters," Romola is forced to see the essential subjectivity of Savonarola's visions as well:

The answer came with painful clearness: he was fettered inwardly by the consciousness that such revelations were not, in their basis, distinctly separable from his own visions; he was fettered outwardly by the foreseen consequences of raising a cry against himself even among members of his own party, as one who would suppress all Divine inspiration of which he himself was not the vehicle. (ch. 52, p. 526)

Just as she apprehended the limits of her father's and husband's authority in defining the secular images embodying perfect womanhood, so she sees now the prescriptive quality of Savonarola's visions. Indignantly, she confronts him:

Do you, then, know so well what will further the coming of God's kingdom, father, that you dare despise the plea of mercy—of justice—of faithfulness to your own teaching? . . . Take care, father, lest your enemies have some reason when they say that in your visions of what will further God's kingdom, you see only what will strengthen your own party. (ch. 59, p. 578)

With this denunciation, Romola claims the right to define God's kingdom as something "wider" than Savonarola, as Church father, would declare. Thus, she rejects the principles he lives by which allow him to divide men into "sheep and goats by the easy mark of some political or religious symbol" (ch. 52, p. 527).

This is the rebellion that allows Romola to claim her own right to define a moral law and her proper relation to it. When she decides to leave Florence a second time, she determines to act in defiance of both civil and religious law, "in the face of a law which is not unarmed with Divine lightnings," just as Savonarola has done. "The law was sacred, but rebellion might be sacred, too. It flashed upon [Romola's] mind that the problem before her was essentially the same as that which had lain before Savonarola— the problem where the sacredness of obedience ended and where the sacredness of rebellion began. To her, as to him, there came a moment when her soul must dare to act on its own warrant" (ch. 56, pp. 552–53). In claiming this freedom, it is important to note, Romola does not rebel in the traditional way allowed women saints—the means the visionary nun and her sisterhood elected. Rather, she claims the right to describe God's kingdom as something "wider" than that envisioned by Christian visionaries and by Dante as well.

Casting aside all the ideals of her culture, however, is an even more terrifying crisis for Romola than accepting her sexuality, and Eliot presents this second existential crisis as a more devastating one for her heroine. Escaping civilization entails more, for Romola, than confronting her relation to nature; it means surviving the moment when all the classical and Christian myths that have shaped her life cease to hold their meaning. Again, Dino's dream foreshadows her crisis of faith and identity:

And thou, Romola, didst wring thy hands and seek for water, and there was none. . . . And the bronze and marble figures seemed to turn into demons and snatch my father's body from thee, and the parchments shrivelled up, and blood ran everywhere instead of them, and fire upon the blood, till they all vanished, and the plain was bare and stony again, and thou wast alone in the midst of it. (ch. 15, p. 215)

Once she rejects the myths defining her role in the city, Romola's anger and despair are all-consuming, as Dino anticipated, but she turns them inward, good daughter of the city that she is, and contemplates suicide.

Romola sets herself adrift in a tiny boat and floats down the Arno, abandoning herself to her own "imagination," but miraculously she retreats beyond both the thoughts of death and the stories of "proud stoical heroism" that provided her first vision of escape. She recalls instead her girlhood daydreams of "floating naiad-like" down the river. She feels the agnostic's despair when she thinks of her past: "Memories hung upon her like the weight of broken wings that could never be lifted—memories of human sympathy that the Great Mother had no milk to still" (ch. 61, p. 590). By this image borrowed from Dante, Eliot reminds us that though Romola has imitated the role of the Great Mother in her work in Florence, she could find no reciprocity in the material world. Though she served the patriarchy by nurturing the poor and the sick, at the behest of the rich and powerful, she was not herself served or satisfied; her "thirst" for human sympathy persisted.

[91]

In recalling Dante's dream vision of the Holy Mother in the Celestial City at this moment of Romola's despair, Eliot discloses the difficulty of her heroine's—and her own—escape. Though Romola yearns for the "milk" of the Holy Mother, like the white radiances in Dante's Celestial Rose that reach ever upward, imitating, in Dante's metaphor, "the infant that stretches out its arms to its mother after it has taken the milk" (*Paradiso*, 23: 121–22), Romola can find no Paradise like Dante's where her desire for perfect love and justice is satisfied. There is no complementing beatific vision for the woman who is defined by her culture as the Other. Thus, Romola is unable to trace the "message of love in the far-off symbolic writing of the heavens" that Dante learned to read when he was instructed by his Beatrice. Instead, Romola feels herself "orphaned in the wide spaces of sea and sky" (ch. 61, p. 590); her wings remain "crushed," and she thus renounces a place in both the earthly and heavenly cities.

Romola looks for meaning, then, in the Terrestrial rather than the other worldly Paradise. In her "cradle of new life" (ch. 68, p. 641), Romola discovers no reconciliation among the celestial spheres; instead, she finds an earthly world outside the city which retains the "awe for noble womanhood" and pays homage to its "primordial power." When Romola leaves her male mentors behind and passes her Lethe, she regains consciousness in a natural world of pregnant silence and primordial beauty. She turns to the past rather than the future and there discovers her fundamental identity among these images of serene beauty: the crescent-shaped valley, the sapphire blue sea, the green luxuriance, and the ripening corn, all symbolizing the attributes of a prehistoric mother goddess predating Florence's icon of the Madonna. The world that Romola retreats to also contains human suffering and is clearly of this world, for here she finds a crying child, a plague-stricken village, and a ruined hovel.

In this primitive, almost prehistoric world, Romola reconstructs a woman-centered culture and exercises her own power as a moral leader in it. In this rural world set apart from Renaissance culture, Romola recognizes the naturalness and power of her own maternal impulses, but she no longer feels obliged to assume the prescribed role of the "Visible Madonna." Though the priest and sick villagers that she meets initially mistake her for the "Mother with the glory about her tending the sick" (ch. 68, p. 646), Romola is no longer willing to cooperate with Christian mythology by acting the part of the divine and disembodied Holy Mother. She is not content with the "aves" of the priest and the villagers; she commands their active help in a way she could not in Florence. Though she cares for a child that she saves from the plague while she is in the village, she leaves him behind when she returns to Florence. Thus, she refuses to reenact the Virgin birth; for Romola, in this primitive world, as in Florence, there are no annunciations to lift her above humanity: "No radiant angel came across the gloom with a clear message for her" (ch. 36, p. 396).

When she departs, Romola leaves behind, as did the patriarchs of Florence, a myth that describes her. But there are no miracles in the many legends that were "afterwards told in that valley about the blessed Lady who came over the sea" (ch. 68, p. 649); there were no visions of supernaturally self-sacrificing Madonnas, no promises of perpetual help. She leaves, instead, "legends by which all who heard might know that in times gone by a woman had done beautiful loving deeds there, rescuing those who were ready to perish." For Romola, as for Eliot herself, such legends must suffice: "If everything else is doubtful, this suffering that I can help is certain: if the glory of the cross is an illusion, the sorrow is only the truer" (ch. 69, p. 650). Ultimately, Romola returns to Florence because Florentine women—and Victorian women writers like Eliot herself—could not imagine living out a utopian separatist vision of a woman-dominated world set apart from male civilization and culture.

Before she returns to Florence, however, Romola recognizes that the "simpler relations of the human being to his fellow men had been complicated for her with all the special ties of marriage, the State, and religious discipleship" (ch. 69, p. 650), and this revelation is like "a new baptism" to her. She does not, we must note, reassume any of her old functions. She returns, instead, to the family who remains, to her cousin Monna Brigida and to her husband's "second wife," Tessa, with her two children. Though her efforts to restore the simpler family-centered values may seem to reflect Eliot's notorious conservatism, we should observe that Eliot has made this saving remnant a community of women. It is a family that defies patriarchal laws of marriage and legitimacy; Romola accepts the responsibility of caring for Tessa's children as warmly as if they were her own. Furthermore, this is a family without living fathers, since both Tito and Baldasarre are dead.[24]

It is Romola who tells Lillo and Ninna about their natural and spiritual fathers' histories. And in repeating this domestic history, Romola reenacts the mother's role that Dante's Cacciguida so beautifully describes; she tends the cradle and soothes the child, using the "tongue that first delights fathers and mothers" (*Paradiso*, 15: 121–26). However, Eliot has moved beyond Dante's vision, beyond the paradisal world he imagines where Church fathers catechize and the lovely Beatrice instructs. She gives us instead a glimpse of a woman-centered world and reminds us that it is woman who first defines the language that delights the child and composes the history of the "things which have not changed" (Proem). Thus Romola asserts the matriarch's power by exercising her right to define such histories and by speaking of its beauty rather than silently representing it.

In the conclusion of *Romola*, Eliot evades all the apotheosis we might expect for a saint or a goddess and insists that we look at Romola's "maimed life" in all its severe grandeur: she renounces Ariadne's crown; she avoids Antigone's self-destruction; she evades Beatrice's transcendence; she rejects the Madonna's motherhood. She comes to recognize the powerlessness of the Madonna's role in Florence, and her perception is clarified and confirmed when she lives, for a time, outside the gates of the city. Because of her splendid classical education and her moral insight into the Christian tradition, Romola is able to attain a more comprehensive understanding of her place in culture and in nature than either Lucy Snowe or Dorothea. She recognizes, at last, a self that transcends not only the legal and social definitions of womanhood constructed by her society but also the female ideals embodied by literature and art in Florence. Thus, she achieves a self-consciousness about urban life and culture that is, of all Eliot's heroines, perhaps closest to her own. We do Romola a great disservice to see her as a "goddess" and not as a woman; we do Eliot an even greater disservice.

NOTES

1. See Andrew Sanders's introduction to *Romola* (Harmondsworth: Penguin, 1980), 10–11. All subsequent citations to *Romola* refer to this edition.
2. *The George Eliot Letters*, ed. Gordon Haight (New Haven: Yale

Univ. Press, 1954–1980), IV, 102. For similar complaints especially relevant to *Romola*, see III, 293, 294, 360, 376.

3. *Letters*, I, 7.

4. John Cross's frankness in *The Life and Letters of George Eliot* (New York: Sproul, 1899) about the isolation Marian Evans faced as a young woman charged with the responsibilities of housekeeping is especially notable because he was otherwise zealous in suppressing evidence that she was less than a Victorian angel.

5. *Letters*, I, 261.

6. See, for example, Gordon Haight, *George Eliot: A Biography* (New York: Oxford Univ. Press, 1968, paper), 122–210; Ruby Redinger, *George Eliot: The Emergent Self* (New York: Knopf, 1975), 226–94.

7. All citations are to *Middlemarch*, ed. W. J. Harvey (Baltimore: Penguin, 1965), 219–35. This scene is, of course, often cited by critics but none has discussed it in relation to women and to *Villette*, to my knowledge.

8. See Charlotte Brontë, *Villette*, ed. Geoffrey Tillotson and Donald Hawes (Boston: Houghton Mifflin, 1971), 171–77. Eliot was deeply impressed by *Villette*; see *Letters*, II, 87.

9. See, for example, Henry James, *Partial Portraits* (London: Macmillan, 1888), 56. Eliot's feminism has been, of course, often debated, but Gordon Haight mentions her support for marriage and divorce reform in *George Eliot*, 204. For a more extended analysis of Eliot's involvement in this and other Victorian feminist causes, see my "Feminism and Positivism in George Eliot's *Romola*," *Nineteenth-Century Women Writers* (Hofstra University Conference, 1980, proceedings forthcoming). John Goode has also confirmed my analysis in his lecture, "The Affections Clad with Knowledge: The Duty of Woman and the Public Life," George Eliot Conference, Nov. 22, 1980, Rutgers University.

10. Eliot's lack of prudishness in her treatment of Tessa reflects her feminist sympathies and her personal experience in sharing the responsibilities of parenting G. H. Lewes's three sons. Eliot seemed to grow more sympathetic to the situation of what Victorians called the "fallen woman," as is evident when we compare her treatment of Hetty Sorrel in *Adam Bede* to Tessa.

11. Gordon Haight seems to have established this tradition in *George Eliot*, 362. See George Levine, "Romola as 'Fable,'" in Barbara Hardy, ed. *Critical Essays on George Eliot* (New York: Barnes and Noble, 1970), 78–98.

12. *Letters*, IV, 42–43.

13. When I consider the frustrations I felt in simply researching the names, dates, and issues of nineteenth-century feminism, I find an entirely new meaning in Eliot's comment that writing *Romola* transformed her into an "old" woman.

14. In *The Earthly Paradise and the Renaissance Epic* (Princeton: Princeton Univ. Press, 1966), 118.

15. Cross, II, 431.

16. See Nina Auerbach's "Artists and Mothers: A False Alliance," in *Women and Literature* (Spring 1978), 6, no. 1, 3–15. Ironically, John Cross

also adopted a nickname for Eliot during their nine-month marriage cut short by her death in December 1880; he called her "Beatrice." This association of Beatrice and Madonna evident in *Romola* is thus borne out by the private mythology shaping Eliot's personal life.

17. Adrienne Rich uses this evocative term in her "Burning of Paper Instead of Children," in *The Will to Change* (New York: Norton, 1971).

18. See Appendix B in Sanders's edition of *Romola*, 683. This is his translation. All subsequent citations from *The Divine Comedy* refer to John D. Sinclair (New York: Oxford Univ. Press, 1939, paper).

19. George Levine's *"Romola* as 'Fable'" presents perhaps the best analysis of Eliot's failures. See also Joseph Wiesenfarth, *George Eliot's Mythmaking* (Heidelberg: Winter 1977), for an excellent summary of this critical tradition.

20. This is Carole Robinson's term from her *"Romola*: A Reading of the Novel," in *Victorian Studies* 6 (1966) 40. I find Dante to be a much less anachronistic parallel for *Romola* than Sartre.

21. Eliot stresses Romola's womanliness, in part, I think, to counter the reactionary Victorian arguments that too much education could "unsex" women. Providing an adequate education, of course, is a complicated problem as Eliot's subsequent treatment of Romola's experience with patriarchal culture reveals.

22. Needless to say, Romola's consciousness that she must wear a costume on the street for her own protection is another element that invites comparison to Victorian—and modern—women's experiences.

23. Eliot's description of Romola's career as a nurse, emphasizing her moral stature and chaste integrity, echoes Florence Nightingale's argument that nursing was a respectable profession for the Victorian woman.

24. The alliance between Romola and Tessa reflects the association that drew middle-class wives and mistresses together later in the agitation to repeal the Contagious Disease Acts in 1871. See Judy Walkowitz's excellent essay, "The Politics of Prostitution," in *Women: Sex and Sexuality*, ed. Catherine R. Stimpson (Chicago: Univ. of Chicago Press, 1980), 145–57.

LOUISE A. DeSALVO

Every Woman Is an Island: Vita Sackville-West, the Image of the City, and the Pastoral Idyll

VITA SACKVILLE-WEST'S *All Passion Spent*, published in 1931,[1] is as astonishingly feminist as Virginia Woolf's *A Room of One's Own* and Rebecca West's *Harriet Hume*.[2] For what it eloquently demonstrates is that the life of a woman without a room of her own, without a work of her own,[3] is the life of a somnambulist—is, in fact, no life at all. And in *All Passion Spent*, the woman's life as somnambulist is lived in the city—that social, political, and economic fortress erected by man to enable him to carry out his work while banishing all things natural, including human affection, and where he incarcerates the woman he has chosen to live his life with him, beside him, while he devotes himself to the task of building the British Empire.

Sackville-West had not always been the egalitarian pacifist feminist she seems to have become (at least for a time) in *All Passion Spent*. Nor had she always defined the city as the place from which men exerted their power; nor always manifested a contempt for the principles of patriarchy which lie at the root of the empire. As a very young child, from one of the noblest and most ancient families in all of England, living at Knole in the Kentish weald, she played very often at being a boy, a soldier, a commander of armies. When her father was in the South African war, she was "always grubby and in tatters."[4] Emulating him, she dug trenches in the garden, raised and commanded an army among the "terrorized children of the neighbourhood," shedding tears of rage when she was not allowed to have her khaki suit made with a pair of trousers instead of a skirt.[5]

In her adolescence, foreign cities became the places where she could have the freedom to act out her lesbian love in a way that was not possible at home. In a letter from Violet Trefusis to her, the allure of a foreign land is described; there one could be lascivious, sensual, even cruel:

I would like to . . . take you on a pleasure-trip with me far away, far from everything. . . . First we must go to Spain. . . . I will show you Manzanares with its winding lanes; Irun, overshadowed by the Pyrenees, with its lovely cruel girls. . . . Follow me everywhere! I will show you eyes of dark velvet, the fandango, undulating bodies, the throbbing castanets, the magpies strutting between the olives, the sad plains, a fluttering mantilla. . . . I will show you treason, infamy, women without scruple, without shame.[6]

According to her son Nigel Nicolson, Vita Sackville-West was a snob, a conforming rebel, a romantic aristocrat: "She attached exaggerated importance to birth and wealth, and believed that while the aristocracy had much in common with working people, particularly those who worked on the land, the middle class . . . were to be pitied and shunned, unless . . . they had acquired dignity by riches."[7] In a letter written to Harold Nicolson before their marriage, she describes a party at the American Embassy in London and she paints ambassadorial life in a very positive light:

I felt a magnificent house wasn't to be despised. I liked it because it was so rich and . . . ambassadorial; and because I am a snob enough to love long dinner-tables covered with splendid fruit and orchids and gold plate, and people whose names I can find in the *Daily Mail* sitting all around.[8]

But her mother Lady Sackville had her doubts about her daughter's ability to carry on the life of an ambassador's wife, and this was the life that Vita seemed destined to live if she married Harold Nicolson.

V. is not suited to diplomacy. . . . She ought to be a *grande dame*, very rich, where she could do what she likes. . . . She told me yesterday she would like to live alone in a tower with her books, and then she threw up her arms and said, "Oh Mama, I really don't know what I want."[9]

When Vita herself contemplated a life in the ambassadorial circles of foreign cities with Harold Nicolson, she confided to her diary:

The very idea of Vienna has appalled me. Am I to pass all my life abroad? I can't do it. I let Mama see how I felt, and this was the first indication she has had of my change of mind. . . . I simply can't leave Knole for Vienna![10]

So that it was not life in a city, or life in a foreign city that appalled her, for with a woman by her side, or alone, she had lived and could live a rich life of freedom and forbidden pleasure. It was the life of a wife in an ambassadorial circle that would curtail her freedom, that would force her to subjugate the lesbian side of her nature,[11] although later in her life she was able to live out both sides of herself. Wifehood became, however, necessary, for she truly loved Harold, believing that marriage to him would be the only way that she could control what she described as the darker side of her nature. Wifehood became, on the other hand, a kind of servitude that she, as an aristocrat, had never before experienced, even if she had been born a noble Sackville, a servitude that seemed to resemble that of the lives of the lower classes.

According to Joanne Trautmann, the fact that Vita Sackville-West, the only child of Lord Sackville, was prevented from inheriting Knole, that 365-room great house with a history that extended far back into the history of England, so wrenched her that she was capable of visiting it only once between the death of her father in 1928 and her own death in 1961.[12] Vita's love for Knole was even greater in many ways than her love for any of the people in her life. On the eve of her wedding, she wrote a poem bidding it farewell:

> To Knole. 1 October 1913
> *I left thee in the crowds and in the light,*
> *And if I laughed or sorrowed none could tell.*
> *They could not know our true and deep farewell*
> *Was spoken in the long preceding night. . . .*[13]

In 1950, the loss still pained her, and she wrote to Harold Nicolson, ". . . my Knole, my Knole! . . . oh God, I do wish that Knole hadn't got such a hold on my heart! If only I had been Dada's son, instead of his daughter!"[14]

Nigel Nicolson has stated that the roots of his mother's feminism can be traced, in part, to her resentment that she would not inherit Knole,[15] gavelkind in Kent stipulating the entail of the house on male heirs only. Her life as a wife, coupled with her inability to inherit Knole, caused her to revise certain of her attitudes toward the aristocracy, toward patriarchal institutions, and, eventually, toward the city and the country as the places in which these institutions made their presences felt.

This change can be easily gauged by comparing *The Heir*, first privately printed in 1922, with *All Passion Spent*, published in 1931. *The Heir*, subtitled *A Love Story*, recounts how Mr. Peregrine Chase, manager of a small insurance office in Wolverhampton, a "sandy, weakly-looking little man, with thin reddish hair, freckles, and washy blue eyes," comes to love and refuse to part with Blackboys, an Elizabethan manor house with a Tudor moat, that has been left to him by an aunt that he has never met. Although he initially had been persuaded by solicitors to sell the house, by the end of the novel, Mr. Chase has developed a sense of the importance of the private ownership of property, of the importance of tradition. He has walked through the manor house, feeling its wood, smelling its smells, hearing its peacocks screeching, walking across its polished oak floors. And he has developed a very new sense of himself that is based upon his inheritance of the tradition of his forebears.

Chase has grown up in a very different world from that of his aunt. She has lived her life in this place with the services of fortune to assist her. Chase, however, has been poor, and has spent his life in factory towns:

> He was poor; and hard-working in a cheerless fashion; . . . and expected nothing further of life. Not very robust, his days in an office left him with little energy after he had conscientiously carried out his business. He lived in lodgings in Wolverhampton, smoking rather too much and eating rather too little. He had neither loved nor married. [16]

Although Sackville-West records the cheerless drudgery of Chase's work, and the dispiriting life of factory towns, the solution that she provides for Chase in *The Heir* is ultimately conservative, far different from the solution that she proposes years later in *All Passion Spent*. Chase falls in love with a place, with Blackboys, and he falls in love with the landholding tradition, the very tradition that denied Vita Sackville-West Knole because she was a woman, the very tradition that had necessitated his drudgery in an office in a factory town, the very tradition that had necessitated the factory worker's spiritless life.

In one sense, *The Heir* is wish-fulfillment, and Chase's inheriting Blackboys represents Sackville-West's wish that she could have inherited Knole. In *The Heir*, she does not criticize the system that had prohibited her inheritance, nor does she investigate the relationship of the private ownership of property to the patriarchal structure of society, as she would, in *All Passion Spent*. In *The Heir* she also establishes the dichotomy between the city and the town as places of working-class drudgery, and the country as an idyllic retreat from those problems into the sanctity and serenity of solitude. But *The Heir* was written before Vita Sackville-West's father died in 1928, before she experienced the loss of Knole that was so devastating, even though it was expected[17]; *All Passion Spent* was written after Vita had lived with the loss of Knole.

The Heir expresses that age-old romantically idealistic pastoral yearning that holds that everything evil exists in cities and everything wonderful occurs in the country where peacocks shriek and sheep graze. At the end of the novel, Chase looks forward to an idyllic life in the country, far away from the pressures and problems of his earlier life in the city.

In *The Land*, published in 1926, Sackville-West explores, as well, the nature of that country life which stands in such sharp contrast to life in the city. In one passage, events in the city are contrasted with the permanence of the land and the work of the yeoman who shapes the "fields, slow-paced, / Into their permanent design."[18] On the one hand, there is the evanescence of the city and diplomacy, carried out by a male elite, the affairs of state changing and shifting with every change in age, point of view, and political philosophy; on the other hand, there is the permanence of the land and humble work, the work of the yeoman, the bee-keeper, the shepherd, the craftsman, in tune with the rhythms of the year which remain the same throughout the ages.

But in this hundred-odd-page celebration of country life, Sackville-West mentions the rightful work of women only a few times, as if women have no place in the country just as they have no place in the political and diplomatic affairs of the city, as if the idyll of life in the country does not extend to women. In one instance, the farmer's wife is depicted as the consumer of the wares of the tradesman who tempts her by asking "What lack you? What d'you lack?"—that age-old appeal to the housewife. In another, Sackville-West states that the very land itself, especially the woodlands, provides no sylvan retreat, no safe and comfortable dwelling place for women. In the "Autumn" section, the relationship of woman to woodlands is described. Although women "still have memories of woods / Older than any personal memories" and although women are themselves "Like trees that fan the air with delicacies":

> Woods are her enemies, yet once she went
> Fleeing before a god, and, all but spent,
> Slipped from his arms, herself become a tree.
> She has forgotten; wood's an enemy. (96)

For Sackville-West, the woods are a place where men victimize women, not a sacred place where women's powerful spirits have been entrapped within trees as nymphs. Although the dichotomy between the evil city and the idyllic country might hold for men, it does not hold for women.

In *The Land*, there is a section entitled "The Island," which describes a garden, made by a woman, as an act of creation and procreation:

> *She walks among the loveliness she made,*
> *Between the apple-blossom and the water. . . .*
> *Each flower her son, and every tree her daughter.*
> *This is an island all with flowers inlaid, . . .*
> *Flowers in their order blowing as she bade,*
> *And in their company by her created.* (45)

This garden is one of the only things over which a woman can have absolute power and control—it substitutes for her lack of control over her own life and her powerlessness, compared to the power of men:

> *Her regiments at her command parade,*
> *Foot-soldier primrose in his rank comes trooping,*
> *Then wind-flowers in a scarlet loose brigade, . . .*
> *There, in the sunlit grasses green as jade,*
> *She walks; she sees her squadrons at attention,*
> *And, laughing at her flowery escapade,*
> *Stretches her hands towards her dear invention.* (46)

There is a curious ambivalence here. The act of creating a garden, usually described in generative life-enhancing terms, is here described as a battle with a woman as commander-in-chief. Described as if it were an act of aggression in which she takes a childlike delight, gardening for a woman is an act of submission. One of Vita Sackville-West's first acts after she and Harold Nicolson went to Constantinople soon after their marriage was to make her first garden on this foreign soil. The garden is the only terrain which a woman is allowed to conquer; the only battlefield upon which she can command regiments. Gardening, therefore, becomes a hostile act, while at the same time it is a pathetic admission of the fact that women have no other arenas (except perhaps the kitchen) in which they can dominate. A woman commandeers her flowers and her vegetables as a man launches warships and begins battles; a woman pulls out the weeds as a man routs the infidel.

Because of the laws of inheritance, because women are excluded from political life, because of the private ownership of land and of property (usually by men), and because women are also out of place in the country, the most a woman can do is to carve out an island for herself to cultivate as a garden on the property which belongs to man, as the woman in *The Land* has done, as Vita Sackville-West herself had done in Constantinople. Metaphorically, she must make of herself an island within the world of men. Life as an island has its rewards in solitude; it has its liability in that the fundamental structure of society is not changed. Life as an island is an admission of failure, an acceptance of dominance, an indication of defeat.

When Virginia Woolf wrote *Orlando*, that mock biography of her friend Vita Sackville-West (published in 1928, two years after *The Land* and three years before *All Passion Spent*), she had the example of Vita's poem *The Land* in mind when she depicted Orlando's centuries-long process of composing "The Oak Tree." Whatever else Orlando may be, it is also a manual of instruction from Virginia Woolf to Vita Sackville-West about the dangers inherent in the way she had been thinking about inheritance, about her ancestry, about the relationship between the classes, about the idyllic nature of life in the country, about the fantasy that foreign cities temporarily can provide a woman with the freedom to be herself.

From the first, Orlando is filled with a sense of awe at his and his family's possessions, as Vita had been as a young woman:

For a moment Orlando stood counting, gazing, recognising. That was his father's house; that his uncle's. His aunt owned those three great turrets among the trees there. The heath was theirs and the forest; the pheasant and the deer, the fox, the badger, and the butterfly.[19]

However much Orlando is smitten by Sasha, the Russian woman who captivates him, he woos her with a recitative of his family's history, and his ardor cools when he suspects that her family is not nearly as illustrious as his. He tells her

> how their house was one of the most ancient in Britain; . . . he would pause and ask her, Where was her own house? What was her father? Had she brothers? (48)

And, when Sasha doesn't answer readily enough, "an awkwardness would come between them" (48).

After Sasha leaves for Russia, Orlando withdraws to the solitude of the country. The first lesson that he learns is about the vanity of earthly possessions—the fact that what one owns is a meaningless indication of worth because all people eventually die:

> Orlando now took a strange delight in thoughts of death and decay, and, after pacing the long galleries and ballrooms with a taper in his hand, looking at picture after picture as if he sought the likeness of somebody whom he could not find. . . . Even this was not enough for him, but he must descend into the crypt where his ancestors lay, coffin piled upon coffin, for ten generations together. . . . "Nothing remains of all these Princes," Orlando would say, indulging in some pardonable exaggeration of their rank, "except one digit," and he would take a skeleton hand in his and bend the joints this way and that. (70–71)

What Orlando, and by extension, Vita Sackville-West herself, must learn, according to Woolf, is that one's ancestry and genealogy do not matter at all compared with the immortality that a writer can achieve through the creation of a work of art. Whom, for example, does one remember—Orlando's forebears or the works of Sir Thomas Browne?

> Standing upright in the solitude of his room, he vowed that he would be the first poet of his race and bring immortal lustre upon his name. He said (reciting the names and exploits of his ancestors) . . . of all that killing and campaigning, that drinking and love-making, that spending and hunting and riding and eating, what remained? A skull; a finger. (81)

Later, when thinking of the possible fame and glory that will be his through writing, Orlando looks at his great house, and contemplates that it was built by anonymous workers, and he realizes that this is more of a permanent creation than anything that has ever been done by his supposedly illustrious family:

Not one of these Richards, Johns, Annes, Elizabeths has left a token of himself behind him, yet all, working together with their spades and their needles, their love-making and their child-bearing, have left this. (106)

Orlando learns that the life of the writer bears more resemblance to the life of the lower classes than it does to the life of an aristocrat. Both writer and worker are, in effect, artisans, joined together by the sanctity of their work. The only difference between the writer and the worker is whether or not their names are attached to the product of their labor. Neither is exploitative; both make solid tangible contributions to the beauty and well-being of humanity.

Better was it to go unknown and leave behind you an arch, a potting shed, a wall where peaches ripen, than to burn like a meteor and leave no dust. (106–107)

After Orlando becomes transformed into a woman, she lives among the gypsies. It is there that she is forced to question her idealistic view of nature.

The English disease, a love of Nature, was inborn in her . . . her soul expanded with her eyeballs, and she prayed that she might share the majesty of the hills, know the serenity of the plains, etc., etc., as all such believers do. Then, looking down, the red hyacinth, the purple iris wrought her to cry out in ecstasy at the goodness, the beauty of nature; raising her eyes again, she beheld the eagle soaring, and imagined its raptures and made them her own. (143–44)

Woolf indicates that this English disease, this love of nature, is worse than an escapist fantasy, for it provides the means by which the aristocracy distort the reality of the hard, gruesome life of peasants. Rustum el Sadi, the old man who brings Orlando out of Constantinople on his donkey, sits silent, watching her, going into raptures over the sights and sounds of nature. "He had the deepest suspicion that her God was Nature" (144). He shows her that she is misguided; he holds out to her "the fingers of his left hand, withered by the frost; he showed her his right foot, crushed where a rock had fallen. This, he said, was what her God did to men" (144).

The message is clear. Behind the privet fences that grew to great heights around the gardens of estates such as Knole, the aristocracy, the landed gentry can indulge themselves in the fantasy that life in the weald, in the wood, in the meadow, is better, for everyone, even the peasant, the farmer, the yeoman, than life can ever be in the city; they can indulge themselves in the self-protective, self-serving fantasy that they share, with the yeoman, a love for their land and that they are, in fact, all brothers and sisters under the skin, united through the commonality of the countryside. By living within this beauty, their aristocratic natures must naturally be transformed, must partake of the glory and the goodness of the countryside. Although the exploitative nature of a stratified society might evidence itself in the city, in the country, the aristocracy can indulge themselves in the hallucination that the yeoman and the farmer are happy, are at peace, are, like themselves, ennobled by their connection with the land. It is, of course, as Virginia Woolf demonstrates, a preposterous delusion, a monstrous hoax.

Looked at from the gipsy point of view, a Duke, Orlando understood, was nothing but a profiteer or robber who snatched land and money. (148)

Back in London, Orlando learns that the exploitation of women is akin to the exploitation of the lower classes; she learns:

The life of the average woman was a succession of childbirths. She married at nineteen and had fifteen or eighteen children by the time she was thirty; for twins abounded. Thus the British Empire came into existence.(229)

If *All Passion Spent* is any indication, Sackville-West learned the most important lessons that Virginia Woolf had taught her in *Orlando*, lessons that extended her consciousness of the exploitation of women beyond that which she had sketched in *The Land*, which is still basically an idyll of country life: that whether a woman lives in the city or in the country, her life is the same; it resembles the life of peasants, of yeomen. As women give birth for the empire, so peasants' limbs are crushed in servitude. And above all is the aristocracy, living a life of luxury, profiteering and plundering, snatching land and money, dominating, ruling.

As *All Passion Spent* opens, the body of Henry Holland, Earl of Slane, career diplomat, former member of cabinet, former Prime Minister, former Viceroy to India, is awaiting burial.[20] His widow, Lady Slane (her name is an apt one), eighty-eight years of age, has yet to live her life. She has, up until now, lived his life beside him. She has followed him to all the capital cities where his career has taken him; she has cared for their children, whom she doesn't very much like; she has received and worn the splendid gifts of jewels, given her by various heads of state, which she doesn't very much value. But she has not yet lived a life of her own. She has never painted the pictures she has dreamed of making.

Duty, charity, children, social obligations, public appearances—with these had her days been filled; and whenever her name was mentioned, the corollary came quick and slick, "Such a wonderful help to her husband in his career!" (50)

Lady Slane's children cannot visualize her anywhere but in the city, "anywhere but in London" (52). And it is in London, in the city, where Lady Slane has "been the life of others" (52), the Angel of Mercy, ministering unto the Battersea Club for Poor Women, the Foundlings' Ward, the Unfortunate Sisters' Organization. It is in the city where she has had her life arranged for her. According to her son, who has inherited his father's place, as well as his attitude:

Of course, she would not question the wisdom of any arrangements they might choose to make. Mother had no will of her own; all her life long, gracious and gentle, she had been wholly submissive—an appendage. It was assumed that she had not enough brain to be self-assertive. . . . She would be grateful to them for arranging her few remaining years. (15)

And it is in London and in other cities where Lady Slane has always been surrounded—surrounded by her husband and her children and servants and diplomats, conducting the affairs of state. In cities, things, concerns, functions, people have always stood between her and the world. She has never been allowed to meet the city or anything or anyone on her own terms. She has, in fact, been made into an island in the middle of the city, an island unto herself, taken care of, isolated, protected from the invasion of insidious influences from the outside, as one would protect and care for a crown colony. And, like a crown colony, Lady Slane doesn't very much like what has happened to her under the dominion of his influence, although she has kept her peace and her place and her silence through these sixty long years of her life with him. Imperialism, it would appear, as Virginia Woolf indicated in *Orlando*, begins at home.

In *All Passion Spent*, the city is associated with the domination of women by men, with politics, with diplomacy, and with the striving ways of the world, which happen to be the striving ways of institutions controlled by men for the greater glory of men. In one memory, from her earlier days, Lady Slane, in reaching back, sees herself in the abandoned city of Fatihpur Sikhri, with a young man named FitzGeorge beside her. This abandoned city becomes the symbol of how vainglorious and unnatural is man's attempt to strive and control and dominate, and is like the scene between Orlando and Rustum el Sadi in *Orlando*:

> She and the young man beside her were isolated from the rest of the world. The Viceroy was away from them, inspecting the mother-of-pearl mosque . . . ; he was pointing with his stick and saying that the ringdoves ought to be cleared away from under the eaves. The young man beside Lady Slane said softly that it was a pity the ringdoves should be condemned, for if a city were abandoned by man, why should the doves not inherit it? . . . There was something unusual, he said, in a city of mosques, palaces, and courts, inhabited solely by birds and animals; he would like to see a tiger going up Akbar's steps, and a cobra coiling its length neatly in the council chamber. They would be more becoming, he thought, to the red city than men in boots. (208–209)

The opportunity to live a life truly her own comes to Lady Slane only with her husband dead and safely stowed under a slab of marble in Westminister Abbey. It is no wonder, therefore, that Sackville-West's husband, Harold Nicolson, himself a diplomat, told his wife that he didn't like *All Passion Spent* very much at all.[21]

In the novel, Lady Slane's life in London and in the cities of her husband's diplomatic career is contrasted with the life she makes for herself in Hampstead Heath, on the fringes of the countryside, after his death, much to the chagrin of her children, who want to continue managing her as their father had managed her before them. Riding on the Underground to Hampstead Heath, to seek out a little house she had seen some thirty years before and remembered through the years, which she intends to let if it is available, she has her first taste of freedom in sixty years, her first taste of anonymity, her first taste of solitude:

> Nor did she look her age, as she sat, swaying slightly with the rocking of the Underground train, very upright, clasping her umbrella and her bag, her ticket carefully pushed into the opening of her glove. It did not occur to her to wonder what her travelling companions would think, could

they know that two days previously she had buried her husband in Westminister Abbey. She was more immediately concerned with the extraordinary sensation of being independent. (71–72)

It is in Hampstead Heath, in that border land that verges on the country, that Lady Slane, at eighty-eight years of age, finally and fully lives a life of her own, on her own.

Hampstead seemed scarcely a part of London, so sleepy and village-like. . . . She walked slowly but happily, and without anxiety, as in a friendly retreat, no longer thinking of Henry's opinions of his children, or indeed of anything but the necessity of finding the house, *her* house, . . . with its garden behind it. (78)

In Hampstead Heath, she now has the solitude and privacy necessary for a life of contemplation; the time to watch the play of the seasons and the workings of the spider. And it is here that she is able to come to know herself as the person she was once, as the person she has become, and as the artist she might have been.

She would be content to stir with the breeze and grow green in the light of the sun, and to drift down the passage of years, until death pushed her gently out and shut the door behind her. She wanted nothing but passivity while these outward things worked their will upon her. (83–84)

What Lady Slane finally comes to realize, from watching the Heath, from being able to take the time to look within herself and to meditate on the significance of her earlier life lived on the fringes of diplomacy and politics, is that the difference between truly living and merely existing is the difference between "striving" and "nonstriving," between acquisitiveness and the renunciation of worldly goods, and, ultimately, between living a destructive life of domination and the life of a creative human being. She concludes that the world is horrible: "It is horrible because it is based upon competitive struggle—and really one does not know whether to call the basis of that struggle a convention or a necessity" (113). She thinks of her children, who have inherited her husband's ways—"trying and striving, not content merely to *be*" (126):

She supposed that party politics and war and industry, and a high birth rate (which she had learned to call man power), and competition and secret diplomacy and suspicion, were all part of a necessary game, necessary since the cleverest people she knew made it their business, though to her, as a game, unintelligible; she supposed it must be so, though the feeling more frequently seized her of watching figures moving in the delusion of a terrible and ridiculous dream. The whole tragic system seemed to be based upon an extraordinary convention. . . . (125–26)

This convention had made men "turn strife into their principle, rather than amity" (126).

In Hampstead Heath, she has what she has never been able to have in the city because of its striving ways. She is able to establish egalitarian relationships with people outside her social class, with Mr. Bucktrout, owner of the house, who, like herself, understands the rhythms of life and the lure of the seasons, the necessity for quietude in old age; with Mr. Gosheron, the fix-it man, who understands that houses have souls, that making and fixing things take a long time; and, at long last, with her maid Genoux who understands how lonely one can be in the midst of people. She is also able, for the first time, to establish a true and deeply felt equality with a man, with Mr. FitzGeorge, who reenters her life, who leaves her his fortune in art, and who provides her with the conditions to choose to renounce that gift and continue to live the quiet life she has decided upon for her last year.

It is no accident that Lady Slane's house is located in the boundary between the inimical city and the hostile country, in the borderland which is neither city nor country, within which she can, at long last, make of herself an invincible island. She allows no incursions from the outside which she herself does not arrange for; tolerates no intrusions—no children, no grandchildren, no great-grandchildren will disturb the equinox of her days.

One of Lady Slane's most cherished memories from her adolescence is her fantasy of a free life in a foreign city, a fantasy that parallels the life that Vita herself had led as a young woman. In a foreign city, she would have had the freedom which would have permitted her to become an artist—but that freedom would necessitate a travestied sex which, in itself, was an allure:

Those ringlets would drop beneath the scissors— . . . that fichu would be replaced by a shirt . . . those skirts would be kicked forever aside. . . . The image of the girl faded, and in its place stood a slender boy. He was a boy, but essentially he was a sexless creature, a mere symbol and emanation of youth, one who had forsworn forever the delights and rights of sex to serve what seemed to his rioting imagination a nobler aim. (143)

[110]

In Lady Slane's recollection, the freedom of life in a foreign city in boy's clothes was a precondition for making art—but that fantasy necessitates a renunciation of the pleasures of sexuality, a denial of one's own sexual nature. She recognizes that the freedom of the transvestite life comes from travesty, from pretending that one is male, so that it is temporary, lasting only as long as one wears men's clothes.

All Passion Spent states that there is a great deal of difference between owning art—which the city fosters (FitzGeorge collects his pieces in the cities of the world and lives with them in London) and making art—which is what Lady Slane had wanted to do. Lady Slane renounces the gift of FitzGeorge's fortune in artistic treasures and gives his collection to the nation and his money to the poor. Lady Slane understands that FitzGeorge

> had tempted her only in order that she should find the strength to reject it. He had offered her not so much a fortune as a chance to be true to herself. . . . It had seemed wrong to her that private people should own such possessions, such exaggerated wealth; therefore she had hastened to dispose of both, the treasures to the public and the money to the suffering poor; the logic was simple though trenchant. (272–73)

Paradoxically, it is because Deborah is no longer an heiress that she is able to refuse the marriage arranged for her and to become a musician—the artist that Lady Slane never was. And times have changed from when Lady Slane was a girl. It is now possible (although frightening) to live alone as an artist, to renounce the economic security that comes with marriage, for the more risky life of a creator. In the closing pages of the book, Lady Slane gives Deborah the greatest gift of all—the support and the courage for her to insist upon the independence and solitude necessary for creation.

> This hour of union with the old woman soothed her like music, like chords lightly touched in the evening, with the shadows closing and the moths bruising beyond an open window. She leaned against the old woman's knee as a support, a prop, drowned, enfolded, in warmth, dimness, and soft harmonious sounds. . . . On some remote piano the chords were struck, and they were chords which had no meaning, no existence, in the world inhabited by her grandfather . . . but in her great-grandmother's world they had their value and their significance. (286–88)

In *All Passion Spent*, Vita Sackville-West states that the city is the symbol of man's domination—not only of women, but also of the lower classes and of nature. In the city, diplomacy and politics prevail; they have been developed as the institutions through which men dominate women; through which the upper classes dominate the lower classes. In the city, materialism and acquisitiveness prevail; they are the outward manifestations of man's perversion of the nonstriving natural order of things; as material goods are the outward symbols of one person's wealth and ascendancy, of another's poverty and subservience. In the city, strife and conflict have become principles of existence—a Darwinian struggle in which the survival of the fittest through the domination or elimination of those defined as the weakest is the theoretical principle which both legitimates and masks the subjugation of one sex by another, one class by another. And the country is no better, except that in the country this struggle is more difficult to perceive because it is hidden beneath the myth of the goodness of the countryside. In the city or in the country, there is no hope for women, just as there is no hope for the poor or for the oppressed, unless the very structure of society is changed.

The conditions necessary to create art, or to create a life of one's own seem in *All Passion Spent* to be incompatible with the institution of marriage, the private ownership of property, and the striving ways of the city. Deborah must, in her youth, make of herself an island, either in a foreign city or in that border land between city and country, as her great-grandmother has done in the closing days of her life—an island unfettered by the ties of affection, ownership, or striving for material goods. Given the conditions imposed upon her by men, every woman, Vita Sackville-West insists, must, with the emotional strength and support of another woman, become an island unto herself if she is to live the life of a creator.

NOTES

1. V. Sackville-West, *All Passion Spent* (Garden City, N. Y.: Doubleday, Doran, 1931). Further references will be to this edition, and page numbers referred to later in the discussion will be placed within parentheses in the body of the text.
2. I would like to thank Jane Marcus for pointing out the correspondence between *All Passion Spent* and West's novel, and for numer-

ous discussions which contributed to this paper, particularly to the sections which treat Sackville-West's attitude to the country. *A Room* and *Harriet Hume* were both published in 1929.

3. See Sara Ruddick, "A Work of One's Own," in Sara Ruddick and Pamela Daniels, eds., *Working It Out* (New York: Pantheon, 1977).

4. V. Sackville-West, "Autobiography," Part I, in Nigel Nicolson, *Portrait of a Marriage* (New York: Bantam, 1973), 11.

5. Ibid.

6. Violet Keppel to Vita Sackville-West in ibid., 78.

7. Ibid., 82.

8. V. Sackville-West to Harold Nicolson, in ibid., 83.

9. Lady Sackville, "Diary," in ibid., 92.

10. V. Sackville-West, "Diary," in ibid., 94.

11. Ibid., 91–97.

12. Joanne Trautmann, *The Jessamy Brides: The Friendship of Virginia Woolf and V. Sackville-West* (University Park: Pennsylvania State Univ. Press, 1973), 5.

13. V. Sackville-West, "To Knole," *Poems of West and East*, in ibid., 99.

14. V. Sackville-West to Harold Nicolson, in Trautmann, 5.

15. Nigel Nicolson to this writer, letter dated 1st November 1980, Sissinghurst Castle, Kent.

I should like to thank Nigel Nicolson for his lengthy response to another essay of mine on Vita Sackville-West which clarified certain of the ideas expressed herein. The ideas expressed are, of course, my own.

16. V. Sackville-West, *The Heir: A Love Story*, (London: Richards, 1949; first privately printed in 1922), 24–25.

17. Michael Stevens, *V. Sackville-West: A Critical Biography* (New York: Scribner's, 1974), 22.

18. V. Sackville-West, *The Land*, with woodcuts by George Plank (London: Heinemann, 1926, 1976), 23. Further references will be placed within parentheses in the body of the text.

19. Virginia Woolf, *Orlando: A Biography* (New York: Harcourt Brace Jovanovich, 1928, 1956), 18–19. Further references are to this edition and are placed within parentheses in the body of the text.

20. This portion of this essay was read at the Modern Language Association Convention at San Francisco, California, in December 1979, in a panel on women and the image of the city, "Cities of Sisterhood," chaired by Susan Merrill Squier. I should like to thank Susan Merrill Squier for inviting me to write the paper for her panel, and for discussions which clarified important issues for me.

21. See Stevens, p. 75.

SUSAN MERRILL SQUIER

Tradition and Revision: The Classic City Novel and Virginia Woolf's *Night and Day*

To VIRGINIA WOOLF, the city of London was the focus for an intense, often ambivalent, lifelong scrutiny. Not only did she make her home there for nearly all of her fifty-nine years, but she found it a powerfully evocative figure in the literary tradition within which she wrote her eleven novels, two volumes of short stories, and countless essays. Yet in March 1915, it seemed to Woolf as if life in London, with its social and intellectual excitement, would no longer be possible for her. Completion of her first novel in 1913 had left her agitated and delusional. When rest, balanced meals, and doses of "Robin's Hypophosphate" failed to cure her, she was sent on doctor's orders to Twickenham convalescent home. There she endured the rest cure developed by Dr. Silas Weir Mitchell: quiet country life, bed rest, and endless glasses of milk.

In March 1915, her progress toward recovery ended. A relapse occurred which raised the possibility that Virginia and Leonard Woolf's temporary residence in Richmond, where they had been living in lodgings since October of the previous year, should become permanent. "Certainly [Richmond] is the first of the suburbs by a long way, because it is not an offshoot of London, any more than Oxford or Marlborough is," Woolf considered in her diary.[1] Yet her attempt to reconcile herself to suburban life, half-hearted as it was, did not disguise London's continuing fascination for her; she was still searching for rooms there on every visit

[114]

to the city. In particular, she was drawn to Holborn and Bloomsbury, enjoying their "tumult & riot & busyness."[2]

It was not London's activity alone which explained her reluctance to leave it for a home in the suburbs, however. Woolf seems to have associated the city with the ability to do serious intellectual work, finding in its "crowded streets . . . the only places . . . that ever make me what-in-the-case of another-one-might-call-think."[3] London was "serious life" to her, unlike Richmond, where she had "always come . . . for an outing."[4] The last entry in her diary before the relapse of March 1915 records a day spent in the city. While it captures London's importance to her life as a writer, it also suggests the city's danger to her tenuous balance of mind. "Then I had tea, & rambled down to Charing Cross in the dark, making up phrases & incidents to write about. Which is, I expect, the way one gets killed."[5] The actual risk Woolf seems to have taken is disturbing, yet what is perhaps even more disquieting is her offhand dismissal of it as "the way one gets killed." London is clearly a source of creative inspiration for her, but at this time in her life it also appears to have been a dangerous environment for her—physically and psychologically. Prudence, it seemed, dictated the move to the more sedate Richmond, which occurred just one day before publication of *The Voyage Out*, just as Woolf began her second—and successful—convalescence.

Although this second cure was successful, a mood of caution lingered, and when Woolf began to plan her second novel a year later, a similar desire to avoid stimulation seems to have shaped that venture. As she confessed long afterward to Ethel Smyth:

After being ill and suffering every form and variety of nightmare and extravagant intensity of perception . . . after all this, when I came to, I was so tremblingly afraid of my own insanity that I wrote *Night and Day* mainly to prove to my own satisfaction that I could keep entirely off that dangerous ground. I wrote it, lying in bed, allowed to write for only one half hour a day. And I made myself copy from plaster casts, partly to tranquillise, partly to learn anatomy. Bad as the book is, it composed my mind, and I think taught me certain elements of composition which I should not have had the patience to learn had I been in full flush of health always.[6]

To understand what Virginia Woolf learned in *Night and Day*, her second novel, we must consider the emotional and aesthetic reasons for what E. M. Forster called her curious condescension

[115]

to classicism.[7] It is generally agreed that the center of the novel was Woolf's beloved sister, Vanessa Bell. In a letter to her Latin teacher, Janet Case, she hinted "try thinking of Katharine [the protagonist] as Vanessa, not me; and suppose her concealing a passion for painting and forced to go into Society by George [Duckworth]."[8] Yet her explanation of the novel's origin, in the letter to Ethel Smyth, suggests that Woolf identified strongly with Vanessa's dilemma: she appropriates the metaphor of the art student to acknowledge the novel's stilted, derivative nature, explaining that it derives from her use of real people and events as "plaster casts" from which to copy.

Those real events and people which formed the original for *Night and Day* were, first of all, the educational divisions of daily life for Vanessa and Virginia Stephen in their years at 22 Hyde Park Gate, Kensington. The novel's title recalls them, thus inverting the culturally established expectations that "night" will be a time of creative fantasy and "day" a time of practical labor. For the Stephen women it was during the day that they were free to engage in creativity, and at night that they found themselves duty bound. "It was when the lights went up in the evening that society came into force. During daylight one could wear overalls; work. There was the Academy for Nessa; my Liddell and Scott and the Greek choruses for me. But in the evening society had it all its own way."[9] Torn between her duties as social hostess around the tea table and her hidden passion for mathematics, Katharine Hilbery in *Night and Day* recalls the conflict Vanessa Stephen felt, between the social duties prescribed by George Duckworth and her own passion for painting.[10] And if the novel originates in that struggle to find the time and place to do serious work, it speaks of a similar struggle on the part of many women in the Victorian and modern eras: to resist the "duty" to serve as "angel in the house" in order to do the work one has *chosen*.

In turning her attention to woman's struggle to work, Virginia Woolf seems to have chosen a topic highly unlikely to provide the "tranquillising influence" for which—as she told Ethel Smyth—she hoped in her second novel. Yet in asserting that she made herself copy from "plaster casts," Woolf was speaking not just of the biographical origins of the novel's theme and characters, but of the novel's form as well. An early scene, in which Katharine Hilbery chooses her parents' postprandial reading, reveals the formal solution Virginia Woolf devised to the problem that had faced her in *Night and Day*: how to express oneself without alienating others or getting onto "dangerous ground." Katharine first tries to interest her parents in modern fiction, but her attempt is futile; her father mocks the authors for being promising children, while her mother dismisses the "light, gold-wreathed" volume of a contemporary author as "too clever and cheap and nasty for words" (ND, 104). They urge her, instead, to read them something "*real*," and she chooses at last a "portly volume in sleek, yellow calf" (ND, 104). Selection of her parents' reading poses risks for Katharine. Choosing the modern novel, she may be judged tasteless; choosing the safer, classical alternative, she may lose her audience. And in fact, she does so, not to clashing tastes but to sleep, for the Fielding novel she finally reads them has "directly a sedative effect upon both her parents" (ND, 104).

I read this early scene in *Night and Day* as a metatextual gloss upon Virginia Woolf's dilemma in writing her second novel. Both the classical and contemporary models which were available to her, writing as she did within the English literary tradition, had certain risks. With the former, she chanced being called derivative; with the latter, she risked alienating her audience or (worse still) being laughed at. Furthermore, there was the overarching risk of losing her sanity, which was perhaps her greatest concern at this time. The reading scene suggests that Virginia Woolf joined her heroine in choosing the sedative restraint, the tranquilizing effect, of the classical model; moreover, it suggests specifically what that model might have been. Katharine ultimately chooses a Fielding novel to read to her parents, and in this essay I will suggest that Fielding offers an important precursor for *Night and Day*. As Irving Howe has pointed out, it was Henry Fielding who originated the classic city novel, with its "dominant literary pattern of discovery and withdrawal in regard to the city."[11] Cautious, concerned with her own mental stability yet convinced that London's crowded streets were "the only places . . . that ever make me what-in-the-case of another-one-might-call-think," Woolf had herself just recently undergone a process of discovery and withdrawal in regard to the city. She had moved, upon her father's death, from the restrictions of Kensington to the spacious squares of Bloomsbury, only to retreat after her marriage to the calm of suburban Richmond. So, she turned to the classic city novel to explore an issue which was intimately related to her own response to the city in 1915: a woman's struggle to do her own work.

Several elements characterize the classic city novel. It is a drama of emotional education whose shape is a spiral journey from country to city and back. Implicitly, it embraces what Raymond Williams has called the "ideology of improvement," since the journey through the city must result, with more or less coincidence as the tradition becomes established, in a good match. Finally, its protagonist learns of life in the city only to live it in the country, since for the youth propelled there by necessity or fortune the city has little appeal in itself, but is only a way station where he may remain until attaining emotional and economic majority, when he may retire gracefully to a comfortable country seat. [12]

Night and Day resembles the classic city novel in a number of ways. Perhaps the shape of Katharine Hilbery's story is the most obvious one; like the Fielding novel which she reads to her parents in Chapter VII, it concerns a marriage choice laced with comic elements. Each principal is identified by geographical coordinates, leading E. M. Forster to observe that the characters "are screwed into Chelsea and Highgate as the case may be, and move from their bases to meet in the rooms and streets of a topographical metropolis." [13] "Katharine Hilbery [of] Chelsea (Cheyne-walk, that is, not the King's Road or the side streets), mellow, august, exquisite" must choose between "Ralph Denham [of] Highgate, strong, raw, ugly" but a hard worker, and William Rodney, the country gentleman who comes "of the oldest family in Devonshire" and places supreme importance not upon work, but on social conventions and family traditions (ND, 68). [14] Despite her Chelsea setting, Katharine's heritage is rural; her family's country seat is Stogden House, home of the passive, prolific Aunt Charlotte. Even the Cheyne Walk drawing-room in which we first meet Katharine has something of the rural retreat about it, at least in the perception of a visitor, Ralph Denham. "With the omnibuses and cabs still running in his head, and his body still tingling with his quick walk along the streets . . . this drawing-room seemed very remote and still; and the faces of the elderly people . . . had a bloom on them owing to the fact that the air . : . was thickened by blue grains of mist" (ND, 10).

Katharine's initial distaste for the city bespeaks her rural origins, too. The view from her Chelsea window reflects an experience of blocked avenues, frustrating enclosures, immobility, for Katharine sees in the city merely a mirror of her life at Cheyne Walk, where she is oppressed by the endless demands of family and friends. "The incessant and tumultuous hum of the distant traffic seemed . . . to represent the thick texture of her life, . . . [which] was so hemmed in with the progress of other lives that the sound of its own advance was inaudible" (ND, 106). Katharine's familial heritage of passivity has made the city horrible to her, because its every connection implies an obligation.

Even now, alone, at night, looking out into the shapeless mass of London, she was forced to remember that there was one point and here another with which she had some connection. William Rodney, at this very moment, was seated in a minute speck of light somewhere to the east of her, and his mind was occupied, not with his book, but with her. (ND, 106)

In short, to Katharine the city is merely the territory for a marriage plot, and its shapeless mass on closer examination will reveal to her not a future, but a future husband, who, at least at the book's opening, seems to be William Rodney.

Under the influence of Ralph Denham, however, Katharine is drawn out of her secluded, "remote" drawing room into the streets, parks, omnibuses, and offices of London, where she comes to question the submission to social and familial obligations which she has always taken for granted. Like the "Young Man from the Provinces" who is the protagonist of the classic city novel, Katharine encounters "pleasures, adventures, and lessons to last a lifetime"; like him, she also chooses her lifetime companion, the man who has educated her emotions so that she can now "read poetry, . . . and feel poetry, and look poetry" (ND, 488). Finally, her adventures in the city over, she plans to return with her husband-to-be to the country, where (we assume) she will study mathematics while he writes his "history of the English village from Saxon days to the present time" (ND, 226).

While Katharine's story recalls the classic city novel in its spiral to and away from the city, and in its stress on emotional education, it is somewhat looser in its enactment of the good match. In one sense, of course, Ralph Denham is the ideal husband for Katharine, since he intuitively grasps her perspective on life. Yet to the more practical mind, like Katharine's Aunt Celia Milvain, his prospects cannot seem ideal: "Hasn't a penny . . . and a family more or less dependent on him" (ND, 462). Mercurial Cassandra Otway's momentous trip from the country to her cousin's city home represents the economic side of that spiral journey, for after some comic contretemps her London visit concludes in the classic good match—her alliance to William Rodney and his exceedingly old Devonshire family. Rodney's appreciation of country society makes him perfect to marry the daughter and rescue the sinking Otway line, while Cassandra's conventional, malleable nature makes her a perfect protagonist for the realistic narrative of economic improvement also a part of the classic city novel. Once married, Cassandra and William will flee the city for their country estate and the spiral journey will be complete.

Night and Day takes an attitude toward country life which is also characteristic of the classic city novel. Nostalgia for a rural, unmechanized past pervades the novel, clashing with an urban world of telephones, motor cars, the suffrage movement, and the elided presence of the Great War. These anachronisms tempted Katherine Mansfield to label the novel "Miss Austen up-to-date," and she raged against it as "a lie in the soul."[15] However, as J. H. Raleigh has pointed out, in "the novel in particular the nostalgic mood is built into the medium, nowhere more so than with the urbanists themselves . . . where the *ubi sunt* theme is in many ways the dominant one."[16] Cassandra and Katharine feel nostalgia for the rural past in part because their mothers are its primary purveyors: Mrs. Hilbery's mental time ranges from Shakespeare's day to the "fair summer of 1853" but is rarely more current, while Lady Otway's way of life revolves around the charming ritual of a carriage ride to Lincoln, in a day of motor cars and railroad trains. Even the forward-looking Ralph Denham seems to be succumbing to the *ubi sunt* emotion as he falls in love with Katharine, for he determines to quit the Bar and retire to the country, where he will write a book celebrating that passing rural world. And although the definition of a good match varies from Cassandra's pragmatic socioeconomic criteria to Katharine's more intangible guides in her search for a soulmate, once the matches are made, the principals plan a retreat to the country. The city may be the setting for their adventures and their search for a mate, but it is never a goal in itself. At the end of the novel, Katharine suggests to Ralph that they take the country cottage he has been dreaming of. "And leave all this?" he protests. To Katharine, however, "all this" is already hers—whether they settle in city or country—for the phrase evokes merely a satisfying domestic prospect mingling mathematics and marriage. "She thought, looking at the sky above Chancery Lane, how the roof was the same everywhere; how she was now secure of all that this lofty blue and its steadfast lights meant to her; reality was it, figures, love, truth?" (ND, 502). The high sky of the city sinks, in this passage, to the snug roof of the connubial home, in much the same way that Katharine's expectations are confined to the happy marriage with which her story ends.

I have been suggesting how, in some important ways, *Night and Day* resembles the classic city novel. However, it is important to note that Woolf's novel diverges from the morality customary in its model in such a way as to accommodate her political and aesthetic vision, and consequently to make the novel more than the uniformly traditional and derivative work some critics have thought it to be.[17] In the classic city novel, the town was associated with worldliness and vice, the country with innocence and virtue. This contrast, Raymond Williams has argued, "depends, often, on . . . the suppression of work in the countryside, and of the property relations through which this work is organised."[18] Yet work, specifically Vanessa Stephen's passion for painting, provided the inspiration for *Night and Day*. It is therefore not surprising that the novel reverses the customary town/country morality of the classic city novel, and instead associates the city with honest work and virtue, and the country with worldly leisure and—if not vice—petty dishonesty. (In Stogden House, for example, Katharine learns that "to marry someone with whom you are not in love is an inevitable step" [ND, 216]). This reversal of values appears in several ways in *Night and Day*, but it can perhaps be seen most clearly in the criteria by which the reader is invited to judge Katharine Hilbery's two suitors.

E. M. Forster wrote that *Night and Day* takes place in a "topographical metropolis"; in this metropolis, topography reveals psychology. I have already described how Katharine's view of the city reflects the immobility and oppression which is her lot when the novel opens; what is even more important is that *in their reactions to the city* her suitors also reveal their characters, in particular their fitness as potential husbands for Katharine. Virginia Woolf uses city scenes to develop a study in contrasts, based on a morality which reverses that of the classic city novel, showing William Rodney and Ralph Denham to be almost diametrically opposed in terms of their attitudes toward the city, toward work and—as a result—toward Katharine herself. The contrasts between Rodney and Denham extend to their origins too. Rodney's country gentry background provides him with a conversational agenda for women which he adheres to in the city as well, with the unhappy result that he invariably underestimates Katharine's abilities and goals. "You talk to them about their children, if they have any, or their accomplishments—painting, gardening, poetry—they're so delightfully sympathetic . . . a woman's opinion of one's poetry is always worth having. Don't ask them for their reasons. Just ask them for their feelings. Katharine, for example—" (ND, 205). Rodney clearly holds little promise to be a husband supportive of Katharine's right to act autonomously; he expects her, like all women, to join in the chorus of his praises. And just as he expects a paper doll woman, his London, too, is merely a toy city, a mock-up, one-dimensional for all its pretensions to culture, "a town cut out of gray-blue cardboard, and pasted flat against the sky, which was of a deeper blue" (ND, 72). Rodney presents himself as passionately involved with Katharine, and with London, when in fact he is merely involved with the pleasant figure of himself—as lover and urban sophisticate—revealed against a backdrop of admiring women in a stage prop city.

In contrast, Ralph Denham sees both woman and city as autonomous and unique, adopting toward each the role of admiring spectator. Perhaps this ability to value and admire London arises from the nature of the comparison he is able to make, for alone among all the major characters in *Night and Day*, Ralph Denham lives in the suburbs. In this, he resembles his creator, who lived in Richmond while she was writing the novel and struggled with the same emotional and intellectual balancing act as her character—the attempt to preserve some independence from suburban values. Virginia Woolf's diary records her distaste for the smug competitions in respectability, the hypocrisy, the hideous taste which she found surrounding her in Richmond.[19] Denham's origins also echo those of Leonard Woolf, whose family still lived in Putney after his marriage. Like Leonard Woolf too, Denham's orientation is deliberately, even defiantly urban. His habit of gazing out over London from his attic window—"The great advantage of Highgate is the view over London," he brags when Katharine visits him (ND, 380)—leads him ultimately to link his admiration for London with his feelings for Katharine, in a revelation scene of compact significance. "'But I'm in love with you!' he exclaimed, with something like dismay . . . looking over the city as she had looked. Everything had become miraculously different and completely distinct" (ND, 386). Denham's response to Katharine, as to London, is affirmative, responsive, admiring. He accepts the innate autonomy of both woman and city rather than attempting to force them to mirror him.

A system of values the inverse of that characteristic of the classic city novel figures in the contrast between Katharine's suitors. Denham is fit to be Katharine's husband precisely because he is a hard-working city dweller who is not afraid of a woman who also works hard, and loves the city. Although styling himself an urbane ladies' man, William Rodney in contrast is revealed as only capable of the most conventional, egotistical response both to Katharine and to London, requiring that they both reflect *his* actions and affirm *his* autonomy. Clearly, the two men would have very different responses to the passion for work which drives Katharine Hilbery, and which was the *donnée* of *Night and Day*: Denham would be likely to support any attempts to study mathematics as a way of "making discoveries," while Rodney's impatience with anything but the role of admiring spectator in the women around him, along with his philosophy upholding marriage as a woman's fulfillment, would make him likely to support Katharine's work only if and as long as it redounded to his credit, and to resent anything which drew her attention away from its "proper" focus on him. If, when the novel opens, Rodney seems destined to be Katharine's husband, he occupies that position only as long as she remains reconciled to the constricted prospect for her future reflected in the city she sees from her Chelsea window.

In fact, the novel's plot turns upon the homonym "prospect." The city reveals all three types of prospect to the characters in *Night and Day*: spatial, mental, and existential. The nature of a character's visual prospect either reflects his or her mental prospect or indicates the existential prospect. Once Katharine abandons her self-abnegating posture as dutiful daughter, she abandons William Rodney as well. Accepting him, she had accepted his prospect: the adherence to social roles and traditions, the roots in country society, the merely superficial understanding both of London and of herself. When her love shifts to Ralph Denham, she then accepts a new prospect which he reveals to her: affirmation of work, innovation, intellectual and social independence. This explains why country gentleman William Rodney, whose work is only a misty backdrop to his carefully cultivated role as *litterateur* (as he describes himself to Denham, "[without a job] I should be ten times as happy with my whole day to spend as I liked"), and dilettante Cassandra Otway are presented with less seriousness and respect than the hardworking solicitor Ralph Denham, who repeatedly defends the merits of work over leisure, and Katharine Hilbery, who at least aspires to do serious work in mathematics (ND, 74, 20). Finally, the turns of the plot itself invert the customary morality of country and city, for both Katharine Hilbery and her friend Mary Datchet are tempted, when in the country, to make fundamentally dishonest decisions about their futures—Katharine to remain engaged to William Rodney, and Mary to become engaged to Ralph Denham—and both recover their ability to act with emotional honesty upon their return to the city.

Yet if *Night and Day* is indebted to its precursor, the classic city novel, a return to the scene from Chapter VII which offers a metatextual commentary on Woolf's strategies of approach to the emotionally charged issue of women's struggle to work, suggests that the novel may also reflect an interest in contemporary fictional models. Katharine's attention is first drawn to the "light, gold-wreathed" volume by a living author, although she ultimately discards that first choice when her father mocks its author and her mother dismisses the book in distaste. This scene suggests that Virginia Woolf too may have yearned to experiment with contemporary fictional forms, to consider not just the struggle of Hyde Park Gate but the joyful creativity of the Bloomsbury years that followed.[20] If Vanessa Bell was central to that first period of time, she was also instrumental in making the second period possible, for it was Vanessa who, "looking at a map of London and seeing how far apart they were—had decided that [the Stephen children] should leave Kensington and start life afresh in Bloomsbury."[21] Fears—of shocking her contemporaries, of being dismissed by the strong literary "fathers" she longed to please, of getting onto mentally "dangerous ground"—may have kept Virginia Woolf from making extended use of contemporary literary models in *Night and Day*, but in its urban iconography as in its system of values the novel reveals evidence of an impulse toward contemporary fiction.

Images of the city as a maze are particularly characteristic of the modern perspective, according to Irving Howe. "If the pattern of 19th-century fiction forms a spiral to and away from the city, it is the sharpest contrast to later novels in which the city becomes a maze beyond escape."[22] The bewilderment, disorientation, and lack of direction induced by a maze typify not only Cassandra's experience of London, but her sense of life itself. In fact, it is in part to escape these feelings that she turns to William Rodney, whose solid center of self promises to stabilize Cassandra's wayward, impulsive nature. Mazes and the experience of the city as a maze punctuate their courtship. Other London excursions originally bring the couple together, but it is a visit to the Hampton Court maze which cements their union, for it is during that absence from Chelsea that Aunt Celia Milvain informs Cassandra's uncle, Mr. Hilbery, of their improper romance. When he, enraged, banishes Cassandra from Cheyne Walk, it is the mazelike qualities of London which save the lovers. Cassandra loses her way to the station in the winding city streets, misses her train to the country, and after "wandering about London all day," is finally forced to return to the Hilbery home (NE, 494). There, William claims her as his own, to protect with his well-meaning paternalism from any future experiments in self-direction.

To Mary Datchet, too, London is a maze, yet unlike Cassandra she finds it "wonderful" because she knows exactly where she belongs in it—"at the very center of it all"—and unlike Katharine she finds her centrality not an oppressive reminder of her obligations to others but an affirmation of her self-sufficiency and personal worth (ND, 49). Mary's centrality seems enviable to Katharine precisely because it bespeaks a control over and distance from the routine familial turmoil from which Katharine suffers. In an image which mythologizes Mary's work in the Suffrage Office, Katharine sees her and her co-workers as "enchanted people in a bewitched tower, with the spiders' webs looping across the corners of the room," and imagines them "flinging their frail spiders' webs over the torrent of life which rushed down the streets outside" (ND, 93–94). This use of web imagery is another characteristic modernist element in *Night and Day*, linking the novel to such important precursors as Samuel

[125]

Butler and Charles Baudelaire. As Allen McLaurin has demonstrated, by "using the image of the cobweb, which was to be one of Virginia Woolf's favorite images," Samuel Butler illustrated "the strange nature of shock."[23] For Baudelaire, too, as Walter Benjamin has observed, "shock experience [lay] at the very center of his artistic work," and he too used the web image to convey the curious nature of that sensation. So, in his dedication to the urban prose poems *Spleen de Paris*, Baudelaire demanded: "Who among us has not dreamt, in his ambitious days, of the miracle of a poetic prose? . . . This ideal, which can turn into an *idée fixe*, will grip especially those who are at home in the giant cities and the web of their numberless interconnecting relationships."[24] Educated by Ralph Denham to "read poetry . . . and feel poetry, and look poetry," Katharine is less able to learn the other half of the lesson: how to cope with the "web of . . . numberless interconnecting relationships" in the "giant cities." From her own position as dutiful daughter and self-abnegating friend and lover, she envies Mary Datchet's firm self-assertion, her "power of being disagreeable to [her] own family," which has yielded a room in which she can "live alone . . . and have parties" (ND, 59).

The distance between Katharine's mythologized, envious perception of Mary Datchet's life and its pleasant but far more complex reality suggests that more than the influence of the contemporary novel is responsible for an interesting imaginative leap in *Night and Day*. "[One] of Woolf's amazing political perceptions," Jane Marcus has observed, was the awareness "that the ideal of the female utopia was to be in paradise alone, to work."[25] Yet curiously enough, only one character attains this female utopia in *Night and Day*, although the novel's stated goal was to explore the conflict between social duties and the passion to do serious work. While both Cassandra and, to a greater extent, Katharine plan to combine marriage and work, at the novel's close those ambitious experiments lie still in the future. Only Mary Datchet is actually alone, working.

What made Virginia Woolf able to imagine Mary Datchet actually attaining her utopia, while Katharine and Cassandra are only shown dreaming of theirs? Clearly, the historical difficulty women have had combining marriage with nondomestic work was an important reason for Woolf's imaginative constraint. In *Moments of Being*, she admits that although Bloomsbury evenings of cocoa and conversation revealed new possibilities of shared intellectual enterprise among men and women, still she felt that if one practiced the "very low down affair" that was marriage, "one practiced it . . . with young men who had been in the Eton Eleven and dressed for dinner."[26] Young men, in short, more like William Rodney than Ralph Denham, who were sure to curtail any unconventional aspirations for privacy and work in their wives and daughters.

There was another reason why Woolf was able to imagine Mary Datchet attaining a solitary dedication to work which neither Cassandra nor Katharine found, one which had to do not with Woolf's own personal experience at 22 Hyde Park Gate, but with the literary model she chose to approach that experience. When she framed Mary Datchet's story, she seems to have understood that—like so many male articulations of human experience—the classic city novel did not easily or entirely express the lives of women, in the lives of its creator Henry Fielding's time or in her own. When one is writing of a woman, the elements of that classic city novel shift: country and city, work and leisure, emotional and economic "improvement," even the concept of a "good match" come to have very different meanings and consequences. Katharine Hilbery's story reflects this difference somewhat, in its departures from the model. Although its shape echoes the classic city novel's spiral journey into and away from the city, as does its resolution in a successful marriage, as I have already demonstrated the values determining Katharine's choice of a husband invert those customary in the classic model, and Katharine herself frequently seems more beleaguered and bewildered than adventuresome and autonomous. Her experiences at her family's country seat, Stogden House, seem to prompt not exploration, but resignation, confirming "the belief that to be engaged to marry someone with whom you are not in love is an inevitable step in a world where the existence of passion is only a traveller's story . . . told so rarely that wise people doubt whether the story can be true" (ND, 216). Furthermore, even when Katharine shakes off the regressive influence of country life and the resignation to a loveless match which it counsels, and plunges instead into adventures and experiments in the city, she does so in defiance both of cultural norms and—at first—of personal inclination. London echoes her experience of familial and social constraint, initially; to young women, urban rambles are more likely to promise social and moral ruination (as a result of the violation of those constraints) than emotional or economic improvement. Such is the serious message underlying William Rodney's superficially silly code that "it was considerably more damning to be seen out of doors than surprised within" (ND, 454). I do not mean here to make the error of oversimplifying Katharine's complex motives and actions: far more than Cassandra, she is autonomous, independent, and concerned with questions of self-fulfillment rather than property or propriety. But even she seems, at the end of the novel, to succumb to society's rule, fittingly if uncharacteristically embodied by Mrs. Hilbery and Ralph Denham, who agree between themselves that a wedding will take place, and that it might even take place in St. Paul's Cathedral. After this surprising reversal of the lovers' earlier agreement that "We don't wish to be married—that's all," we are rather less surprised to find Katharine deferring to Denham's preference on the question of their future home. If his character promised affirmation of her autonomy, the form of the fiction in which that character dwelt promised to limit that affirmation to the customary domestic retreat of the novel's conclusion (ND, 466, 489, 502).

Virginia Woolf could imagine Mary Datchet attaining the urban utopia of privacy and work because in Mary's story she avoided the flaws of the classic city novel as a vehicle for female characters. Several factors made it difficult for a woman to attain her utopia by that spiral journey from country to city and back again. First, the story invests its protagonist with a degree of autonomous agency which has rarely been available to women, thus implicitly excluding female characters from the position as protagonist. Then, its resolution in a "good match" and a return to the country would, for women, have meant surrender of whatever powers of self-determination had been acquired in the city. Finally, for women to assert themselves in choosing to engage in urban adventures, as the story requires of its protagonist, would most likely have resulted not in a triumphant, enlightened return to the rural bosom of the family, but—at best—in estrangement from that family forever, and—at worst—in moral ruin, perhaps even death. Virginia Woolf herself would trace the realistic consequences of a woman's attempt to adapt this masculine plot to her life in her tale of the fictional Judith Shakespeare, whose desire to write drew her to London from the provinces, yet who ended up not a celebrated playwright like her brother, but pregnant, unmarried, ultimately dead by her own hand.[27]

Mary Datchet's story turns the spiral journey inside out, transforming the elements of the classic city novel and, ironically, adapting modernist urban images to feminist themes as well. Drawn first into London by her "determination to obtain education" and her "power of being disagreeable to [her] family," Mary expands her schooling in self-determination and emotional honesty during a rural retreat at Disham, where she is tempted momentarily by Ralph's dishonest offer of marriage. Instead of taking the opportunity to return to the country, by accepting a proposal of marriage she knows to be spurious, Mary chooses to remain a single woman in the city. If the climax of Katharine's story is her discovery of "the existence of passion" in her feelings for Ralph Denham, Mary's tale turns on the subtler realization that "[there] are different ways of loving," that her feelings for Denham have paled beside her more lasting passion for work (ND, 447). A socially sanctioned, if self-consciously experimental happy marriage provides the resolution of Katharine's story, while Mary's tale, in contrast, features a socially anomalous conclusion: her dedication not to a man, but to work "for the good of a world that none of them were ever to know" (ND, 506).

Although the dramatic vertical contrast of Chapter XXXII, in which Katharine and Ralph pause to gaze at the light burning high above in Mary's window, valorizes Mary's decision, it also removes it from the experience both of the engaged couple, who can only wonder "Is she alone, working . . . What is she working at?," and of the reader as well (ND, 505). Mary's story transcends the terms established by the classic city novel, and so makes possible its own utopian ending. Resolution is transformed into an acceptance of continuing struggle; the "good match" into a harmonious blending of work and self rather than lover and self; the country-city-country spiral into a trajectory culminating in the triumphant possession of a room of one's own in which to work, in the city. So identified is Mary with the London in which she lives that by the novel's end, the city's electric glow seems the same as the light in her window, symbolizing the vitality of women working in that public arena.

Throughout this discussion of *Night and Day*, I have approached Katharine Hilbery's story as, in some sense, a representation of Virginia Woolf's own *as she was writing the novel*. In doing this, I have taken my cue from Woolf's choice of the art student metaphor in describing the novel's composition (in her letter to Ethel Smyth), and from the important metatextual scene in Chapter VII in which Katharine Hilbery is forced to choose between two fictional forms. Adopting this approach one last time, I want to consider the novel's opening for what it reveals of Virginia Woolf's strategies in *Night and Day*. Marooned at the tea table, a young woman is struggling to assimilate a difficult new-comer into a comfortable conversation between old friends. The group has been considering the fate of a cousin who has married and moved to Manchester: will it be possible for her to find a "retired schoolmaster or man of letters" from whom she can learn Persian, and so create for herself some intellectual compan-ionship" (ND, 10). When her opinion of the situation is re-quested, the young woman replies "at random," "I should think there would be no one to talk to in Manchester" (ND, 11).

Of course neither Katharine Hilbery's metaphor nor her use of it in this particular social situation *is* random. Rather, this initial interchange reveals Katharine's strategy for coping with the prob-lems she faces in *Night and Day*. Trapped in a stultifying drawing room where she must observe social propriety and fill the role of Angel in the House, Katharine longs for freedom to study math-ematics, which is her passion. In speaking of her cousin, she in fact speaks of herself: she might as well be in Manchester, for she has no one to talk to in the Chelsea drawing room where the novel opens. Yet Katharine has had the same social training as her creator, and she knows that to complain of her solitude would strain the conversation even more.[28] So, Katharine gives veiled public voice to her private anxiety: that she may never find a man with whom she can learn to speak the exotic language of authen-tic feeling (both for him and for her work) rather than the custom-ary banalities of teatime gossip. And, by chance, there is a man present just as she speaks who can hear what she is actually saying beneath her social manner, as Ralph Denham's musings make clear. "It struck him that her position at the tea-table, among all those elderly people, was not without its difficulties, and he checked his inclination to find her, or her attitude, gener-ally antipathetic to him" (ND, 13). Soon, he is urging her to break free of her familial constraints, and then is breaking free of his own to find himself not merely not antipathetic, but actually in love with her.

The elements of this initial scene resonate beyond Katharine Hilbery's character to reveal the anxieties which faced Virginia Woolf as she began to write *Night and Day*, and the strategies she evolved to allay them. Like Katharine, she worried that she would be unable to assimilate the difficult newcomer, her novelist-self, to the comfortable conversation between old friends which was the English novelistic tradition.[29] Only recently married, and newly moved from London to a suburb which was as far from being "an offshoot of London" as any provincial city, Woolf shares with the imaginary Manchester cousin the anxiety that she will be unable to find intellectual companionship. Finally, there was the further anxiety that work itself would be impossible, if there was no one for her to talk to. So, she adopted the strategy of her heroine in her second novel, using her training in social decorum to express her most deeply held feelings while protecting herself from the charge that she has failed in her social duties by breaching a social code or by offending others. Like Katharine Hilbery in its opening scene, Virginia Woolf uses the city in *Night and Day* to approach an issue indirectly. By adopting, transforming, and transcending her traditional literary model—the classic city novel first framed by the father of the English novel, Henry Fielding—she was able to address the question of woman's struggle to work while avoiding a risky incursion into the socially and psychologically "dangerous ground" of direct self-expression.

NOTES

1. *The Diary of Virginia Woolf, Volume One: 1915–1919*, edited by Anne Olivier Bell (New York: Harcourt Brace Jovanovich, 1977), 31.
2. Ibid., 9.
3. Ibid.
4. Ibid., 29, 30.
5. Ibid., 35.
6. *The Letters of Virginia Woolf, Volume Four: 1929–1931*, edited by Nigel Nicolson and Joanne Trautmann (New York: Harcourt Brace Jovanovich, 1978), 231.

7. Forster wrote, "*Night and Day* . . . is the simplest novel she has written, and to my mind the least successful. Very long, very careful, it condescends to many of the devices she so gaily derides in her essay on 'Mr Bennett and Mrs Brown.' . . . In view of what preceded it and of what is to follow, *Night and Day* seems to me a deliberate exercise in classicism." "The Novels of Virginia Woolf," *New Criterion*, April 1926, 277–86, collected in *Virginia Woolf: The Critical Heritage*, edited by Robin Majumdar and Allen McLaurin (London: Routledge & Kegan Paul, 1975), 171–78, 173.

8. *The Letters of Virginia Woolf, Volume Two: 1912–1922*, edited by Nigel Nicolson and Joanne Trautmann (New York: Harcourt Brace Jovanovich, 1976), 400.

9. Virginia Woolf, *Moments of Being* (New York: Harcourt Brace Jovanovich, 1976), edited by Jeanne Schulkind, 129.

10. Virginia Woolf, *Night and Day* (New York: Harcourt Brace Jovanovich, 1948). Further references will follow the text in parentheses, taking this form: (ND, 00).

11. Irving Howe, "The City in Literature," *Commentary* 51, no. 5, (May 1971), 60–68, 62.

12. Raymond Williams, *The Country and the City* (New York: Oxford Univ. Press, 1973), 62; Howe.

13. Forster, 173.

14. Harold Child, "Unsigned Review, *Times Literary Supplement*," in *Virginia Woolf: The Critical Heritage*, 77.

15. Katherine Mansfield, "Review," *Athenaeum*, 21 November 1919, 1227, in *Virginia Woolf: The Critical Heritage*, 80; Quentin Bell describes Mansfield's "private opinion" of *Night and Day*: "It was 'a lie in the soul.' 'The war has never been: that is what its message is . . . I feel in the *profoundest* sense that nothing can ever be the same—that, as artists, we are traitors if we feel otherwise: we have to take it into account and find new expressions, new moulds for our new thoughts and feelings.'" *Virginia Woolf: A Biography* (New York: Harcourt Brace Jovanovich, 1972), II, 69.

16. John Henry Raleigh, "The Novel and the City: England and America in the Nineteenth Century," *Victorian Studies*, II, no. 3 (March 1968), 291–328, 306.

17. See, for example, the reviews by E. M. Forster and Katherine Mansfield already cited.

18. Williams, 46.

19. As Woolf's diary pictured it, Leonard's mother lived in a cheap and sordid setting of dismal villas in dismal streets, each with its dismal, fiercely pruned tree in its square of concrete. Woolf admitted that she was a snob on the subject; she found setting and inhabitants horrifying in their coarse respectability. Yet this snobbery is one which discriminates not between class origins or material possessions, but states of consciousness. Woolf prefers the lower classes because of the vital freedom she found in their self-expression. Her quarrel lies with the type of soul which she felt was usually produced by the suburban environment, that soul which Leonard Woolf saw reflected in the stucco home of his

sisters and mother, and which is exemplified by Mrs. Denham. Her history has shown the same restriction and gradual narrowing of prospect as her house. "'When I first married,'" she tells Katharine," 'Highgate was quite separate from London . . . and this house . . . had a view of apple orchards. That was before the Middletons built their house in front of us.'" Middle-class suburban life with its economic straits and its deadly respectability, represented by the appropriately named Middletons, has gradually cut Mrs. Denham off from any avenues for action. Now, all that remains for her to do is to defend her present way of life, to "prove that [Highgate] was healthier, more convenient, and less spoilt than any suburb round London," and to remember the apple orchards of the past (ND, 374–75).

20. See *Moments of Being*, 162, for discussion of the differences between life at 22 Hyde Park Gate, where Virginia Stephen lived until her father's death in 1904, and at 46 Gordon Square, where the Stephen children then moved. The contrast between Kensington and Bloomsbury, she wrote in October 1918, as she was writing *Night and Day*, "was the gulf between respectable mum[m]ified humbug & life crude & impertinent perhaps, but living." *The Diary of Virginia Woolf, Volume One: 1915–1919*, 206.

21. *Moments of Being*, 162.

22. Howe, 64.

23. Allen McLaurin, *Virginia Woolf: The Echoes Enslaved* (Cambridge: Cambridge Univ. Press, 1973), 10–11.

24. Walter Benjamin, *Illuminations*, edited by Hannah Arendt (New York: Schocken, 1969), 163, 165.

25. "Enchanted Organs, Magic Bells: *Night and Day* as Comic Opera," *Virginia Woolf: Revaluation and Continuity*, edited by Ralph Freedman (Berkeley: Univ. of California Press, 1980), 96–122, 109.

26. *Moments of Being*, 169.

27. *A Room of One's Own* (New York: Harcourt, Brace & World, 1957). For further discussion of the ways that fictional forms constrain real lives, and fictions constrain fictions, see Margaret Homans, *Women Writers and Poetic Identity: Dorothy Wordsworth, Emily Brontë, and Emily Dickinson* (Princeton: Princeton Univ. Press, 1980), especially the introductory chapter, and Jean Strouse, *Alice James: A Biography* (Boston: Houghton Mifflin, 1980).

28. As Virginia Woolf explained in *Moments of Being*, she had learned "the rules of the Victorian game of manners" by "tea-table training . . . this surface manner [which] allows one to say a great many things which would be unaudible if one marched straight up and spoke out" (129).

29. In this anxiety, of course, Virginia Woolf was far from alone, as contemporary feminist scholarship reveals. See particularly, Margaret Homans, *Women Writers and Poetic Identity: Dorothy Wordsworth, Emily Brontë, and Emily Dickinson*; Sandra Gilbert and Susan Gubar, *The Madwoman in the Attic* (New Haven: Yale Univ. Press, 1979).

JANE MARCUS

A Wilderness of One's Own:
Feminist Fantasy Novels of the Twenties:
Rebecca West and Sylvia Townsend Warner

Wish in Spring

To-day I wish that I were a tree,
And not myself,
Confronting spring with a neat little row of poems
Like cups and saucers on a shelf.

For then I should have poems innumerable,
One kissing the other;
Authentic, perfect in shape and lovely variety,
And all of the same tireless green colour.

No one would think it unnatural
Or question my right;
All day I would wave them above the heads of the people,
And sing them to myself all night.

But as I am only a woman
And not a tree,
With piteous human care I have made this poem,
And set it now on the shelf with the rest to be.

Sylvia Townsend Warner, *Espalier*

A writer's country is a territory within his own brain; and
we run the risk of disillusionment if we try to turn such
phantom cities into tangible brick and mortar.

Virginia Woolf, "Literary Geography"

[134]

Seldom it is that Artemis goes down to the town.

Callimachus, *Hymn to Artemis*

You take delight not in a city's seven or seventy wonders,
but in the answer it gives to a question of yours.
Or the question it asks you, forcing you to answer, like
Thebes through the mouth of the Sphinx.

Italo Calvino, *Invisible Cities*

What is the question?

Gertrude Stein

THE CITY IN MUCH OF OUR LITERATURE is a moral landscape, a place for posing serious questions, a space either inner or outer, depending on the author's perspective, a view of life within the walls as everything from a landscape of desire to a landscape of death. The wilderness, desert, or forest beyond the walls takes on the opposite moral meaning. The city and the country are then locked into a dialectical relationship to the writer as question and answer.

The ancient world poses the question for women artists in terms of two goddesses: Athena, the guardian of the city, and Artemis, the Lady of the Wild Things. The historical questions and answers also shift according to geography, gender, race, and class, particularly in relation to violence and rape. Perspectives vary on whether the city or the country is safer. Notions of either the city or the country as the space of freedom or the protected space also vary. One is always the answer to the other.

In view of the oddly recurring theme of rape and female flight from male violence in Greek mythology and classical literature, it is interesting to note the ancient equation of chastity with female freedom. Chastity is not an absence of experience or sexuality or a state to be pitied or abhorred. It is a positive state of wholeness, and the gods are shown in pursuit of virgins and reluctant maidens as if it is natural for a woman to prefer virginity to heterosexual experience, and as if they were, in raping the nymphs, depriving a natural enemy of a prized possession. It seems natural that a woman who is hunted as prey wishes to escape to the wilderness to join Artemis, the huntress, divine

[135]

protectress of women and animals, who also has the power to kill the assaulters. Artemis represents independent female identity and selfhood. She also represents an ideal of sisterhood.

What I am suggesting is that there is a female version of pastoral which posits chastity as freedom in a wilderness presided over by Artemis. This ideal exists in relation to its normative opposite, heterosexuality and motherhood within the family and the city. Female literary nostalgia for the lost wilderness is not only a longing for personal freedom, but a longing for a lost sisterhood under the protection of the goddesses. British women's travel literature aches with this nostalgia, as in Ethel Smyth's *A Three-Legged Tour of Greece*, Rose Macaulay's *Towers of Trebizond*, and Vita Sackville-West's Persian memoirs. The Eastern city haunts the Western female imagination as the home of the goddesses. Other cities—the Leipzig of Henry Handel Richardson's *Maurice Guest*, the Edinburgh of Rebecca West's *The Judge*, the London of Elizabeth Robins's *The Convert*—echo with exhilarated claims to public space by the emancipated student or political activist.

In modern British fantasy novels, an imaginary mythological wild space is sought by women as a source of creativity and selfhood in response to the phallocentric city. It is a women's Walden, a gynocratic green world. Rebecca West and Sylvia Townsend Warner in *Harriet Hume* and *Lolly Willowes*, are, in a sense, rejecting domestic space as the territory of the nineteenth-century female novelist. They are also rejecting the feminist realist appropriation of public space in the city in the hopeful novels of the first two decades of the twentieth century, when the suffrage struggle seemed to promise women some space of their own in the city, which was public, not private. In contrast to Virginia Woolf's demand for a room of one's own in a domestic space which has usurped female privacy, West and Townsend Warner envision a wilderness of one's own, away from family control of domestic space and male control of public space. Central to the concept of female wilderness is the rejection of heterosexuality. In the dream of freedom, one's womb is one's own only in the wilderness. It is a flight into a pre-patriarchal magical world of trees and transformations, animals and plants, and proud inviolateness. In this mythology, the actors return to the prelapsarian world of preclassical feminine power. It is the myth of the fall of the goddess which is important here. The imaginary primal scene is not the Christian garden of Eden with Adam and Eve and the serpent. It is rather Delphi, Apollo's killing of the python, and subsequent usurpation of the powers of the earth mother.

I would like to suggest that in Ovid's rendering of the myth of Daphne[1] there is a subtext which dramatizes for women readers the fall of the mother goddess, and that the resonance of the myth of "lady into tree" is due to the deep and moving fantasies of both sexes about her fall.[2]

Ovid's story of Daphne purports to tell us two things: the origin of the Pythian Games, and the source of the laurel used to crown the victors. Cupid's revenge for being laughed at when he draws his bow after Apollo has slain the python is to shoot a love arrow at Apollo and its opposite at Daphne. Hence her aversion and his passion are not their own, but the result of a quarrel between two young men about who has slain the dragon. The winner is sexually punished for insisting that the victory is his alone. Next we see Daphne begging her father Peneus, the river spirit, to allow her to remain a virgin in the service of Artemis. This gives us a nonmagical reason for her chastity of choice—but no such reason for Apollo's lust. Her father agrees after she cites Diana's father as precedent, and Daphne dons animal skins and does not dress her hair. Apollo pursues her and she flees. His love song is a boast of his powers—the gift of poetry, the gift of prophecy—and he claims to be the world's first healer.

The text does not tell us where Apollo got these gifts. But they are all the attributes of the Great Mother.[3] By slaying the python at Delphi, he has usurped her powers. What else then are the Pythian Games but a male celebration of the overthrow of the Earth and her maternal power? To save his daughter from rape by Apollo, Peneus turns her into the evergreen laurel tree. Peneus remains loyal to the old order, for the river is in the domain of Artemis. Apollo's embraces are repelled by Daphne, but he claims the leaves to crown both his lyre and his bow. The myth is really about an imagined transition from a matriarchal order to a patriarchal one. The rivers and trees resist and remain in the domain of Artemis. When women writers recall the myth of Daphne, they too resist Apollo's violent patriarchal mode of civilization.

In a famous modern essay,[4] Norman O. Brown appears to have chewed a great many narcotic laurel leaves to celebrate the myth

[137]

as Apollo's birth as a poet, in which Brown reads attempted rape as the sublimation of desire and the source of civilization. Like Geoffrey Hartman's reading of the Procne and Philomel myth as the story of the artist as truth teller,[5] the critic's gender bias represses the message of the power of sisterhood and ignores the key elements of woman's revenge for male violence and rape. What Hartman misses is the story of a woman who kills her own son and serves him to his father to eat in revenge for her husband's rape of her sister. What Brown misses is that nature rebels at Apollo's desecration of Delphi and asserts its elemental transformative power to turn a girl into a tree, *virgo* into *virga* (neither of which equals virility, despite Brown's insistence). But Brown attributes metamorphosis to men, as Hartman forgets the sex and circumstance of the "voice of the shuttle." I resist seeing Daphne as Apollo's phallus, or the reading of Procne's *peplos* as unrelated to her rape. If the Christian story of the fall of Adam and Eve leaves Eve henceforth to bear her children in sorrow, this subtext story of the fall of the Earth Mother leaves Apollo forever chasing a still unravished bride with woman as his sexual enemy, not his mate. Let us explore the way two women writers recall the wilderness where chastity is power and resistance is made against Apollo, the civilizer and rapist.

In male discourse the city is a female body. In women's fantasy novels the city is a hostile male body, and the heroines of Rebecca West's *Harriet Hume*[6] and Sylvia Townsend Warner's *Lolly Willowes*[7] retreat to nature, the garden or the forest to find nature and the body of the mother. Judith Gardiner has argued that the crucial scene in women's novels takes place at the mother's deathbed.[8] In West's earlier novel *The Judge*,[9] Ellen Melville's mother's death is the most powerful scene. In *Harriet Hume*, the heroine's mother is not dead but absent. She exists in a photograph which Harriet's lover fantasizes about. Harriet reads his mind. It is a typical male rape fantasy in which he imagines he is rescuing a lonely woman from an unhappy sex life. His rape of the mother is also a rape of the country, Cumberland, as his real relationship with Harriet and with London politics are rapes of the city.

In *Lolly Willowes* Laura restrains her grief at her mother's death and only breaks down when she finds a gardening glove of her mother's which still holds the shape of her hand. The rest of her life is spent getting back in touch with Mother Earth. The city's hostility to her spinsterhood and nature itself isolate her from the natural female world. When her nephew violates her space in the wilderness, he is driven away by a swarm of bees, the creatures Erich Neumann describes as sacred to the mother goddess, not only because of the nourishing quality of their honey, but because of the minimal role the male plays in their community life.

The anti-Apollonian discourse of the feminist fantasy narrative reproduces the magical lost woman's wilderness. Feminist fantasy fiction recovers the song of Daphne and speaks with the rustling tongues of laurel leaves. Like Joyce's "leafy speafing," it releases the maiden imprisoned in the lettering leaves. The discourse of Artemis is pure, savage, and antiurban, signifying both selfhood and sisterhood and a powerful sexuality in virginity. Artemisian discourse is directed against male desire.

One of Natalie Barney's most famous witticisms was that nothing in London was made for women, not even the men. I have argued that for women artists like Virginia Woolf, London was the capital of the patriarchy in the same way that Paris was, for a Jewish exile like Walter Benjamin, "the capital of the nineteenth century."[10] The position of the woman artist in relation to male hegemony over culture clearly expressed in intellectual life among the city's monuments to patriarchal imperialism and capitalism is paralleled by the role of the Jewish intellectual in Weimar Germany. The artists are in the untenable role of administering a culture for those who deny them the right to do so. The same is true for blacks in the arts in the United States.

I have described Virginia Woolf's ambivalent relationship to patriarchal London, her feminist attacks on all its monuments from Big Ben to Westminster Abbey in her London novels. And Susan Merrill Squier has analyzed Woolf's relation to the city in a series of fine essays.[11] If a city can be said to have a sex, London was, and is, unmistakably male. Since the city in history and in literature is almost always female, this is an oddity in itself. Raw power and sophisticated power sit side by side in phallic imperialist monuments, all-male clubs, the Houses of Parliament. The best shops and services are for men; even intrepid women are made to feel inferior. "As a woman I have no country," Woolf wrote. But as a woman she did have a city. She had it, however, in that state of wary truce that a feminine woman has in marriage to a very masculine man. Like an attractive but dangerous lover, London was vital in a way she desperately needed to experience, but it also oppressed her.

In Western literature the city is almost always a woman. The male writer perceives the city as subject or object, as mother or whore, through the subjectivity of his sex. The city is to be conquered, raped and subjugated, or idealized in a quest, captured in a war, wooed like a lover, spurned like a wife. He bedecks it with jewels to reflect his own glory; he masks his own aggression by claiming that his battles for cities were fought for women instead of power. He lies ("Was there another Troy for her to burn?") about woman's complicity in his actions. He moans at her unfaithfulness, weeps patriotically over the city, his mother. Like Titus in Sylvia Townsend Warner's *Lolly Willowes*, he loves it as a body.

Women writers have not seen the city as a female body, and London in particular has had the fearful phallic dominance of masculine power. In their realistic documentary portrayal of the suffrage movement (1906–13), women novelists began to show an unmatched exhilaration about the city which was directly derived from their own experience of marching in forbidden streets by the thousands. This political power was short-lived, and fantasy novels of the twenties were the result of frustration and disappointment at the city's refusal to accept women in the centers of patriarchal power. In *The Convert* (1907) Elizabeth Robins reveals the suffragettes' thrilling Trafalgar Square demonstrations as opening up London to women. Edinburgh is portrayed in Rebecca West's *The Judge* as a glorious scene for the drama of women's liberation. Bloomsbury offices bloom with ardent young women in Woolf's *Night and Day*. Only in May Sinclair's *The Tree of Heaven* does the suffrage novel suggest something sinister in the suffragettes' assimilation into city life and politics. Sinclair is anxious that women not lose their spiritual connection with nature in their adaptation to male urban culture.

I want to argue that the feminist fantasy novel of the twenties (including *Orlando*)[12] is the direct result of political disappointment in the power of the struggle for the vote to change anything. A limited franchise was offered in 1918, and the majority of women got the vote when all men were enfranchised in 1928, exactly as the Liberal party had planned in 1832. The brilliance of American feminist fantasy novels in the past few years (Joanna

Russ's *The Female Man* is one of the most powerful) is a result of similar frustration with the political process. The feminist fantasy novel of the twenties is a response to realism's failure to make permanent female space in the citadels of male power. It is a retreat to the garden and the forest to lick wounds from those earlier battles and to reenact the myth of Daphne—lady into tree.

Rebecca West's *Harriet Hume: A London Fantasy* (1929) opens with a line from Dryden ". . . And like white witches, mischievously good," and the tapping of branches on the window, warning that the trees "will get us yet." It is Kensington just after the war, and Harriet's house must be entered by the garden, a partitioned corner of old Blennerhasset House produced in the postwar building boom. Arnold Condorex, her lover, dislikes women with occult gifts who remember being Egyptian princesses in an earlier life. Harriet is a "birdwoman built by a magician" ethereal and artistic: "Loving her was like swathing oneself with a long scarf of spirit" (5). But he sees her as a witch and her success as a pianist a result of being "in league with formidable forces."

Harriet Hume is indeed "mischievously good," like a fairy princess. Her twinkling feet and hands and wraithlike beauty seem out of sympathy with her masculine-derived name. One expects a female Scotch philosopher in heavy brogues (perhaps a Cicely Fairfield transformed into Ibsen's Rebecca West).[13] But Harriet is a Scheherazade who beguiles her lover with fairy tales. He is obsessed by the openness of her house, the little gate which opens into a glorious garden in the middle of the city, the French doors which open directly into her sitting room dominated by her magnificent piano. West captures in Arnold's suspicion of the openness of Harriet's house male suspicion of the woman artist's refusal to enclose herself in domestic space. As the novel opens, the lovers ritually walk the length of the garden three times, and Harriet tells the tale of the three trees at the end of her garden, three ladies, Ladies Frances, Georgiana, and Arabella Dudley, from a painting by Sir Joshua Reynolds in the National Gallery called "The Three Graces Decorating a Statue of Hymen." This is an Artemisian tale of sisterhood, of sworn chastity.

The three infants were abducted overnight, Harriet begins, and found in the morning bound together with a garland of flowers. They would not be separated from each other or their garlands of flowers throughout their youth until forced to marry. Their immortal beauty began to fade at marriage and separation from their sisters. They meet in their forties under one roof (a townhouse in Portland Place which Arnold later occupies as a cabinet minister), weave a garland, are transformed into goddesses again, and escape. But they are pursued by a band of "Mohocks" bent on rape as they cross the park, the Brompton Road and the outskirts of Chelsea—on their way to Knole. (This is clearly a reference to Virginia Woolf's *Orlando* [1928] and Vita Sackville-West's ancestral home. But Woolf's Three Graces transform Orlando from male to female, while West's goddesses transform the ladies into trees. Rebecca West, in her powerful role as reviewer on both sides of the Atlantic in the twenties and thirties, reviewed all of Woolf's books as they appeared in the *New York Herald-Tribune* Sunday book supplement and contributed to the making of her reputation. She praised "the high fountain of genius" in *Orlando* and was the only critic to see that it was a myth of English history and not simply a "Sapphist pastiche.")

The Three Ladies pray to Mother Earth and are swallowed, their upper bodies extending into trees in the corner of the garden, and all the flowers burst into bloom at once. Then they "know the calm integrity of being trees" (40). Arnold says "I would like to be a tree in your garden," but Harriet can read his mind. He is bent on fame and fortune, the ruthless climbing of a political career necessary for a man without blue blood or family connections. He will lie, cheat, and steal, make an unhappy marriage, win a cabinet post and a title, and fall in disgrace. Her clairvoyance rattles him, and her acceptance of genteel poverty in Kensington, modest fame, and the dedicated life of an artist distresses his conscience. In the course of years, as Harriet moves from solo performances to orchestral appearances and then chamber music, Arnold suspects her career has gone downhill, since he can only conceive of success as individual showing-off, like his own speeches in the House, his use of party politics for personal ends. He is sorry that Harriet's small hands mean she will never be the "best" pianist in the world. But she's content with her achievement and considers the great old men who ask her to join their quartet real masters from whom she learns the serious pleasure of the discipline of art. The making of chamber music in concert with her fellow musicians is more demanding and invigorating than solo playing. Like Apollo, Arnold is jealous of her power.

Harriet's fantasy of ladies into trees is a modern version of the myth of sisterhood. It invokes both the eighteenth century and ancient Greece, a classical invocation of the female spirits in triumph over patriarchal rape and marriage. The sisters are reunited in death and reborn in nature. Harriet, the artist, in touch with these spirits daily in her mysterious Artemisian woodland in Kensington, never marries, is very happy, and remains beautiful. She will not leave Kensington, though she gives concerts in cities all over the world, for she loves its decayed beauty, like a lilac bursting from the crack in a decayed tombstone. Arnold is afraid of the garden and its lush fertility as he fears Harriet's sexuality and calls her slut, jade, wench, trollop, though she walks the London streets and all the parks in chaste tranquillity, dressed always in a thin white muslin dress with a small waist and a pleated skirt or else a white Greek gown and a black opera cape. She seems immune to the dangers of the streets, and Arnold so fears her powers that when she leaves his Portland Place house late at night he is sure she will mount a broomstick to fly home.

Harriet's sensual garden is a trap which Condorex rejects. He gives up sexual happiness for a cold marriage of convenience to a woman he describes as a "limp anchovy." To the male bent on "repression of nature" and ruthless climbing, Harriet's enchanted garden is like Klingsor's magic garden in Wagner's *Parsifal* where the flower maidens seduce the seeker for the Grail. While Harriet is a "white witch," Arnold sees her as like Kundry and her "gifts" of understanding are seen as evil wishes for his downfall. When she tells him the plots of his evil thoughts, Arnold denies thinking them.

While all of London belongs to the musician, from the Queen's Hall where she performs to Kensington Gardens where she feeds the ducks, Arnold is offended by her intrusion into public space. Her youth and beauty should not enjoy this freedom. Because of her openness, he thinks she is "loose" like the latch on her garden gate. When he encounters her in a residential street between his Portland Place home and her workplace, Queen's Hall, he fantasizes that she is the wife of a "jolly waterman" or a housepainter, not a lady. He is even more shocked that the "saucy wench" is eating cherries out of a bag in a public street. In an earlier fantasy at the sight of photographs of her parents from Cumberland, he dreams of being the romantic prince who will rescue Harriet's mother, the beautiful lady, from the proud patriarch, in fact that he will comfort all the sad ladies of the North.

Arnold's career begins with a lie, a speech in which he saves his master's face by describing Mondh, a city in India which doesn't exist. He rises to become Lord Mondh and gets entangled in a scheme to borrow money from an Indian prince, Camaralzaman. After Harriet's warning he backs out, but Camaralzaman has his revenge by announcing that Mondh has fallen to the Russians. The cabinet is in a bind. Since Mondh does not exist, how can it fall or be taken again? As his career has progressed, Arnold has become less and less in touch with London and its people. He rides in a closed car like the Prime Minister in *Mrs. Dalloway* and lives as Lord Mondh in the invisible imperial city of his imagination. Rebecca West's critique of imperialism is shattering. The Victorian imperialists have left a legacy of exploitation. A young man can rise out of the class of the exploited by doing the dirty work of the aristocracy. He becomes one of them, complicit in their guilt by maintaining the empire their fathers built, and cannot represent the will of the people or the class he has left behind. West shows us the handsome, self-deceived Arnold in several narcissistic conversations with his mirror (his looks and his role playing have made his career), a nice feminist reversal of fiction's recurring feminine scene.

When he feels like a prisoner in his own house because he cannot pay the servants, he blindly walks the streets on a hot, dusty day and sees a matron dead among the shoppers in Oxford Street. Then he encounters Harriet with her cherries and insists on showing her his eighteenth-century Adam house in Portland Place. He shows her the marks of the Adams brothers, the lacy ironwork, the ram's heads, the arches and alcoves "like an altar to some austere god of Greece" (123). After his next political intrigues are foretold, Harriet tells another story about a woman who lived in a mean street in this grand neighborhood. She wakes up one morning to see a flock of headless sheep being led by the three Adam brothers in expiation of their offenses to the gods. "Apollo is particularly bitter at the time he has spent in an alcove in the dining room of Syon House in Isleworth, watching the Percy family at meat" (144). The decapitated sheep are very happy, she says, "glad to be rid of the rash captaincy of the head." They become enchanted and turn into people, so that both Harriet and Arnold recognize their audiences.

After Lord Mondh's fall (which is like the fall of the invisible Indian city of British imperialism and the patriarchal city of the male world of money and power) he dreams that the Three Ladies in their garland descend the stairs and abandon his house. He shoots himself. But this is a fantasy, and there's a fourth act to West's comic opera. In fact it is impossible to read the last section of *Harriet Hume* without visualizing it as a modernist eighteenth-century masque-opera in the style of the Sitwell-Walton *Façade* or Dame Ethel Smyth's *Fete Galante*. Condorex blames Harriet (always described as his enemy, his "opposite"), and his spirit stalks across London to shoot her. Rebecca West's career-long concern with duality surfaces here in the exploded oppositions of male/female, city/country, matter/spirit. The independent woman artist gets her lover at last in the spiritual world after foiling his plot to kill her, preparing her house for a marriage feast and dying herself—a wry comment on what happens in real life.

The spirit of Arnold Condorex walks a mad walk through London, lost, not knowing what season it is. The scene recalls Septimus Smith's conversation with the trees in *Mrs. Dalloway*. He wanders from Portland Place to Oxford Circus. In a florist's shop he sees a vase of lilies and longs to crush them, to stamp out all flowers and vegetables. In the part he envisions "a conflagration which shall turn every man and every woman in London to ashes by morning" and beats and kicks the trees. "There are thousands of them," he thought furiously, "they drive avenues into the darkness every way, and they are all my enemies" (238). Like Septimus, he has a mission: "Oh, I must instantly relieve humanity of its sufferings, which must be immense" (238–39). He determines to end "the infernal pull of opposites" by killing Harriet. In the opening scene of the novel, Harriet read Arnold's mind, his fantasy of the two children they never have, whom he has named Andrew and Phoebe. As he nears Harriet's Kensington garden he hears two children called by those names. Consumed by hatred, he goes to destroy his "opposite" in high delusion as a bridegroom going to his wedding chamber. But she has read his mind again, and two comic policemen clap him on the shoulder and disarm him.

By now the reader is thoroughly confused. The lightness of

fantasy has been dispelled by the heavy-handed Freudian mad scene (Rebecca West was an early and important champion of Freud in England). Harriet comes down off her pedestal as Art, Womanhood, Life, Nature, and Spirituality, and says to her opposite:

"Why, what was the use of me being so innocent in this g-g-garden," she bleated into her handkerchief, "when I had no power to impose my state on the rest of society? I may have been innocent, but I was also impotent. If I had derived a comprehension of harmony from my art, it was a grave lack in me that I could not instill it into others and establish it as the accepted order of life, and I should be churlish if I blamed those who have the power I lacked, and went out into the world, and did what they could on what they knew to govern it." (253)

So the opposites are resolved, and one may note that the sometime "churlish" socialist-feminist Rebecca West of the essays in *The Freewoman* and *The Clarion* from 1911 through the twenties[14] has ceased to fly her flags. Harriet forgives her would-be murderer. She flutters about, cleaning the house and serving a wedding feast to Arnold and the policemen while all the flowers and trees burst into bloom before their eyes. Harriet conducts a musical botany lesson from her window, and one must acknowledge Rebecca West's debt to Gilbert and Sullivan in the final scene, where Arnold stands beside Harriet in the threshold of the house, now lighted like a Christmas tree. West has joined man and woman, materialism and nature, but at what cost? The suburb has had its domestic triumph over the city. Harriet's London, pastoral and artistic, has taken Condorex from his identification with the mythical imperialist city of Mondh. Her ending suggests that both women and men are at fault in the battle of the sexes and that women will always surrender.

There are some elements of wish-fulfillment and autobiography in the novel. In *1900*, published in her ninetieth year,[15] Dame Rebecca recalls the Edenic (or Artemisian) pleasures of the Kensington of her first eight years. She and her mother and two sisters were abandoned by her father, and her mother gave up her career as a pianist to support her girls in genteel poverty in Edinburgh. The novel is, in some sense, a tribute to her mother and her music, with the daughter giving the mother back in fiction the career she never had, and even restoring the lost husband, albeit after death. The exploration of the problem of how the woman artist finds a fit mate is probably also behind the fiction, as West tried to imagine the return of her lover, H. G. Wells.[16] Even in imagination he comes to murder and is enchanted into staying. Condorex's fixation on upward mobility and his unacceptable social origins is distinctly like Wells.

Harriet Hume divides London into public space and private space, the green world of the woman artist and the gray world of the male politician, separated by the dusty world of ordinary people in Oxford Street. Clearly she cannot imagine Harriet transforming the cabinet, and so her resolution is still a romantic one in which the female world accepts and forgives the death-dealing destructive male. It is as if she is saying that men will destroy the world with their imaginary empire building if we let them. It was just over twenty years later, reading Freud, that Virginia Woolf wrote of women, "We must compensate the man for his gun."[17] The fantasy of *Harriet Hume*'s sunny opening turns to leaden farce, just as *The Judge* went from Austen to Brontë, comedy to tragedy. It may be significant to Rebecca West's view of life that policemen are always called in at the end, that her comedies and fantasies end with suicide and murder. The dualism she damns in her critical writing informs her own fiction. If one can imagine such a thing as a Calvinist fantasy, that is *Harriet Hume*'s genre. Her myths have a moral: women turn into trees to escape male violence, and men kick the trees. Marriage, the tale tells us, destroys sisterhood and art for women. They are only possible in death.

The city has its separate spheres in West's novel, just as Victorian men and women were assigned to limited roles. Art and nature, the concert halls and parks, belong to women. The clubs and houses of Parliament, the City and the law courts, money and power, to men. There is a clear Kensington/Westminster opposition, a war between the city's sections which mimics the sex war, and woe betide the creature who trespasses on the enemy's territory. Some unseen hand crashes down on the piano keys at the end of Harriet Hume's London sonata. Not only are the woman artist's hands too small to stretch across the keyboard of musical genius, they are too delicate to handle the keys of the city. The suffragettes may have stormed the London streets and wrested the keys of the city from men through militancy, but all to no avail, West seems to say. Only continued vigilance and the threat of violence on woman's part will allow them to be anything more than trespassers on male territory. As for the keys to men's

hearts, the invisible city of human affection, Harriet's clairvoyance tells her that her lover blames her for his actions because
of her knowledge. The false city of Mondh, men's dream of imperialism, is more real to him than Harriet's love. She does indeed put on his "knowledge" with his power, and becomes the
guilty cause of his downfall in his deranged mind. London remains the capital of the patriarchy, with Kensington a docile isle
of femininity within its borders; an occasional timid trespasser
enters the fastnesses of Westminster, broomstick in hand for a
fast flight back to the forest. *Harriet Hume* is Artemis's lament that
her suburban wilderness is only an island in a patriarchal imperialist state. Earlier, the young Rebecca West had written an-
grily at a political situation which denied the young artist the
conditions in which to write. The government's opposition to
suffrage forced her to march with the suffragettes, to write political essays and propaganda for feminism instead of novels. Harriet's plight proves her point. She has ignored politics for art and
now must accept the world that men have made, comfort the
killer-lover, since she has not been willing to fight to impose her
own values on the world and to govern it according to the order of
nature.

The prophecy in *Harriet Hume* that "the trees will get us yet"
was fulfilled in Sylvia Townsend Warner's *Lolly Willowes* (1926).
There is no need to ask who is Sylvia, for she has created a world
of trees and given her heroine to the forest as heartily as other
authors give them in marriage. There is no more exquisitely powerful evocation of the joys of spinsterhood in print. The rapture of
St. Teresa as the bride of Christ matches Lolly's rapture at her
dance with the devil. The prose is as sharp and delicate as Lolly
Willowes's nose and chin. The single woman's passion for adventure and her flight into freedom are portrayed without guns and
policemen in the plot. The humor is not that bitterly intellectual
Scotch brew of Rebecca West, but a lighter and more domestic
concoction like the dandelion wine Laura sips with her landlady,
Mrs. Leak. Feminists have complained that Jane Austen never
left us a portrait of the joys of her own happy spinster's life. But
the spirit of Jane Austen has bewitched Sylvia Townsend
Warner's pen and inhabits it as the devil inhabits Lolly's cat, as a
familiar. She is as enchanting in her evocations of the natural

world as the greatly gifted children's story writer, Alison Uttley. A dry feminist wit undercuts any sentimental effect, and family life, religion, and society are wryly wrung out like dishrags and hung on the bushes to dry in the open air.[18]

If *Harriet Hume* is a London piano sonata which turns into a Gilbert and Sullivan comic opera, *Lolly Willowes* is a fantasia. In the first movement, soprano and flute are shored up by her father's low bass and the voices of the Somerset woods. In the second movement, the soprano is swamped by the family chorus and London's rhythmic demanding rounds. In the third, the single voice breaks free to the accompaniment of the songs of birds, wind, trees and the devil's trill on violin. *Harriet Hume* does not record the heroine's fight for freedom. But we see Lolly Willowes in the bosom of her family, passed from father to brother as she changes from daughter to aunt. The rejection of aunthood is as passionately played a drama as Elizabeth Barrett Browning's rejection of permanent invalid daughterhood.

London is Lolly's prison. Her brother has even paved the back garden, and she does not flourish as a houseplant, but needs wild earth and forest beneath her feet. As a brewer's daughter at Lady Place in Somerset, Laura leads an eccentric childhood and youth. Nannie Quantrell teaches her the lore of herbs and simples. With her own little still, she brews concoctions while the family brews beer. She reads and studies and wanders the fields and woods according to her own whims. She wants to brew mugwort as well as nettles, quoting Pliny on Artemis revealing the virtues of mugwort to Pericles, but Nannie forbids it. She publishes anonymously a little book called *Health by the Wayside* at the local press. It falls flat, and her father buys up the remainders, but modern readers recognize Lolly as a precursor of the women's health movement. Lolly's niece Fancy finds her aunt unenterprising and unemancipated. But London has deprived Lolly of her contact with the earth, seeds and bulbs and fruit and flowers. To her father, Laura is an ermine, a vixen, a weasel and she is just as uncomfortable in London as they would be.

When her brothers tie her up in a game, she waits contentedly to be rescued, singing a song about a snake with no mackintosh (a lament for the death of the Delphic python). Her education consists of reading in her father's library, Locke on understanding and Glanvil on witches, and being a comfort to her father after her mother's death. Her happy solitariness is spoiled at her father's death, and she goes to Apsley Terrace to be aunt to her brother's children.

This ten-year limbo is rendered with chilling eloquence. London is colder than the country. The water is hard. Laura's hands roughen, and her face hardens. Patriarchal time is shown as oppressive, like Woolf's depiction of Big Ben in *Mrs. Dalloway*. The weights of the grandfather's clock droop "sullenly over the abyss of time wherein they were to make their descent during the seven days following" (50). She is bored by church and drawn toward Jews, Catholics, and mystics, but Henry forbids adventures. She doesn't like the lawyers Henry brings home as prospective suitors—"their jaws were so many mousetraps, baited with commonplaces" (55). They give up when she suggests to Mr. Arbuthnot that he might be a werewolf. Laura's face loses its expressiveness and becomes "nut-crackerish," and her sister-in-law feels "emotionally plumper" than Laura because of her wife and motherhood. Townsend Warner clearly sees the city as hospitable only to the bourgeois family. Lolly is an outsider and only fits by forming herself to aunthood. The single woman is better off in a village:

But when Laura went to London she left Laura behind, and entered into a state of Aunt Lolly. She had quitted so much of herself in quitting Somerset that it seemed natural to relinquish her name also. Divested of her easily-worn honours as mistress of the household, shorn of her long meandering country days, sleeping in a smart brass bedstead instead of her old and rather pompous four-poster, wearing unaccustomed clothes and performing unaccustomed duties, she seemed to herself to have become a different person. Or rather, she had become two persons, each different. One was Aunt Lolly, a middle-aging lady, light-footed upon stairs, and indispensable for Christmas Eve and birthday preparations. The other was Miss Willowes, "my sister-in-law Miss Willowes," whom Caroline would introduce and abandon to a feeling of being neither light-footed nor indispensable. (61)

The novel captures the transitional period in the history of the family—as the ideology of the natural duty of a daughter to nurse her parents in their old-age and deathbed illnesses was replaced by a pathology of the single, self-sacrificing woman. Lolly's nieces will want to know why she hasn't made something of herself, as Peggy is impatient with her Aunt Eleanor's outmoded gentility in *The Years*. *Lolly Willowes*, one guesses, must have been one of Virginia Woolf's few models for *The Years*, where the relationships between aunts and nieces and nephews are a primary affront to the patriarchal genealogical imperative of the English novel. In Lolly's relationship with her nephew, Titus, there is a parallel to Sara Parigiter's relationship to North. Sara is also something of a white witch, a crippled prophetess who mumbles spells and rhymes. But she belongs to the city as strongly as Laura belongs to the country. Like Woolf, and her friend the composer, Ethel Smyth, and many other twentieth-century feminists, Sylvia Townsend Warner attacks Milton—

She thought of *Paradise Lost* with a shudder, for it required even more constancy to write someone else's book. Highly as she rated the sufferings of Milton's daughters, she rated her own even higher, for she did not suppose that they had to be forever jumping up and down to light the poet's cigarette; and blank verse flowed, flowed majestically, she understood, from his lips, whereas Titus dictated in prose, which was far harder to punctuate. (210)

When Laura's brother James dies, Lady Place and the brewery are leased until Titus is of age to inherit the property, and so Laura cannot even return to her own fields and forests on holiday. She suppresses the pain this causes her and makes no remarks on the injustice, but "it seemed as though some familiar murmuring brook had suddenly gone underground" (63). As war breaks out her niece Fancy marries and has a daughter. Her husband is killed and she goes to France to drive a lorry, much to the disapproval of her mother—"The married nun looked at the widowed amazon and refused battle" (69). Laura spends the war years doing up parcels in a room plastered with fading recruiting posters—"Laura watched them discolour with a muffled heart" (69). She faints on Armistice Day and slowly her new life begins. She hallucinates herself into imaginary woods in the country while pretending at comfortable aunthood in London:

Her mind walked by lonely sea-birds, in marshes and fens, or came at nightfall to the edge of a wood. She never imagined herself in these places by daylight. She never thought of them as being in any way beautiful. It was not beauty at all that she wanted. . . . Her mind was groping after something that was shadowy and menacing, and yet in some way congenial. . . . Loneliness, dreariness, aptness for arousing a sense of fear, a kind of ungodly hallowedness—these were the things that called her thoughts away from the comfortable fireside. (76–77)

What Lolly wants is *der Wald*, the primeval forest where Hecate and Artemis rule the forces of life and death and a deeper spirituality is possible than in orderly Apsley Terrace and middle-class London.[19] She wants magic and mystery and finds the alien places in London where she can feel natural magic at work. She imagines a London like Defoe's, on the docks, in the city churches, among the graves at Bunhill Fields. Her first "epiphany" is a moment of being, to use Woolf's term, in the goods yard of the G.W.R., where she has gone to buy a crate of apples. Rotherhithe, Kew, and the Jews' Burying Ground are the London places where ancient mystery reveals itself to her. The old maid brightens her life in the spare room with gorgeous, expensive exotic flowers. Henry and Caroline do not approve. The grand illumination comes in a greengrocer's in the Moscow Road where Lolly is overcome by the sight of jars of glistening red plums, home-made jam and nuts and eggs from the country. She has a vision of the greengrocer's mother and then of herself as a tree:

A solitary old woman picking fruit in a darkening orchard, rubbing her rough fingertips over the smooth-skinned plums, a lean wiry old woman, standing with upstretched arms among her fruit trees as though she were a tree herself, growing out of the long grass, with arms stretched up like branches (83)

She buys a huge bunch of mop-headed garnet and yellow chrysanthemums, and the grocer wraps them with sprays of beech. The grocer says they're from the Chilterns in Buckinghamshire. She rushes out to find a map and guidebook and in her sylvan ecstasy settles on Great Mop (227) as the very place to become the village witch. The family is not amused, but she is adamant. Henry has lost a good deal of her money and she is forced to rent rooms from Mrs. Leak. "If she were not to pick fruit from her own trees, there were common herbs and berries in plenty for her growing wherever she chose to wander. It is best as one grows older to strip oneself of possessions, to shed oneself downward like a tree, to be almost wholly earth before one dies" (105–106).

Great Mop's name is obviously a play on a witch's broomstick, that phallic object of domestic service which links the repeated acts of bringing order and cleanliness with the power to fly. The mop is merely a magical tree brought from the woods to exercise its natural magic in the house, as the village of Great Mop is an enclave of domestic order surrounded by the great mysterious beech forest—reverse of the city where nature is paved over and pushed out except for contained gardens and parks. Lolly has several flashes of illumination during her excited prowlings of the woods and hills. She reads Mrs. Leak's old books on folk medicine, and the two women share their love for "distillations" over black currant tea and elderberry wine. Mrs. Leak and Lolly are both brewers, natural witches: "The lamplight shone upon the tidy room and the polished table, lighting topaz in the dandelion wine, spilling pools of crimson through the flanks of the bottle of plum gin. . . . When Mrs. Leak smoothed her apron the shadow solemnified the gesture as though she were moulding a universe. Laura's nose and chin were defined as sharply as the peaks on a holly leaf" (118). Mrs. Leak described to Laura the eccentricities of the villagers: "she called them up and caused them to pass before Laura, but in a dispassionate way, rather like the Witch of Endor calling up old Samuel" (125). Music in the night and late-burning lights suggest that the village has a mysterious life, and eventually Laura is initiated into its mysteries.

She begins by sacrificing her map and guidebook at a lonely well, feeling one with the spirit of the place. On her way to regain paradise, she apprentices herself to saunter the poultry farmer, and Milton is again mocked by Warner's wry feminist humor:

Till now, Laura had rejected the saying that man is the noblest work of nature. Half an hour with Mr. Saunter showed her that the saying was true. So had Adam been the noblest work of nature, when he walked out among the beasts, sole overseer of the garden, intact, with all his ribs about him, his equilibrium as yet untroubled by Eve. She had misunderstood the saying merely because she had not happened to meet a man before. Perhaps, like other noble works, man is rare. Perhaps there is only one of him at a time: first Adam, now Mr. Saunter. (131–32)

Lolly's next "moment of being" is a wave of terrible fear when she is on top of Cubbey Ridge and hears a goods train penetrating the beech woods on its way to Paddington: "It expressed something eternally outcast and reprobated by man . . . loud, separate, and abrupt, each part of the engine trampled down her wits" (143). In rejecting the city and its "iron hunter," the train, Lolly rejects phallocentric culture for "the secret country of her mind." "The country was desolate and half-lit, and she walked there alone, mistress of it, and mistress, too, of the terror that roamed over the blank fields and haunted round her" (135).

A train soon brings Caroline to visit, and Laura enters the village church for the first time, and identifies with a carved Foolish Virgin shaking an empty oil flask close to her ear. Watching Saunter and his hens from the hillside, she sees him as Adam and herself as God: "Did God, after casting out the rebel angels and before settling down to the peace of a heaven unpeopled of contradiction, use Adam as an intermediate step?" (141). She shapes a batch of scones into likenesses of the villagers (usurping God's powers yet again) and butters them and eats them with Mr. Saunter. As his apprentice, she goes from Foolish Virgin to Wise Virgin, as potent as the henwife in fairy tales who "hatched the future in her apron":

Laura knew that the Russian witches live in small huts mounted upon three giant hen's legs, all yellow and scaly. The legs can go; when the witch desires to move her dwelling the legs stalk through the forest, clattering against the trees, and printing long scars upon the snow. (147)

Henwifery transforms her, rids her of her anger against her family for keeping her from the world of women's natural magic. She finds release face down in a field of cowslips: "She knelt down among them and laid her face close to their fragrance. The weight of all her unhappy years seemed for a moment to weigh her bosom down to the earth; she trembled, understanding for the first time how miserable she had been" (149). She does not forgive the patriarchal institutions which have oppressed her, but she begins to forget them, listing the enemy in capital letters as Virginia Woolf does in *Mrs. Dalloway*, to exorcise their evil spells— "Society, the Law, the Church, the History of Europe, the Old Testament, great-great-great-aunt Salome and her prayer-book, the Bank of England, Prostitution, the Architect of Apsley Terrace and half a dozen other useful props of civilization" (150).

Lolly Willowes, self, witch, tree-woman, is born again, but her nephew Titus, Bloomsbury writer (much like Lytton Strachey), bursts into Great Mop like Apollo chasing the nymphs of Artemis. He decides to write his biography of Fuseli as far as possible from the reading room of the British Museum. He wants to capture "the real man," and doesn't care for Fuseli's pictures. But Lolly's awakening to witch-womanhood seems to be Warner's dramatization of Fuseli's famous painting *Nightmare*. Lolly's dream is not of the ugly smug incubus-devil perched on Fuseli's sleeping woman's belly. Her first familiar is a black cat, named Vinegar after Vinegar Tom in Glanvil's book of witches. Her nephew is an "infant Bacchus" in the village—"All the white-aproned laps opened to dandle him" (157) as he charms the village that Lolly has treated so discreetly.

Warner's portrait of Titus is much like Woolf's portrait of Jacob Flanders. We see him through objects and the eyes of others— "He left his pipe and tobacco pouch on the mantelpiece. They lay there like the orb and sceptre of an usurping monarch" (158). He is oblivious to her pain at his presence and insinuates himself into the hearts of the villagers, as Lolly gets angrier. His love of the country horrifies her: "It was comfortable, it was portable, it was a reasonable appreciative appetite, a possessive and masculine love. . . . He loved the countryside as though it were a body" (160). She hates him for this possessive love, basking in the "green lap" of the country. In a sour field she acts out her rebellion against Titus and what he represents, the power to repress her real self into docile aunthood. She finds the cat on her return and realizes that she has made a pact with the devil:

If she had been called upon to decide in cold blood between being an aunt and being a witch, she might have been overawed by habit and the cowardice of compunction. But in the moment of election, under the stress and turmoil of the hunted Lolly as under a covering of darkness, the true Laura had settled it all unerringly. (175)

In using the word "election" Warner makes Lolly's witch-hood a vocation. Nun's ecstasies as brides of Christ are the counterpart of her fantasies of the devil as "loving huntsman." The novel not only dignifies spinsterhood. It mocks the patriarchal God whom Virginia Woolf called "Milton's bogey,'" and allies Milton's Satan with women and the old natural magic of the religion of outcasts in the forest. She goes to a Witches' Sabbath in the woods with Mrs. Leak where the dancers leap to odd music by candlelight. A masked young man with the face of a girl licks her cheek while dancing, and she retreats into the woods. (This recalls the seduction of Artemis by Lencipus dressed as a girl.) A new Satan appears as a gamekeeper-guardian. She returns to discourage Titus from disturbing her peace, and Titus begins to be afraid in the woods; mice disturb his sleep; the milk curdles. In a comic scene she watches Titus attacked by wasps on a hill opposite where she sits and returns to find his stings being nursed by Pandora Williams, whom he asks to marry him. "One has to offer marriage to a young woman who has picked dead wasps out of one's armpit" (221). In Folly Wood, Titus had met Beelzebub and decided to leave Great Mop. Lolly thinks that the devil has helped her to find a female inheritor for Lady Place. She sees them to the train and finds herself in an odd funereal place on the walk back, Maulgrave Folly, full of minarets and obelisks, built by the "Satanic Baronet." She has a conversation with Satan, now a gravekeeper, and gives him an apple. "Once a wood, always a wood," he says, and she thinks of the savage sacred places in London where she had the first intimations of her vocations:

> The Vatican and the Crystal Palace, and all the neat human nest-boxes in rows, Balham and Fulham and the Cromwell Road—he saw through them, they went flop like card-houses, the bricks were earth again, and the steel girders burrowed shrieking into the veins of earth, and the dead timber was restored to the ghostly groves. Wolves howled through the streets of Paris, the foxes played in the throne-room of Schonbrunn, and in the basement at Apsley Terrace the mammoth slowly revolved, trampling out its lair. (231)

It is remarkable how similar this vision of the destruction of the patriarchal city and the return of the power of nature is to Lucy Swithin's visions in *Between the Acts*, of London as a swamp with rhododendrons growing in Piccadilly. It represents a fierce feminist commitment to the life-giving principles of nature, the common urge to wipe out men's cities of oppression and start again. Townsend Warner's devil is "a kind of black knight, wandering about succoring decayed gentlewomen." Lolly says that women are sticks of dynamite longing for the concussion which will justify them. Women are dangerous, incalculable and extraordinary. They are witches in their hearts. She makes a passionate speech to the devil:

> When I think of witches, I seem to see all over England, all over Europe, women living and growing old, as common as blackberries and as unregarded . . . Nothing for them except subjection and plaiting their hair. . . . (234–35)

Satan calls them to a life of adventure, not to do harm or good. She doesn't want to be "a district visitor on a broomstick," but "to have a life of one's own, not an existence doled out to you by others." The devil is the emancipator of women. The novel ends with Lolly sleeping in the woods "a hind couched in the devil's converts" under "his undesiring and unjudging gaze, his satisfied but profundly indifferent ownership" (247), a free woman.

There is a dry irony here, similar to Virginia Woolf's, which allows Sylvia Townsend Warner to carry off this novel, while Rebecca West fails in *Harriet Hume*.[20] Everything that happens in *Lolly Willowes* can be explained naturally, if the mind is so inclined. But *Harriet Hume* mixes melodrama and magic to spoil the tone. And Rebecca West is angry with women for not having imposed their own natural values on culture. Lolly's separation from male values is complete. She mocks Milton and Fuseli, but is kind to Saunders and her nephew.

West still seems to admire the Adam houses and the Reynolds painting which inspire her tale. She makes the reader uncomfortably guilty, while Sylvia Townsend Warner's fiction affords the relief of guilt in the knowledge that there have always been subversive women like us. There are two notions of women's transformative magic or spiritual power at work here. One blames our mothers for not making the world a better place for women, and the other celebrates that they survived at all in the patriarchy. *Harriet Hume* and *Lolly Willowes* are two versions of female pastoral where the feminist imagination grapples with women's marginal place in the city. One survives by escape to a forest, the other is killed by a lover jealous of her powers. The male principle (Satan) is a fantasy for Lolly, not a reality she has to live with. West's dualistic vision assumes that male jealousy of women's power can never be overcome and that she is doomed eternally to know and to forgive. Sylvia Townsend Warner's solution, the creation of Eros, the devil, the green-world lover who protects the heroine without the sex/death power struggle of *Harriet Hume*, is the woman artist's hope. Satan does not pursue Laura to rape her. Consequently, she never has to take Lady Mary Wortley Montague's advice: "We harden like trees, and like rivers are cold." Laura never gives her laurels to crown male civilization and his cities. She sleeps with the trees, her own woman.

NOTES

I am grateful to my colleagues Louise DeSalvo, Kay Turner, and Larry Carver for their comments and suggestions about this essay.

Jane Marcus

1. *The Metamorphoses of Ovid*, trans. A. E. Watts (San Francisco: North Point, 1980).
2. Annis Pratt, *Archetypal Patterns in Women's Fiction*, (Bloomington: Indiana Univ. Press, 1981). Pratt calls the use of this myth in women's fiction the "rape-trauma archetype." See pp. 4 and 5 for definition, though the whole book is full of references to the myth and its modern appearances.

In a review essay covering several critical books on fantasy literature (*TLS*, May 13, 1983) T. A. Shippey raises the theoretical question of "whether modern fantasy does not have a more than coincidental nexus with modern fascism," in view of the violence and degradation of women and slaves in contemporary (male) science fiction texts. It is clear that female fantasy is often written by those with "strong belief systems" for moral and political ends. Both West and Warner were active in left-wing politics, attracted by utopian social projects, and strongly disappointed in the amount of *real* change they were able to effect in the lives of women and working people. Colin Manlove's *The Impulse of Fantasy Literature* (Macmillan, 1983) argues that the theme of all fantasy is "its insistence on and celebration of the separate identities of created things," which is true of both novels under discussion here. Evil is then shadow or non-being, as in Warner's devil figure or West's life-destroying male. Alfred Habegger argues in *Gender, Fantasy and Realism in American Literature* that the realistic novel springs from the rejection of the fantasy implicit in popular fiction, not, as I argue here that, for women, the fantasy novel rejects realism as inadequate to convey the female sense of "life!" as Orlando says.
3. Erich Neumann, *The Great Mother* (Princeton: Bollingen, 1963). See also Joan Bamberger, "The Myth of Matriarchy" in *Women, Culture and Society*, ed. Michelle Zimbalist Rosaldo and Louise Lamphere (Stanford: Stanford Univ. Press, 1974); and Tom Moore, "Artemis and the Puer," *Puer Papers*, 1979 (Irving, Texas: Spring Publications).
4. Norman O. Brown, "Daphne, or Metamorphosis," in *Myths, Dreams, and Religions*, ed. Joseph Campbell (New York: Dutton, 1970).
5. Geoffrey Hartman, *Beyond Formalism* (New Haven, Yale Univ. Press, 1970). I discuss Hartman's patriarchal misreading in "Liberty, Sorority, Misogyny," paper delivered at the English Institute, 1981, in *The Representation of Women in Fiction*, ed. Carolyn Heilbrun and Margaret R. Higonnet (Baltimore: Johns Hopkins Univ. Press, 1982).
6. Rebecca West, *Harriet Hume: A London Fantasy* (New York: Doubleday, 1929). All quotations are from this edition. It has now been reprinted as a Virago Modern Classic (London) and by Dial in the U.S.
7. Sylvia Townsend Warner, *Lolly Willowes or The Loving Huntsman* (London: Chatto and Windus, 1926). Rpt. 1980, London: Women's Press (not, at this writing, in print in the U.S.).
8. Judith Kegan Gardiner, "A Wake for Mother," *Feminist Studies* 4 (June 1978), 145–65. In folktale and myth, the tree is often the mother. See Jack Zipes, *Breaking the Magic Spell: Radical Theories of Folk and Fairy Tales* (Austin: Univ. of Texas Press) p. 172, on the origin of *Cinderella*, "the tale revolves around a female who receives help and gifts from her

dead mother, who continues living in the form of a tree, and from animals." I am indebted to Beverly Stoeltje for this observation. The "flamboyant tree" and the tree in the forest serve the same function in Jean Rhys's *Wide Sargasso Sea*. Note also the real oak tree and Orlando's poem of that name in Woolf's *Orlando*. Contemporary feminist novelists, in particular Margaret Atwood, deny the proposition that "women have no wilderness in them." And Djuna Barnes's *Nightwood* in the character of Robin Vote reiterates the savage woman of the Artemisian sisterhood in the wilderness of Parisian night-life, ending in the animal before the altar of the goddess in a forest in up-state New York.

9. Rebecca West, *The Judge* (New York: Doran, 1922). Reprinted as a Virago Modern Classic with new introduction by Jane Marcus, Dial in U.S.

10. Jane Marcus, "Thinking Back through Our Mothers," in *New Feminist Essays on Virginia Woolf* (Lincoln: Univ. of Nebraska Press, 1981), 1–30.

11. Susan Merrill Squier, "The Politics of City Space" in *The Years: New Feminist Essays on Virginia Woolf* (Lincoln: Univ. of Nebraska Press, 1981), 216–37, and "A Track of Our Own," in Marcus, ed. *Virginia Woolf: A Feminist Slant*, 1983, in press.

12. Virginia Woolf, *Orlando* (London: Hogarth, 1928); see particularly pp. 123–28, the transformation, or sex change scene, attended by three ladies, Purity, Chastity, and Modesty. In Lady Purity's hand "reposes the white quill of a virgin goose." Womanhood and writing seem to require chastity. It is an odd scene, even for a fantasy, for Woolf seems ambivalent about whether the graces are goddesses or "Horrid Sisters." "The Sisters try to cast their veils over the mouths of the trumpets so as to muffle them" is a remarkably aggressive sexual metaphor in which Woolf tries to capture women's theft of art from the male. The goddesses are also witches, and these pages are extremely ambivalent.

13. See Jane Marcus, *The Young Rebecca: Writings of Rebecca West* (New York: Viking, 1982) for the story of this transformation.

14. Ibid.

15. Rebecca West, *1900* (New York: Viking, 1982).

16. See Gordon Ray, *H. G. Wells and Rebecca West* (New Haven: Yale Univ. Press, 1974).

17. Virginia Woolf, "Thoughts on Peace in an Air Raid," *The Death of the Moth* (New York: Harcourt Brace, 1942), 243–48.

18. John Updike complains about Townsend Warner's "weak endings," "erratic sense of form, enigmatic and sentimental style." Clearly it is simply not a style based on the model of male sexual experience. "Her stories tend to convince us in process and baffle us in conclusion; they are not rounded with meaning but lift jaggedly toward new, unseen, development." *Picked Up Pieces* (New York: 1976), 231–36.

19. In Townsend Warner's autobiographical collection of stories, *Scenes of Childhood* (New York: Viking, 1982), there are many references to trees and her mother. Her mother grew up in India and remembers the Sanskrit story of the mouse that gnaws the root of the world tree and the connection between this and the Scandinavian story of Ygdrasil (35).

She describes trees as characters in her stories, as minutely as people, and infuses them with a brew of natural myth. See "Being a Lily," and "Deep in the Forest," which tells the tale of her German lessons from a young woman whose conversation was only from fairy tales.

There is now an edition of Townsend Warner's *Collected Poems* (Manchester: Carcanet New Press, N.Y.: Viking, 1982, ed. Claire Harman) revealing Townsend Warner as a tart Hardyesque poet. Trained as a musicologist, Townsend Warner was also a dedicated communist. Her letters to her lover, Valentine Ackland, will be published separately, but Viking has just issued a volume of *Letters* (1983, edited by William Maxwell, Warner's editor at the *New Yorker*), an astonishingly vivid and moving record of a writer's life. She reveals here that the character of Mr. Saunter was based on her stepfather, and tells David Garnett of her pleasure at meeting Margaret Murray, the author of an important study of witchcraft, who liked her witch but was "doubtful" about her devil. She describes Reynolds Stone—"He looks at trees with an astonishing degree of love and trust and penetration; almost as though he were exiled from being a tree himself." In 1965, she wrote to her friend Bea Howe, "Did you know that poor Jane Welsh Carlyle brought back *a nettle* from her mother's grave and cherished it in the Cheyne Walk garden—till a hireling gardener dug it up?"

20. Rebecca West did not abandon her fantasy of chaste sisterhood. It is retold in "Parthenope" (1959) in *Celebration* (New York: Viking, 1977) as the story of seven "mad" sisters in Victorian England who have Greek names and wear Greek dresses and frolic in a garden. They are forced into marriage by their father but are rescued from their husbands and children by their sister, Parthenope. She is boyish and also sane, and hides the mad nymphs in a small town in France. Her anger at spending her life as the guardian of her sisters may be taken as an allegory of Rebecca West's resentment at her position as the lone outspoken feminist writer in England for so many decades. For a discussion of modern novels on this theme, see Carol Pearson, "Women's Fantasies and Feminist Utopias," *Frontiers* 2, no. 3, 1977. For the most successful visionary treatment of the fantasy of the recovery of women's lost power, see Leonora Carrington, *The Hearing Trumpet* (New York: Pocket, 1977) and Gloria Orenstein's discussion in *The Theatre of the Marvelous* (New York: New York Univ. Press, 1976) and her "Leonora Carrington's Visionary Art for a New Age" in *Chrysalis*.

SYDNEY JANET KAPLAN

"A Gigantic Mother": Katherine Mansfield's London

Here in my room, I feel as though I was in London. In London! To write the word makes me feel that I could burst into tears. Isn't it terrible to love anything so much? I do not care at all for men, but *London*—it is life. (Wellington, Oct. 21, 1907)[1]

NOT LONG AFTER KATHERINE MANSFIELD had read aloud T. S. Eliot's *The Love Song of J. Alfred Prufrock* to the guests at Lady Ottoline Morrell's party at Garsington, in June 1917, she was introduced to the poet himself, and recorded in a letter to Lady Ottoline the following description of the conclusion to another party:

I came away with Elliot [sic] and we walked past rows of little ugly houses hiding behind bitter-smelling privet hedges; a great number of amorous black cats loped across the road and high up in the sky there was a battered old moon. I liked him very much and did not feel he was an enemy.[2]

They had, in fact, some important things in common: they were exactly the same age and they were both outsiders in London— he an American, she a New Zealander. I wish we could know their conversation during that walk, because Mansfield's picture of "ugly houses," "amorous black cats," and "battered old moon" evokes a London not completely unlike Prufrock's "certain half-deserted streets" and "yellow fog that rubs its back upon the window-panes." I do not want to suggest imitation on

[161]

Mansfield's part, however. While her interest in *Prufrock* and its author might result in echoes or ironic references in her own writing from time to time (the comment in her journal of 1917: "Is that all? Can that be all? That is not what I meant at all,"[3] is the most obvious), most similarities appear to be more the result of parallel development than influence.

Katherine Mansfield's enthusiasm for Eliot subsided, however, as we see in these comments she made to Virginia Woolf after the publication of Eliot's *Poems* by the Hogarth Press in 1920:

Eliot—Virginia? The poems *look* delightful but I confess I think them unspeakably dreary. How one could write so absolutely without emotion—perhaps that's an achievement. . . . I don't think he is a poet—Prufrock is after all a short story. I don't know—These dark young men—so proud of their plumes and their black and silver cloaks and ever so expensive pompes funèbres—I've no patience.[4]

But is it the "dreariness" of the male point of view that really marks her divergence from Eliot? If we pay attention to Mansfield's *tone* when she describes urban details similar to those of Eliot, we may approach their differences in response. The few lines from the letter to Lady Ottoline give us a clue: Mansfield nearly *delights* in the squalid features of nighttime London. She views them with affection and humor. Her description emphasizes the diminutive: "rows of ugly little houses *hiding*," the "battered old moon" is far away, and all true danger and threat seem absent. For Mansfield, it is a relief to be out in the streets and away from the party; for it, rather than the streets, is the locus for social hostility and competition, the real limitations of city life.

Earlier in the same letter to Lady Ottoline she had complained how most parties are "too infernally boring," and was upset that one man there was "so stupidly callous about the war." But the streets for Mansfield—even this night with Eliot—the streets themselves are a source of creative energy. She would use the "amorous cats" some months later in "Bliss" ("A grey cat, dragging its belly, crept across the lawn, and a black one, its shadow, trailed after"[5]), and simultaneously take the opportunity to satirize the London avant-garde, and the absurd young poet, Eddie Warren, with his exaggerated city metaphors: "I saw myself *driving* through Eternity in a *timeless* taxi" (343).

A letter to John Middleton Murry on November 4, 1917, provides another illustration of Katherine Mansfield's ironic, *energetic* response to the city at this time, a city undergoing the trauma of World War I:

> By the way, isn't *Furnished Rooms* a good title for a story which plays in the Redcliffe Road? I can't resist it. . . . The meeting on the dark stairs—you know, someone is coming down and someone is coming up. . . . Then the whole street. And for backcloth, the whole line of the street—and the dressmakers calling to the cat, the Chinamen, the dark gentlemen, the babies playing, the coal cart, the line of the sky above the houses, the little stone figure in one of the gardens who carries a stone tray on his head . . . the lamenting pianos, and all those faces hiding behind the windows—and the *one* who is always on the watch.[6]

A journal entry nearly six months later expresses her continued interest in the same setting:

> If I had my way I should stay in the Redcliffe Road until after the war. It suits me. Whatever faults it has it is not at all bourgeois. There is "something a bit queer" about all the people who live in it; they are all more or less "touched." They walk about without their hats on and fetch and carry their food and even their coal. There are nearly four bells to every door—the curtains are all "odd" and shabby. The charwomen, blown old flies, buzz down each other's basements.[7]

There simply is not the same quality of hopeless impersonality in Mansfield's "there are nearly four bells to every door—the curtains are all 'odd' and shabby" as in Eliot's lines from "Preludes": "One thinks of all the hands / That are raising dingy shades / In a thousand furnished rooms."

It was during the time of Mansfield's acquaintance with Eliot that she wrote a brief story called "The Common Round," which appeared in *The New Age* on May 31, 1917, and was later revised as "Pictures" in *Art and Letters* in 1919. This story gives us a superb example of Mansfield's use of the city to both determine and reflect the main character's dilemma. Miss Ada Moss is an unemployed singer, middle-aged and overweight, out of place as an operatic contralto in the new world of popular entertainment: the cinema. The story takes us through one day of her life: a regular little "voyage" about the city as she searches for work in order to pay her landlady, who threatens to kick her out of her seedy Bloomsbury room that "smelled of soot and face powder and the paper of fried potatoes she brought in for supper the night before" (393). There are Prufrockian echoes in Miss Moss's impression of the street, when she descends to it to begin her series of futile rounds from one theatrical agent to another:

There were grey crabs all the way down the street slopping water over grey stone steps. [Eliot's "pair of ragged claws" comes to mind here.] With his strange hawking cry and the jangle of the cans the milk boy went his rounds. Outside Brittweiler's Swiss House he made a splash, and an old brown cat without a tail appeared from nowhere, and began greedily and silently drinking up the spill. It gave Miss Moss a queer feeling to watch—a sinking—as you might say. (396)

There are more reasons for that "sinking" feeling as the day goes on. When she stops first for a cup of tea (planning to use her last few cents), she finds that she is too early:

. . . when she came to the ABC she found the door propped open; a man went in and out carrying trays of rolls, and there was nobody inside except a waitress doing her hair and the cashier unlocking the cash-boxes. She stood in the middle of the floor but neither of them saw her.
"My boy came home last night," sang the waitress.
"Oh, I say—how topping for you!" gurgled the cashier.

Miss Moss is only an object of indifference to them—"neither of them saw her"—and the repetitive, mindless dialogue which continues between them establishes a rhythm which points ahead to Eliot's later use of the bar-room conversation in *The Waste Land*. "Pictures" is a perfect, modernist city piece in miniature, with its use of the stream-of-consciousness, its rhythms of London waking up, its snatches of conversation overheard. Ada Moss is also much like Joyce's Leopold Bloom walking through *his* frustrating morning rounds. Also like Bloom she is a city person, one totally without status or power. A taxi driver yells at her as she crosses the street: "Look out, Fattie; don't go to sleep!" Her movement through the city is marked by such indignities, and she suffers them with remarkably good humor and with considerable courage. Miss Ada Moss ends her day by allowing a "stout gentleman," who tells her "I like 'em firm and well covered," to pick her up, and we assume, to help her pay her rent that evening. Mansfield's last words in the story remind us, with disturbing irony, of Miss Moss's "voyage": "And she sailed after the little yacht out of the café" (401).

It is troubling to find Miss Moss defeated by the end of the story, especially by a victimization that is ultimately sexual. Yet

Mansfield's awareness of what produces Ada Moss's desperation is precisely the point where she reveals her greatest difference from Eliot. It would be hard to imagine Katherine Mansfield describing the young typist in *The Waste Land*, who "lights / Her stove, and lays out food in tins," with such cruel disdain. [Neither would she phrase a line like Eliot's reference to the typist's "carbuncular" lover: "one of the low on whom assurance sits / As a silk hat on a Bradford millionaire."] Rather than use her alienated city characters as symbols of the breakdown of Western civilization or as contrasts with the great figures of the past, Mansfield identifies with them. Her stories are much more likely to turn upon an instance of inhumanity or social injustice (see in particular "Miss Brill" and "The Life of Ma Parker").

Katherine Mansfield's initial affinity with Eliot derives from similarities in their stylistic evolution, especially in their common inheritance from the symbolists.[8] Mansfield's treatment of the city clearly demonstrates the evolution of her style from nineteenth-century aestheticism to modernism. It is an evolution comparable to other major modernists, especially Eliot and Joyce. As an example, consider the following "vignette," one of Mansfield's earliest published writings (October 1907). Note its over-obvious personification, romantic sense of correspondences, and stilted diction:

It is at this hour and in this loneliness that London stretches out eager hands towards me, and in her eyes is the light of knowledge. "In my streets," she whispers, "there is the passing of many feet, there are lines of flaring lights, there are cafes full of men and women, there is the intoxicating madness of night music, a great glamour of darkness, a tremendous anticipation, and, o'er all, the sound of laughter, half sad, half joyous, yet fearful, dying away in a strange shudder of satisfaction, and then swelling out into more laughter. The men and women in the cafes hear it. They look at each other suddenly, swiftly, searchingly, and the lights seem stronger, the night music throbs yet more madly.

Out of the theatres a great crowd of people stream into the streets. There is the penetrating rhythm of the hansom cabs.

Convention has long since sought her bed. With blinds down, with curtains drawn, she is sleeping and dreaming.

Do you not *hear* the quick beat of my heart? Do you not *feel* the fierce rushing of blood through my veins?

In my streets there is the answer to all your achings and cryings. Prove yourself, permeate your senses with the heavy sweetness of the night. Let nothing remain hidden. Who knows that in the exploration of your mysteries you may find the answer to your questionings.[9]

[165]

Mansfield's persona and the personified city of London merge voices here. (Mansfield even forgets to include a closing quotation mark!) This London is archetypically feminine—"she stretches out eager hands," "she whispers," and she is passionate: "the quick beat of my heart," "the fierce rushing of blood through my veins."

Compared with Mansfield's later, sharp-edged, unembellished depiction of the London streets in "Pictures," the vignette seems embarrassingly histrionic, but it is important to remember that its impressions of London are those of the eighteen-year-old Kathleen Beauchamp, who had only just assumed the pen name "Katherine Mansfield." She recently had returned to Wellington after three years as a student at Queen's College in London. During those years (1903–6) she dreamed of an artistic career, either as a musician—for she played the cello—or as a writer. From the protected environment of the college, London had suggested tentative adventures, moments of intrigue whose dangers were cushioned by the rules and regulations of the school. While Kathleen and her friends might venture forth from the college on their way to music lessons wearing large artist hats and ties, they invariably had to return to their rooms on time. The darker sides of life in London appeared to them as romantic and exciting, images of bohemia caught in glimpses. Through their professor of German, Walter Rippmann, they were introduced to the art and literature of the nineties: Beardsley, Symons, and Wilde. These "chosen" pupils were invited to tea and enjoyed their taste of "decadence" in the comfortable surroundings of their professor's artistically decorated flat.

In contrast with her classmates, this devotion to the nineties went deeper than fashionability for Kathleen Beauchamp. It continued after her return to New Zealand, where she longed for London from her room in her parents' expensive Wellington house. It provided her with an ideal of the city that was linked with her own urge toward sexual experimentation. One of the many Wilde epigrams that she copied into her notebook in 1907 was: "For we castrate our minds to the extent by which we deny our bodies."[10] The world of the decadents was one of sexual ambiguity, a place where sexual boundaries break down for the pure artist, where experience leads to artistic creation. The Wildean aesthete is a curious model for a young woman, however, for the aesthete—especially in his "decadent" pose—is, after all, a *male* figure, even with his supposed androgyny (although that certainly appealed to a young woman troubled by her own bisexuality). Such an example finally leads only to the worship of the male body and the exclusion of the female altogether.

The Wildean aesthete proved to be too limiting a model for Mansfield. But as the style of the London vignette suggests, it provided a temporary justification for a growing sense of sexual division in herself, a realization at about this time that she was "child, woman, and more than half man."[11] Sexual ambivalence is also apparent in the quotation at the beginning of this essay, with her unconscious remark: "I do not care at all for men, but *London*—it is life." Mansfield's sense of self-division affects her attitudes towards the city—her simultaneous longing for and rejection of London. It also relates to a characteristic feature of her style. Antony Alpers observes that in a considerable number of early Mansfield sketches and stories we can see the author or her persona at a window, either longing for greater life or observing others experiencing it. (The London vignette is a good example.) Alpers remarks: "a trick of her mind is evident: she is constantly inhabiting one space while observing another, and has her characters doing the same."[12]

In addition to Mansfield's initial devotion to the symbolists, her career corresponds with Eliot's and other male contemporaries' in another way. Malcolm Bradbury makes the point in his discussion of the modernist writer and the city (although he does not include Mansfield in his discussion) that "frequently it is emigration or exile that makes for membership of the modern country of the arts."[13] Mansfield's impulse to escape the provincialism of New Zealand and the bourgeois values of her parents was as significant as her need for sexual expression. Surely Katherine Mansfield can be grouped with those other modernists as one who "perceives from the distance of an expatriate perspective of aesthetic internationalism."[14]

That she also felt confused by her decision to leave New Zealand and take up life as an "independent" woman in London is reflected in an entry in her journal, written in December 1908, a few months after she had arrived in England. It shows how much she was torn between her attraction to London and her fears of failure there. It also gives evidence of her attempt to combine the stylistic features of aestheticism with a psychological projection of her own life (in retrospect, of course, it is painfully prophetic).

I should like to write a life much in the style of Walter Pater's *Child in the House*. About a girl in Wellington; the singular charm and barrenness of that place—with climatic effects—wind, rain, spring, night—the sea, the cloud pageantry. And then to leave the place and go to Europe. To live there a dual existence—to go back and be utterly disillusioned, to find out the truth of all—to return to London—to live there an existence so full and strange that life itself seemed to greet her—and ill to the point of death return to W. and die there. A story—no, it would be a sketch, hardly that, more a psychological study—of the most erudite character—I should fill it with climatic disturbance—and also of the strange longing for the artificial. [15]

The same problem had faced her in 1906, when, as a seventeen-year-old student, she attempted to write a novel. *Juliet*, an unfinished *Bildungsroman* that survives only in fragments, exemplifies Mansfield's difficulties in imagining a life in the city for an ambitious young woman like herself. The choices for such a woman were simple:

On one hand lay the mode bohème, alluring, knowledge-bringing, full of work and sensation, full of impulse, pulsating with the cry of Youth Youth Youth. . . . On the other hand lay the Suitable Appropriate Existence, the days full of perpetual Society functions, the hours full of clothes discussions, the waste of life. [16]

Juliet wins the battle for independence from her family and escapes to London long before her author was able to do so. In this respect the novel is a projection, an exploration of a life not yet lived.

Juliet's choice of London is in accord with Bradbury's remarks on the vital link between artistic emancipation and the drift toward the city in the fiction of this period:

If one theme of Modernist literature is disconnection and loss, then another is that of artistic emancipation—so that not only Dedalus in *A Portrait of the Artist as a Young Man* but Paul Morel in *Sons and Lovers*, George Willard in *Winesburg, Ohio*, and many another literary hero all stand at the end of their novels on the edge of some urban redefinition of themselves—as if the quest for self and art alike can only be carried out in the glare and existential exposure of the city, where, as Julius Hart puts it in a compelling phrase in his poem *Journey to Berlin*, one is "born violently into the wild life." [17]

But Bradbury neglects a most crucial point. While it is abundantly clear if we look at Mansfield's diaries, letters, and early writing that she was seeking "artistic emancipation" for *herself* in moving to London, it would be hard to find examples in her fiction of female heroes standing "on the edge of some urban redefinition of themselves" who actually achieve it. One by one Mansfield's city women retreat into fantasy and personal isolation. The "wild life" degenerates into disappointment, as well as an alarmingly female sense of terror.[18]

Obviously, as the works Bradbury mentions so boldly announce, the literary "hero" is only defined as masculine. Stephen, Paul, and George face very different futures from that of Juliet. Mansfield, in a sense, begins where the others—Joyce, Lawrence, and Anderson—leave off. She gives us Juliet's life *in* the city. Juliet emerges as a completely self-supporting "new woman," who lives in a dreary room "up five flights of stairs," where she reflects upon:

The horror of the long white day. She could not endure another. Here in this twilight, shaking off her great chains of Commerce, London shone, mystical, dream-like. . . . This struggle for bread, this starvation of Art. How could she expect to keep art with her in the ugliness of her rooms, in the sordidness of her surroundings.[19]

Juliet has moments of triumph over "her fatigue, her doubts, her regrets," and expresses her author's own youthful wish for independence:

"How weak I am. How I ought to be full of strength, and rejoicing all the day. Relations at the other end of the world who have, thank Heaven, cast me off and my wish fulfilled. I'm alone in the heart of London, working and living."[20]

Juliet also asserts her rejection of women's traditional roles, her distrust of marriage, and her respect for work. Living happily for a time with a woman friend, who remarks that they have "all the comforts of matrimony with none of its encumbrances," Juliet spiritedly agrees:

"As it is we are both individuals. We both ask from the other personal privacy, and we can be silent for hours when the desire seizes us. . . . I loathe the very principle of matrimony. It must end in failure, and it is death to a woman's personality. She must drop the theme and begin to start playing the accompaniment."[21]

While a contemporary feminist might end her novel at this point, the seventeen-year-old author must have felt too threatened by the implications of Juliet's independence, feeling the need to punish herself for her own assertions. As the novel continues, Mansfield does not allow Juliet the fulfillment she seeks in the city. She closes off all possibilities for her, instead, taking her through a tragic course of events including seduction and betrayal, pregnancy, abortion, and death. Although Kathleen Beauchamp was making plans for her own escape into an independent life at the same time as she was writing *Juliet*, she could not imagine what independence might really mean. She could only envision a typically *female* tragedy. This is not surprising; neither in life nor in literature did she have any other models for the woman artist she longed to become. What she did surmise was that London would be the one element essential for her own development in that direction.

Although *Juliet* was never completed, even its sketchy outline gives us some wonderful, unguarded glimpses into Mansfield's early, highly romanticized conceptions of the city and the hopeful artist's place in it. Moreover, *Juliet* illuminates Mansfield's awareness of a special dimension of the city—that is, its potential as a catalyst for sexual release. The London vignette, quoted earlier, with its sexualized language: "intoxicating madness," "strange shudder of satisfaction," "swelling out into more laughter," "penetrating rhythm of the hansom cabs," came to its climax with "in my streets there is the answer to all your achings and cryings." Katherine Mansfield must have been aware of the sexual implications of her language in the vignette, since in *Juliet*, which was written earlier, she stated them explicitly. When Juliet's roommate informs her that her restless mood has a physical cause: "'You feel sexual,'" Juliet responds with: "'Horribly— and in need of a physical shock or violence. Perhaps a good smacking would be beneficial.'" Juliet also explains:

"I am in need of exercise. I shall go out, I think, for a walk, despite the fact that I shall become physically, mentally, and psychically damped. . . . I feel a need of a big grey sky, and a long line of lights. Also a confused noise of traffic, and the sense of many people—you know?"[22]

All of this helps us to interpret a characteristic feature of Mansfield's later fiction, where she portrays a female character rushing outside, or desiring to be caught up in the rapid movement of life in the London streets. In "Revelations" (1920), Monica Tyrell, who "suffered from her nerves," feels "she could not stand this silent flat . . . this ghostly, quiet, feminine interior. She must be out; she must be driving quickly—anywhere, anywhere" (428). And in "Bliss" (1918), Bertha Young asks: "What can you do if you are thirty and, turning the corner of your own street, you are overcome, suddenly, by a feeling of bliss . . .?" (337). An unrecognized, or at least undefined sexual restlessness affects a good number of Mansfield's city women, and that restlessness often is both a symptom of rebellion against confinement in stereotypically female spaces and a clue to the diction and rhythm of her prose in evoking women's responses to the city.

Nevertheless, the example of Katherine Mansfield's own first experiences in London—both imaginatively and literally—may lead a feminist to question the effects of aesthetic doctrine on the art and—even more significantly—the life of the *female* artist. The aesthetes' emphasis on the pursuit of sensual gratification, their belief that the artist's duty is to experience *more* than the ordinary person—experience cultivated for its own sake—may have pernicious consequences for women who seek such experience. What Katherine Mansfield feared, as is clearly evidenced in Juliet's defeat, became all too true in her own life. This is not the place to describe the tumultuous events of Mansfield's early years in London. Antony Alpers's biography is a reliable source for details. It is enough to say that she underwent numerous disillusioning experiences, including those of misplaced trust, loss of love, pregnancy, abortion, and illness. A few lines from an unfinished story of 1909 allow us a glimpse of her growing disenchantment:

"Surely after my terrible sorrow, London seems to lose all her reality. I had thought of her as a gigantic mother in whose womb were bred all the great ones of the earth—and then—suddenly—she was barren, sterile."[23]

Katherine Mansfield's vulnerability as a woman alone in London surfaces in several stories in which a young woman is victimized by predatory males: "The Swing of the Pendulum" (1911), "The Little Governess" (1915), and, of course, "Pictures" (1919). There is also the unmarried pregnant woman in "This Flower" (1919), who is attended by a "leering" doctor with "a rather shady Bloomsbury address."

Some of the disappointments Mansfield experienced during her first years in London may have been temporarily submerged during the better stages of her relationship with John Middleton Murry,[24] when she was caught up in the enthusiasm over new friendships (Lawrence, Woolf, Eliot) and new discoveries in technique and conceptualization as her skills as a writer increased. Later, those disappointments would resurface, intensified by the suffering and despair resulting from her worsening tuberculosis. Her illness forced a change in her viewpoint from an emphasis on experience to one of observation. In this respect, Alpers's comment about Mansfield's use of the window as both an opening into the world and symbol of her own self-division is particularly relevant. As her illness progressed, the window nearly became her only way to connect with the city outside. With more distance in feeling between herself now and what she could observe, she gave expression rather to her delight in the city as *spectacle*, such as the following in a letter to Virginia Woolf in April 1919. Here Mansfield captures moments almost cinematic in their quick-flashing movement:

> But what I chiefly love, Virginia, is to watch the people. Will you laugh at me?—it wrings my heart to see the people coming into the open again, timid, airing themselves; they idle, their voices change and their gesture. A most unexpected old man passes with a paper of flowers (for whom?), a soldier lies on the grass hiding his face, a young girl *flies* down a side street on the—positive—*wing* of a boy—[25]

I also notice a resemblance in tone and phrasing between this letter to Woolf and the passage, a few years later in *Mrs. Dalloway*, where Clarissa expresses *her* own delight in city people and the city panorama: "what she loved was this, here, now, in front of her; the fat lady in the cab."[26]

In moments of despair and depression Mansfield might turn against her pleasures in the real city and try to invent an ideal one—but not very often:

> Why isn't there some exquisite city where we all have our palaces—and hear music—and walk in heavenly landscape and look at pictures and where all the people are beauties—moving in the streets as it were to a dance. I am quite serious. I *pine* for lavishness. For the real fruits of the earth tumbling out of a brimming horn (perhaps it is four years of Khaki).[27]

Mansfield would ultimately reject London, but not completely by free choice. To escape London's cold and dampness she was uprooted over and over again as she moved from pension to hotel, hotel to pension, in France and Italy and Switzerland. It is no wonder that her nostalgia for New Zealand intensified. Her longing for "lavishness" blurred with memories of Wellington's crisply blue harbor, the dense bush surrounding its hills of wooden houses. Many of her greatest stories are set in New Zealand rather than London: "Prelude," "At the Bay," "The Garden Party."[28] In the last year of her life she wrote to her father about her memories and the pain of separation:

> The more I see of life the more certain I feel that it's the people who live remote from cities who inherit the earth. London, for instance, is an awful place to live in. Not only is the climate abominable but it's a continual chase after distraction. There's no peace of mind—no harvest to be reaped out of it. And another thing is the longer I live the more I turn to New Zealand. I thank God I was born in New Zealand. A young country is a real heritage, though it takes one time to recognise it. But New Zealand is in my very bones. What wouldn't I give to have a look at it![29]

(This is as close as she would get to the fate of the "girl in Wellington" projected in her journal, who would finally return to Wellington to die.)

Yet it would be a mistake, I believe, to consider London the destroyer of Katherine Mansfield. She was one of our first true contemporaries, one of the first notable women writers who attempted to live on equal terms with men *in* the city at a very young age. It was, after all, the only place she could have lived that way at all; such a life would have been impossible in Wellington, with its cultural isolation and with her socially minded parents always on watch. If she failed it was because her *body* failed, not because her ideal of independence was wrong. As much as she turned against London, she still knew the secret of its attraction for her and its power to inspire her. It was in London that her talent was ripened and sharpened; it was there she developed the techniques that allowed her to express her unique vision. Her role as an outsider in the city strengthened her powers of observation. Mansfield knew how to look at people and see what is important in their lives, but she knew also: "One wants to feel a stranger, for these things to have their charm."[30] She questioned herself about her interest in charwomen, shabby streets, coal buckets: "But do you like this sort of talk? This kind of thing? What about the Poets and—flowers and trees?" Her answer comes from the real Katherine Mansfield: "As I can't have the perfect other thing, I *do* like this. I feel, somehow, free in it. It has no abiding place, and neither have I. And—and—Oh well, I *do* feel so cynical."[31]

NOTES

1. *Journal of Katherine Mansfield*, ed. J. Middleton Murry (London: Constable, 1954), 21.
2. Quoted by Antony Alpers in *The Life of Katherine Mansfield* (New York: Viking, 1980), 244.
3. *Journal*, 124.
4. "Fifteen Letters from KM to Virginia Woolf,'" *Adam International Review*, Nos. 370–75, 19.
5. *The Short Stories of Katherine Mansfield* (New York: Knopf, 1954), 341. Hereafter, page references to this collection will be included parenthetically.
6. *Katherine Mansfield's Letters to John Middleton Murry, 1913–1922*, ed. John Middleton Murry (New York: Knopf, 1951), 95.
7. *Journal*, pp. 132–33. Mansfield was no stranger to the concept of the transiency of urban life; Alpers notes that she "had amassed a total of twenty-nine postal addresses since coming to London in 1908," 201.
8. For a useful discussion of Eliot's "process of modernization," see Monroe K. Spears, *Dionysus and the City: Modernism in Twentieth-Century Poetry* (New York: Oxford Univ. Press, 1970), 138–43.
9. Katherine Mansfield, "Vignettes," *The Native Companion* 2 (Oct. 1, 1907), 129–30.
10. *Journal*, 11.
11. Ibid., 13.
12. Alpers, 53.
13. Malcolm Bradbury, "The Cities of Modernism," *Modernism: 1890–1930*, ed. Malcolm Bradbury and James McFarlane (Penguin, 1976), 101.
14. Ibid.
15. *Journal*, 37–38.
16. Margaret Scott, ed. "The Unpublished Manuscripts of Katherine Mansfield. I. *Juliet*," *The Turnbull Library Record* 3 (n.s.) (March 1970), 25.
17. Bradbury, 100–101.
18. See especially, "'Rosabel'" (1908) and "The Little Governess" (1915) for examples of disappointment and fear.
19. *Juliet*, p. 13; another influence on Mansfield was the fiction of the naturalists, who offered many examples of women struggling amidst the sordidness and hopelessness of the city. Bradbury comments on the merging of influences in turn-of-the-century literature: "The London of strange, unreal contrasts and encounters had been in fiction since Dic-

kens; it certainly has much to do with those strange exchanges between Naturalism and Impressionism, Realism and Surrealism, Determinism and Aestheticism that make up the turn-of-century mood." Bradbury, 181.

20. *Juliet*, 13.

21. Ibid., 16–17.

22. Ibid., 16.

23. Quoted in Ruth Elvish Mantz and J. Middleton Murry, *The Life of Katherine Mansfield* (London: Constable, 1933), 321.

24. For J. Middleton Murry's own account of his impressions of London during this time, see *Coming to London*, ed. John Lehmann (London: Phoenix, 1957), 94–107.

25. *The Letters of Katherine Mansfield*, ed. J. Middleton Murry (New York: Fertig, 1974), 201. In the same letter, incidentally, Mansfield tells Woolf that she had read her "article on Modern Novels."

26. Virginia Woolf, *Mrs. Dalloway* (New York: Harcourt Brace, 1925), 12.

27. *Letters of Katherine Mansfield*, 189.

28. For an extensive collection of Mansfield's writings about New Zealand, gathered from her journals, letters, sketches, and stories, see Ian A. Gordon, ed., *Undiscovered Country: The New Zealand Stories of Katherine Mansfield* (London: Longmans, 1974).

29. *Letters of Katherine Mansfield*, 456.

30. Ibid., 408.

31. *Journal*, 133.

CHRISTINE W. SIZEMORE

Reading the City as Palimpsest: The Experiential Perception of the City in Doris Lessing's *The Four-Gated City*

Kevin Lynch in *The Image of the City* implies that a city is a text. He says it has "legibility." Like the "printed page . . . [which] can be visually grasped as a related pattern of recognizable symbols, . . . a legible city [has] . . . districts or landmarks or pathways [that] are easily identifiable and . . . grouped into an over-all pattern."[1] Lynch's terms are particularly useful for an analysis of the city's linear elements, but the city has other dimensions too and in that sense it is not just any text; it is a specific kind of text. Another urban planner suggests that a city is a palimpsest, a text that is built up layer after layer, each layer preserved partially, or wholly underneath the others.

> A city . . . is the pulsating product of the human hand and mind, reflecting man's history, his struggle for freedom, his creativity, his genius—and his selfishness and errors. It is the palimpsest on which man's story is written, the record of those who built a skyscraper or a picture window, fought a pitched battle for a play street, created a book-shop or a bakeshop that mattered. It is a composite of trials and defeats, of settlement houses, churches, and schoolhouses, of aspirations, images, and memories.[2]

Whether one thinks of the seven layers of Troy or of the contemporary city of Atlanta, whose district "Underground Atlanta" flourished on the level of the railroad in the 1890s, was covered over by expressways in the twentieth century, was uncovered and flourished again as an entertainment district in the 1970s, only to be buried again by the economic forces accompanying another layer of circulation, rapid transit, the analogy of the city as a layered text that can be read by those with skill and trained perception is equally apt.

To those familiar with women's studies, the image of the palimpsest recalls another application. Women's novels have been called palimpsests because the real story about women is hidden beneath the surface text.[3] Women have a long heritage of writing and of reading beneath the surface and of being aware of the layers of meaning. If both the tradition of the city itself and of women novelists is "palimpsestic," then women ought to be particularly capable "urban novelists." Novelists who themselves can decipher and portray the multiplicity of layers in their own lives and histories ought to be those who can portray the experience of the city.

Doris Lessing is such a novelist, and she herself uses the image of the city as a palimpsest, a layered text built up over time, perceived by women, early in *The Four-Gated City*. Martha Hesse, the protagonist, has arrived in London just after World War II. She walks around London, noticing its districts and boundaries and its bombed out buildings. As she walks, she notices the details of the city herself and she thinks of how her landlady, Iris, who runs "Joe's Fish and Chips" would view these sights:

Iris, Joe's mother, had lived in this street since she was born. Put her brain together with the other million brains, women's brains, that recorded in such tiny loving anxious detail the histories of window sills, skins of paint, replaced curtains and salvaged baulks of timber, there would be a recording instrument, a sort of six-dimensional map which included the histories and lives and loves of people, London—a section map in depth. This is where London exists.[4]

The city here is portrayed as multilayered. It exists not only in three dimensions of space, but in three additional dimensions, perhaps of time: the *histories, lives,* and *loves* of people. This concept of the city is symbolized by a fragment of thirteen layers of wallpaper all fused together, a miniature palimpsest, that Martha scrapes off the wall of a bombed house and puts in her pocket as she starts thinking about the nature of the city. Furthermore, this miniature palimpsest of wallpaper fits into a pattern of actual palimpsestic texts that occurs throughout the novel: Thomas Stern's ant-eaten testament with his own "additions and riders, in red pencil" and Mark's insertions layered over those in red pen (176), Dorothy's diary (413–14), Mark's layers of clippings on his walls (282–83), and even the "appendix" itself in which the accounts and letters of several characters overlap (560–614). The piece of wallpaper, however, is a particularly significant "text" here because it is an image of the city and a statement of how to read the city.[5]

The piece of wallpaper is an appropriate image of the city and of a method of perceiving the city because it is both layered and a fragment. As Kevin Lynch emphasizes, "Most often, our perception of the city is not sustained, but rather partial, fragmentary, mixed with other concerns."[6] This kind of perception, partial, fragmentary, and mixed with other concerns, is precisely the kind of perception that women are good at, as Nancy Chodorow implies in *The Reproduction of Mothering*. She argues that because women go through a less clear-cut oedipal stage than men, women "define and experience themselves as continuous with others; their experience of self contains more flexible or permeable ego boundaries." This results partly because mothers "tend to experience their daughters as more like, and continuous with themselves. Correspondingly, girls tend to remain part of the dyadic primary mother-child relationship itself. This means that a girl continues to experience herself as involved in issues of merging and separation."[7] Because women do not separate out the sense of self as rigidly as men do, they are more comfortable with seeing the city as mixed and partial, as districts overlapping one another, rather than definite precise areas. Perhaps it is also because of this fluid ego boundary that they do not feel so threatened by fragmentation.

Martha herself becomes an astute observer of the city not only just because she is a woman, but also because for her this exact issue of merging with and separation from her mother and acceptance of a fragmentary identity is what she must work out in *The Four-Gated City*. Martha has been struggling with psychic separation from her mother throughout the *Children of Violence* series. She doesn't even read her mother's letters because they seem to threaten her so much. Her mother seems to Martha to be able to invade Martha's ego boundaries not only in person but even in her letters. Finally when Martha comes to London alone, she experiences freedom and begins to accept herself.

For a few weeks she had been anonymous, unnoticed—free. Never before in her life had she known this freedom. Living in a small town anywhere means preserving one's self behind a mask. Coming to a big city for those who have never known one means first of all, before anything else, . . . that freedom: all the pressures are off, no one cares, no need for the mask. (4)

In the freedom and anonymity of the city Martha recognizes the various personas and masks she has worn in the past and she realizes that she can control them. She is no longer forced to be "Matty," the clowning persona she adopted to fight her mother. She accepts herself as having many personas and as being multi-layered.[8] This recognition of herself as multilayered allows Martha to read the city, and finally after she has come to understand the city which gives her freedom, she comes to terms with her own mother. She reads all the letters and allows her mother to come to visit. Martha finally develops an ability to feel comfortable with fluid ego boundaries and is even later in the novel able to cross Lynda's ego boundaries and understand the nature of madness. Her development of this ability, however, starts with her reading of the city.

It is precisely Martha's focus on boundaries and her growing acceptance of fluidity and fragmentation that allow her to read that fragment of wallpaper and the city. When she learns about the people of the city, she does not restrict herself to a single class or layer of society any more than she restricts herself to a single persona. Nor does she feel that she must stay with any one person long enough to learn his or her entire life story. She accepts knowing people as fragments. When Martha observes the spatial qualities of the city, she does not focus on the "landmarks" or "nodes . . . the strategic spots" that are the two broadest elements of a cityscape according to Lynch. Rather she focuses on boundary areas, more fragmentary areas that Lynch calls "districts," "paths," and "edges."[9] It is in the variety of overlapping districts connected by paths and edges that Martha constructs her section map of the height, width and depth of the city.

The final dimension in which Martha has to learn to read the piece of wallpaper and the city is that of time. After Martha has scraped her piece of wallpaper off the wall and observed it spatially, noting the "thick sog of papers: layers of it . . . fused together, like a kind of felt" (73), recognizing the overlapping pieces, and identifying the boundaries and layers, she reads it in terms of time:

Picking at the layers, she counted thirteen. Thirteen times had a man stood on trestles, . . . and stretched new clean paper over the stains and dirts of the layer beneath. Thirteen times had a wife or children said, Yes, that's very nice, I like that, Dad; or had said, No, we chose wrong. The two papers at the very bottom were rather beautiful, . . . they got progressively uglier as the decades slid by. The one at the top was hideous, must have been an acid green, with a bad jangling pattern. In the middle was a rather pretty sprigged pattern, like a Victorian young lady's morning dress. (74)

The incorporation of the aspect of time is perhaps another important reason why Lessing said that cities are recorded in "women's brains." This sense of historical time is not for instance strongly present in Dickens in spite of his intense visual imagination and his tremendous scope and breadth as an urban novelist. Although Dickens captured the movement of the city[10] and "the city dweller's experience of architectural change," Alexander Welsh says that Dickens had "little historical imagination."[11] John Raleigh puts it even more strongly:

I think . . . that London or any of the new large cities must have been equally disturbing at almost a subconscious level, for two other reasons (not that the squalor was to be disregarded): one, it was so large that no one could grasp it; and, second, it was always changing and growing, so that it constituted a new paradox in man's history: a huge "thing" that was "alive." And in some ways it is these aspects that were finally to defeat the imagination even of a Dickens or a Balzac.[12]

What stands out strongly in Raleigh's comment is that something "changing and growing . . . constituted a new paradox in *man's* history." For any parent who has watched a child grow, it is not a paradox at all. In fact, as Sara Ruddick argues in an essay on "Maternal Thinking," a mother's "realistic appreciation of a person's continuous mental life allows a mother to expect change, to change with change" and furthermore that "if we attend to maternal practices, we can develop new ways of studying . . . the changing natures of all peoples and communities, for it is not only children who change, grow."[13] Doris Lessing expresses the idea that "maternal thinking" colors perception in *The Golden Notebook* when she asserts that it was written with "that filter which is a woman's way of looking at life."[14] In *The Golden*

Notebook Anna says to Tommy, the adolescent son of her close friend, that women do see their children in phases, but that it is not belittling as he might think.

But I think that's how women see—people. Certainly their own children. In the first place, there's always been nine months of not knowing whether the baby would be a girl or a boy. Sometimes I wonder what Janet [Anna's child] would have been like if she'd been born a boy. Don't you *see*? And then babies go through one stage after another, and then they are children. When a woman looks at a child she sees all the things he's been at the same time. When I look at Janet sometimes I see her as a small baby and I *feel* her inside my belly and I see her as various sizes of small girl, all at the same time.[15]'

Because of motherhood women are trained in seeing many different ages or layers all at the same time. Ruddick agrees that this interconnectedness is also an aspect of maternal thinking: "The agents of maternal practice, acting in response to the demands of their children, acquire a conceptual scheme—a vocabulary and logic of connections. . . . Intellectual activities are distinguishable, but not separable from disciplines of feeling. There is a unity of reflection, judgment, and emotion."[16] It is perhaps this unity as well as the acceptance of change over time that explains why, in Lessing's view, women can record "in such tiny loving anxious detail the histories of window sills, skins of paint . . . the histories and lives and loves of people, London—a section map in depth" (10), why women can read palimpsests.

Martha starts her reading of the city by learning about and experiencing fragments of the lives of urban characters. In fact this is what she says London is to her when questioned seriously by Phoebe, the earnest Labour party worker and sister of Martha's friend in the colonies:

And now, because it was Phoebe who sat there, opposite, the past weeks changed their aspect and presented "London" to Martha as a series, containing dockland Stella, the café and Iris; Jack; Henry; and the people in the streets and pubs. Fragments. (79)

Stella and Iris are particularly important characters for Martha not only because they take her in, but also because they are lower-class women and represent the variety of social classes Martha gets to know. Stella, who first befriends Martha, is "the matriarchical boss of her knot of streets, among the body-proud, work-proud men who earned their wages by physical strength and who judged everyone by strength and their capacity for work—was Stella the only Boadicea among the masculine communities of the river's edges" (15). Iris, "a small fattish smeared woman . . . [who] wore an overall washed so often it had gone a greyish yellow" (4) runs a small grimy cafe and rents a room to Martha after Martha leaves Stella. Like Stella, Iris takes care of Martha and values her:

> Iris felt for Martha, or rather Martha's experience that enabled her to drop into the life of Joe's café like a migrating bird, exactly the same emotion as she felt for a baulk of timber hauled up out of the tides of the river. . . . Martha had been something extra, something given, something unearned. . . . Treasure. (18)

Martha has to leave Iris and she feels guilty about that, but she feels that Iris's very kindness might threaten her new-found freedom. Martha can't afford to take on a new mother in Iris just at the moment when she most needs her experience of separation, of anonymity and freedom. Nonetheless, Iris has given Martha a treasure she can take with her. It is Iris who has taught Martha how to read the "histories and lives and loves" of people in the details of the London street. Martha can now walk "in a double vision, as if she were two people: herself and Iris" (10).

Iris and Stella do not reappear in the later three parts of the novel. Even Henry Matheson, who is upper class and might know the Coldridge family with whom Martha goes to live, does not reappear after Martha has lunch with him at Baxter's and turns down his offer of a secretarial job. These characters do not reappear because their lives have only intersected with Martha's in fragments. Their stories are soon to be papered over by lives of other characters Martha will meet, but Martha has learned from them all. She knows London in a way that the London journalists editorializing about socialism do not: "Had the editors and journalists never met Iris . . . and Stella, did they know nothing of what they could find out by getting onto a bus, crossing the river, and living for a week or so with Stella or with Iris? It seemed not" (15). For Martha a very significant dimension of the city is made up of its urban characters, "that current of people, that tide, which always flows in and out of London" (6).

For most urban novelists, however, the city is not just a group of urban characters; the spaces of the city, its physical presence, are an equally significant aspect. Martha brings the same concern for variety, interest in boundaries, and tolerance of fragmentation which allowed her to learn about the people of the city to the reading of the spatial qualities of the city. Here the variety and fragmentation are like a collage; sometimes a new structure is superimposed on an old district, sometimes boundaries are clearly observable as one area barely overlaps or is merely contiguous to the next. Kevin Lynch's five categories of cityscape, as mentioned earlier, are useful in defining the nature of Martha's spatial perception. Lynch's five elements are defined as follows: the *landmarks* are those well-known buildings or "reference points" that give a city "imageability"[17]; the *nodes* are "strategic spots," places of "junction," "concentration" or "convergence of paths"; the *districts* are "two dimensional," "recognizable" sections of the city; the *paths* are "streets" and "walkways"; and the *edges* are "linear elements not . . . considered as paths," "boundaries . . . barriers . . . or seams, lines along which two regions are . . . joined together."[18]

Martha is aware of the landmarks and nodes of London. She listens to Big Ben chime (72), she looks at the bomb damage to St. Paul's (17), and she rides the bus up to Piccadilly Circus, but because her mother spent so much time trying inauthentically[19] to instill the values of British culture into her colonist child by repeatedly mentioning these landmarks, they only evoke alienation and pain for Martha now. As the bus goes past Trafalgar Square, Martha thinks of "the haphazard insignificance of it, and the babyish statue," and begins to laugh. She tries to explain her feelings to her upper-class companion, Henry. "This . . . is the hub of the Empire" (22), but he doesn't understand. Her laughter subsides into pain. She recognizes the significance and power of the landmarks and nodes; for her, however, they evoke not identification and pride but only pain: "all kinds of half-buried, half-childish, myth-bred emotions were being dragged to the surface: words having such power! Piccadilly Circus, Eros, Hub, Centre, London, England . . . each tapped underground rivers where the Lord only knew what fabulous creatures swam! She tried to hide pain, Henry not being a person who knew how to share it" (22). As both a woman and a colonist, Martha is unable to identify with the battle of Trafalgar, and she does not glory in Britain's colonial past. She considers herself an "alien," and despite Henry's offer of a job, she realizes she will never fit into his society. "She had discovered, swapping notes with other aliens in pubs, that it was not only she who had to fight paranoia, so many invisible rules there were to break, rules invisible to those who lived by them, that was the point" (22). As an alien, however, Martha is able to see other elements of the city that remain invisible to men like Henry, men who are too blinded by the landmarks and the power they represent to see the districts and paths and edges that thread through a city as invisible rules thread through a society.[20]

Because Martha rejects the vision of the city as a single towering landmark, she is able to notice the variety of districts within London. When she first gets to London, she wanders around both the district of the dockyards, "a world of black greasy hulls" (13), and the district of fashionable Oxford Street with its "lit glass" and "dark weights of masonry" (32). She often walks the districts of the many small shops "passing shop fronts, each one the face of a low oblong room like Joe's café: haberdasher, grocer, chemist, greengrocer, hardware, fishmonger, then all over again, chemist, grocer, hardware, grocer, laundry, a pub. All over London: millions of little shops, each one the ground floor of an old house. On either side of her the terraces: damp. Stained with damp. Under her feet, a damp concrete." (8) As Martha moves from one district to another, she notes the boundaries of the districts, both the paths she walks on, the "damp concrete" under her feet, and the edges, the terraces on either side of her.

The paths and edges of the city are those elements that are most often completely invisible to those like Henry who see a city in terms of landmarks and who restrict themselves to certain fashionable districts. Martha, however, is sensitive to boundary areas both in human relationships like that with her mother and in spatial perception. She noticed that the fragment of wallpaper that seemed like felt was actually thirteen overlapping pieces. In the same way, as Martha walks around London, she notices boundaries between districts, whether they are specific streets or merely linear seams. One particularly vivid portrayal of these elements of the city occurs as Martha walks one night from Baxter's, the fancy upper-class restaurant, to Jack's house by the canal. First she walks down Oxford Street. When the shops that form the edge of Oxford Street end, Hyde Park becomes the new edge on one side.

She walked down the pavements at the Bayswater Road, with the park on one side, balances and patterns of leaf dramatically green where the

street lights held them, retreating into mysterious shadow beyond. . . .
On her right hand, the great ponderous houses that stood so assertively
on damp soil. Great ugly grey houses. They were boarded up or empty
or in makeshift use. (32)

One edge is the park; she sticks close to it walking "under the
trees that edged the pavement." The other edge is "the grey cliff
of buildings on her right" (32).

As Martha observes the edges, the linear forms stretching between districts, she also observes the subtle boundaries between
districts:

There had begun, from the moment she had left Oxford Street and the
shops, that heightened wary atmosphere which meant she must walk
careful of her eyes, because in this stretch of the Bayswater Road, men
prowled after women. Invisible boundaries, invisibly marked
territories—just as, across the river a boundary could be marked by an
old hulk of timber with river salt in its seams . . . here the corner of a
street or the hour of a day could say: Here a certain kind of order ends.
(32–33)

She walks fast until she passes "another invisible boundary.
From here until past Queensway, the pavements were lined with
prostitutes. . . . But Martha was freer here than she had been in
that other territory she had only just left, whose boundary was
simply a bisecting street. She was protected precisely by the line
of girls for sale, who knew she wasn't one of their trade union" (33). The boundaries are subtle. Sometimes they are just
a bisecting street; at other times they are invisible because they
are signaled not by a change in structure but by a change in the
groups of people in the street. A sensitive observer, and a woman
walking alone in a city at night susceptible to being accosted at
any time automatically becomes such an observer, can thus perceive these subtle changes in district.

After Martha leaves the prostitutes, she reaches Notting Hill
and braces herself "before turning off . . . into an area which was
worse than anything" (34). Even in the squalor of the area and the
stench rising from the refuse thrown into the canal, Martha acknowledges the value of the city to herself: "Far from being an
enemy . . . [London] was her friend. This was the best thing she
had known, to walk down streets interminably, to walk through
mornings and afternoons and evenings, alone" (35). Although
Martha has to be wary as she walks around the city, she experiences a heightened level of consciousness as she walks be-

cause of the freedom in the city and the intense powers of observation that being in the city requires and evokes. During this walk Martha is able to think back to her childhood and accept some of her personas. She gets a glimpse of the fluidity and boundlessness of consciousness that she will later explore more systematically.

Before Martha descends into the depths of consciousness, however, she must explore the depth of the city. Her attitude toward the depths of the city reveals that she is not afraid of this dimension. She does not see in the lower layers of the city the sewers of Victor Hugo or the eerie subway tunnels of T. S. Eliot and Robbe-Grillet (Martha never rides the subway). Rather, Martha sees riches and treasure:

The great market that was London had opened . . . where it seemed as if wealth had swum together just here, to offer congealed money, furs, carpets, silver, gold, robes, but like icebergs, only a fraction of them visible. . . . Above all, it was a sense of hidden wealth: and walking over the damp grey pavements it was to feel that under one's feet stretched invisible warehouses of luxury and richness and beauty—miles of them, caverns of them. . . . A secret city. A hidden city. And, if instead of walking past . . . one pushed open a door . . . suddenly, hey presto! a great descending stairway to the underground city beneath London where were stored for miles and miles the most fabulous carpets and tapestries and silks in the world. (77)

It is perhaps this conviction of the richness rather than the terror of depths that later allows Martha to descend to the basement of the Coldridge house and enter into Lynda's madness.

Martha also keeps with her a sense of the passage of time in the city. When she first scraped the piece of wallpaper off the bombed-out house, she projected back into time thinking of the stories that could accompany each layer. Ten years later after Martha sees the rebuilding of London, she still remembers the earlier bombed city, maintaining the simultaneity and layering of different points of time:

The city had lost its grey shoddiness; that dirty, ruinous war-soaked city . . . it was gone. A fresh soft air moved through it. . . . She walked through this [rebuilt] city and kept that other one in her mind, so that a long street of fashionably bright buildings had behind it, or in it, an avenue of nightmare squalor, a darkness and a lightness together. . . . London heaved up and down, houses changed shape, collapsed, whole streets were vanishing into rubble, and arrow shapes in cement reached up into the clouds. . . . It seemed as if the idea of a city or town as something slow-changing, almost permanent, belonged to the past. (287–88)

The city is in constant flux literally as well as in the eyes of the single perceiver walking through it, but the past of the city is not lost. It is preserved, even if covered over with a layer of paint like a palimpsest, by one who can read it carefully.

By the end of Part I, Martha must leave the multitude of people and the spaces of the city, to continue her education by exploring one family in depth and learning about the spaces within a single house and within herself.[21] She takes with her, however, the knowledge of people, and of districts, boundaries, and edges that she has gained from walking through London and an acceptance of fragmentation and layering that both comes with and is necessary for the experience of perceiving the city. As Dagmar Barnouw points out, "Martha's 'education' in . . . [the rest of the novel] is toward the conscious recovery of that space with its pictures and voices that she received here by chance, made sensitive, receptive by her 'aimless' walking"[22] through the city of London and her observation of it.

The ability to read even the most challenging of texts, however, is no guarantee that one can preserve them. By the end of the novel, London has been bombed again, this time in some kind of nuclear holocaust from which only a few characters have escaped. Mark went to Africa, but he never was able to build his ideal city; he was too busy administering a refugee camp. His last notes before his death say pessimistically: "Nineveh and Tyre, and Sodom and Gomorrah, and Rome, Carthage, Balkh, and Cordova—but that never meant anything. A desert which was a graveyard becomes a place where cities are not built" (611). Mark's word is not the last one, however. His comment is only one in the palimpsestic appendix that closes the novel. The last layer introduces a new symbolic character. On top of the stack of documents that comprise the appendix is an official note saying that Joseph Batts, a young boy whom Martha recognizes as having superior sensitivities, has come to Nairobi to Francis, Mark's son, to work as a gardener. This event recalls a symbol from Part I of the novel, that baulk of timber which survived the first bombing of London:

The door to this bomb site was . . . held shut by a bolt or a baulk of timber. . . . It was splintered, eaten, beaten, battered. Touching it was not touching wood, but nearer to water-eaten stone. . . . "They" had pulled this great beam out of the river at some point. . . . It had . . . been used as a base for a stair . . . before the bomb had destroyed [the] house . . . though not the timber itself. . . . In the hulk of timber was a cleft, more like a crack in rock than a split in wood. Moss grew in it. Salt lay seamed in finer cracks, salt from the salty, tide-washed river. Iris said the timber was probably part of a ship once. (9)

That hulk of timber that has been reused again and again and has survived both water and fire is referred to several times throughout Part I. It is one of the details of the city recorded "in women's brains" (10); it is a treasure to Iris, like Martha's own arrival (18); it marks boundaries between districts (33) like the other visible and invisible edges. It is an urban artifact that has survived many uses, but at first it seems barren. When Martha returns to it after her night with Jack, however, she "greet[s] . . . the slab or hulk of timber. In the less than two days since she had seen it, a minute yellow flower had emerged from a crevice. That great salty, sour, more-stone-than-wood monument had put out a coronet of green leaves and a flower. A small wind tugged at it, but the flower held firm, its roots being well dug in" (73). The old hulk of timber "with river salt in its seams" that has marked "invisible boundaries" (33) is another palimpsest. Seasoned wood is made up of layers and seams itself, and the hulk was used to mark boundaries that were invisible to those who were blinded by landmarks and could not read palimpsests. This wood, however, is not just a fragment; it has also served as soil for a flower, a new order. In spite of the seeming destruction of the novel's ending, there is hope that people with a new kind of consciousness, people who can read palimpsests, can survive. If that old splintered, battered, seamed timber can put out a flower, perhaps a city too can be rebuilt, maybe not an ideal city, but perhaps an ordinary, many-layered city with many districts, edges and pathways and multitudes of urban characters. And perhaps it can be recorded again in the minds of women who "passing a baulk of timber remember, smiling, how it came rolling up out of the Thames on that Thursday afternoon it was raining, to lie on a pavement until it became the spine of a stairway" (10).

NOTES

1. Kevin Lynch, *The Image of the City* (Cambridge, Mass.: MIT Press, 1960), 3.

2. Charles Abrams, *The City Is the Frontier* (New York: Harper and Row, 1965), 16.

3. Sandra Gilbert and Susan Gubar, *The Madwoman in the Attic: The Woman Writer and the Nineteenth-Century Literary Imagination* (New Haven: Yale Univ. Press, 1979), 73.

4. Doris Lessing, *The Four-Gated City* (1969; rpt. New York: New American Library, 1976), 10. All subsequent references to the novel will be to this edition.

5. Mary Anne Singleton in *The City and the Veld* points out that the city functions as two separate symbols in Lessing's work: the new Jerusalem or ideal city and the city of the plains or the fragmented modern consciousness. My emphasis in this work is not on Lessing's use of the city as a metaphor for something else but on Lessing's portrayal of the experience of the city. *The City and the Veld: The Fiction of Doris Lessing* (Lewisburg, Pa.: Bucknell Univ. Press, 1977).

6. Lynch, 2.

7. Nancy Chodorow, *The Reproduction of Mothering: Psychoanalysis and the Sociology of Gender* (Berkeley: Univ. of California Press, 1978), 169, 166.

8. Claire Sprague focuses on the multilayered quality of Martha and her acceptance of a variety of roles for herself. She sees the piece of wallpaper as an image of Martha herself. " 'Without Contraries Is No Progression': Lessing's *The Four-Gated City*," *Modern Fiction Studies* 26, no. 1 (Spring 1980), 102.

9. Lynch, 46–47.

10. Raymond Williams says that this movement of the city, this "random passing of men and women" is actually Dickens's "fictional method" and this is one of his great strengths as an urban novelist. *The Country and the City* (New York: Oxford Univ. Press, 1973), 154–55.

11. Alexander Welsh, *The City of Dickens* (Oxford: Clarendon Press, 1971), 7.

12. John H. Raleigh, "The Novel and the City: England and America in the Nineteenth Century," *Victorian Studies* 11, no. 3 (March 1968), 307.

13. Sara Ruddick, "Maternal Thinking," *Feminist Studies* 6, no. 2 (Summer 1980), 353. She bases the argument that maternal thinking will help better to study communities on Jean Baker Miller's *Toward a New Psychology of Women* (Boston: Beacon Press, 1976).

14. Doris Lessing, "Preface to *The Golden Notebook*," in *A Small Personal Voice: Essays, Reviews, Interviews*, ed. Paul Schlueter (New York: Knopf, 1974), 29.

15. Doris Lessing, *The Golden Notebook* (New York: Simon and Schuster, 1962), 229.

16. Ruddick, 348.

17. Yi-Fu Tuan picks up Lynch's terms and discusses people's ten-

dency to define a city in terms of landmarks in *Topophilia: A Study of Environmental Perception, Attitudes, and Values* (Englewood Cliffs, N.J.: Prentice-Hall, 1974), 204–6.

18. Lynch, 46–48.

19. Ruddick mentions the dangers of "inauthenticity" in mothering: "Maternal thought embodies inauthenticity by taking on the values of the dominant culture. . . . Inauthenticity constructs and then assumes a world in which one's own values don't count" (354). Ruddick bases her ideas about inauthenticity on Adrienne Rich, *Of Woman Born: Motherhood as Experience and Institution* (New York: Norton, 1976).

20. Hana Wirth-Nesher stresses that the city is best portrayed in its real heterogeneity, mysteriousness, and fragmentation in novels by outsiders who personally have experienced these aspects of the city. She focuses on male Jewish writers, but Doris Lessing as a woman and a colonist fits Wirth-Nesher's theory as well. "The Modern Jewish Novel and the City: Franz Kafka, Henry Roth, and Amos Oz," *Modern Fiction Studies* 24, no. 1 (Spring 1978), 91–109.

21. Roberta Rubenstein has an interesting interpretation of *The Four-Gated City* in which she sees Erich Neumann's three dimensions of psychic and physical life, the domain of the outside world, the domain of the community, and the domain of the self, as being three concentric circles in each section of the novel. The domain of the outside world would thus be London for Part I of the novel, but the "repressive political and social atmosphere" in Part II, "the Alderston march" in Part III and the desensitization of the sixties in Part IV. Rubenstein concentrates more on the sphere of the community (the Coldridge household) and Martha's "self," but her interpretation does show the connection with Lessing's vivid portrayal of London in Part I and later parts of the novel. *The Novelistic Vision of Doris Lessing: Breaking the Forms of Consciousness* (Urbana: Univ. of Illinois Press, 1979), 138–39, 149,151. The imagery of the "house" is also discussed by Sprague, 101, 109–14.

22. Dagmar Barnouw, "Disorderly Company: From *The Golden Notebook* to *The Four-Gated City*," in *Doris Lessing: Critical Studies*, eds. Annis Pratt and L. S. Dembo (Madison: Univ. of Wisconsin Press, 1974), 87. All the articles here originally appeared in *Contemporary Literature* 14 (Fall 1973).

Part III

North American Writers

SHERRILL E. GRACE

Quest for the Peaceable Kingdom: Urban/Rural Codes in Roy, Laurence, and Atwood

DISCUSSING THE CHARACTERISTICS of pastoral myth in his "Conclusion to a *Literary History of Canada*," Northrop Frye argues that

the nostalgia for a world of peace and protection, with a spontaneous response to the nature around it, with a leisure and composure not to be found today, is particularly strong in Canada.[1]

If Frye is correct, as I think there is little doubt he is, then one would expect Canadian literature to be dominated by natural or small town settings, by images of the wilderness or rural life, and by a consciousness shaped by an experience of the land. Such a literature is not, at first glance, a likely place to find strong city portraits or powerful urban settings, let alone metaphors of cities as consciousness. Indeed, our major writers create out of a profound and pervasive awareness of the natural landscape—prairie, Northern Shield, mountain, seashore. In Robert Kroetsch's words, we seem most drawn imaginatively by the great, silent, unstructured spaces surrounding us.[2]

When human habitations appear in the literature, they are more often small towns than large cities. Whatever the reason for this predilection, whether the topographical fact that the largest cities—Montreal, Toronto, and Vancouver—are stretched along a three-thousand-mile latitude with vast, sparsely populated areas between them, or because these cities are relatively new and raw, ungraced by the centuries of tradition that inspire poets, or because there is something in the Canadian psyche that finds the city an uncongenial metaphor or landscape—it is a rural, rather than an urban, perspective that governs much of our best writing.

I say rural *perspective* because this preference for nature or small towns is part of an old and complex convention that functions by oppositions: adoption of a rural perspective assumes rejection (at least, conventionally) of an urban perspective.[3] Arising from this basic opposition, with its shifting parameters that are as old as pastoral myth itself, is a set of expectations and values, which are represented by the semantic codes governing a particular literary system.[4] To the degree that nature and the small community are peaceful, the city is not; to the degree that the natural wilderness stimulates the imagination, the urban wilderness does not. But this constant opposition between city and country is not a simplistic matter of good and bad, positive and negative. Concepts of human identity and community, and the nature of both, are defined by the articulation of these codes.

In part as a result of the fact that the three writers to be examined are women, a further aspect of these codes warrants attention. Sexual stereotyping of city and nature, whether obvious or implied, has long been an element in literature, myth, and thought; hence, the city, like nature, is usually viewed as female. According to Jung, the city "is a maternal symbol, a woman who harbours the inhabitants in herself like children. . . . The Old Testament treats the cities of Jerusalem, Babylon, etc. just as if they were women."[5] Certainly, cities are often spoken of as female, or described in terms used for women, by male writers, especially when the city represents a negative, threatening presence. Striking instances of this can be seen, for example, in Joseph Conrad's *The Secret Agent*, Italo Calvino's *Invisible Cities*, and in much American literature, notably Pynchon's *V.* and *Gravity's Rainbow*.[6] The question to be asked here is whether or not the three women writers under discussion—Gabrielle Roy, Margaret Laurence, Margaret Atwood—adhere to this sexual stereotyping, and it would appear that they do not. Consistent with the *opposition* of urban/rural codes, as outlined below, is the designation of the city as male in opposition to a female nature— implicitly in Roy and Laurence, explicitly in Atwood.[7]

In the following discussion of these three Canadian writers, I hope to illustrate the significance of urban/rural codes by examining their portrayal of the three largest Canadian cities. In doing so, it should be clear not only how these women perceive cities and nature as women, but also how they express a Canadian sensibility. As female writers, and as Canadians, they seem doubly drawn to the natural world, expressing through that affinity their resentment and fear of a perceived patriarchal civilization, symbolized so well by the city, that conquers the landscape "by imposing an alien and abstract pattern upon it."[8] Furthermore, Roy, Laurence, and Atwood, like the majority of Canadian writers, male or female, "tend increasingly," as Frye suggests, "to see much of this [civilizing] process as something that is human but still dehumanized, leaving man's real humanity a part of the nature that he continually violates."[9]

In 1945 when Gabrielle Roy published her first novel, *Bonheur d'Occasion*, translated as *The Tin Flute*, she was immediately acclaimed as a striking new Canadian voice for two reasons: first, because the novel embodied an unrelenting social realism and, second, because of its urban setting, both of which were uncommon in Canadian literature at the time. *Bonheur d'Occasion* is set in a poor *quartier* of Montreal, and the desperate lives of its characters are seen not only against, but also in terms of, St. Henri's dirt and imprisoning boundaries. As Roy herself has said, however, *Bonheur d'Occasion* is not simply social documentary about the French Canadian urban poor; it is "the study of the human condition as well."[10]

Implicit in the setting and in the fates of the characters, Florentine Lacasse, her mother Rose-Anna, Jean Lévesque, and Emmanuel Létourneau, are the larger questions of the nature and value of human relationships and the possibilities for human happiness—questions largely explored in terms of urban/rural codes. An emphatic polarity of setting is, in fact, characteristic of Roy's writing. Thus, after writing *Bonheur d'Occasion*, Roy turned to an idyllic natural world for her next work, *La Petite Poule d'Eau* (1950) (translated as *Where Nests the Water Hen*), while her third novel, *Alexandre Chenevert* (1955) (translated as *The Cashier*), involves a return to an especially grim, annihilating Montreal.[11] She has felt compelled to look separately and, in turn, at the rural and urban worlds because, as both *Bonheur d'Occasion* and *Alexandre Chenevert* make clear, a harmonious combination of the two worlds seems impossible.

[195]

St. Henri in *Bonheur d'Occasion* is a slum, a low lying area of stone, cellars, and tenements hemmed in by factories and a walled canal, and crisscrossed by wires and railway tracks. To further emphasize the hopelessness of the place, the narrator explains that,

Autrefois, c'étaient ici les confins du faubourg; les dernières maisons de Saint-Henri apparaissaient là, face à des champs vagues; un air presque limpide, presque agreste flottait autour de leurs pignons simples et de leurs jardinets. De ce bon temps, il n'est resté à la rue Saint-Ambroise que deux ou trois grands arbres poussant encore leurs racines sous le ciment du troittoir.

(In other days this was where the suburb stopped. St. Henri's last houses had stood there facing waste fields, and an almost limpid, rustic air hung about their simple gables and tiny gardens. From those better days St. Ambroise now has no more than two or three great trees, their roots still digging in beneath the concrete of the sidewalk.)[12]

If one looks up the mountain, slightly to the north-west of St. Henri, one can easily see the prosperous urban domain of the wealthy Montreal English in Westmont. Within this almost allegorical urban world, young Florentine Lacasse and her family struggle to survive. Florentine, frivolous and shallow as she is, is frantic to escape the poverty and degradation of St. Henri personified in her mother, Rose-Anna, who every May 1st is pregnant and moving from one cramped lodging to a still smaller one. Like Crane's Maggie, Florentine places her hopes for escape in lipstick, silk stockings, flimsy garments, and a young man, Jean Lévesque. Jean, however, is also intent upon escaping St. Henri for the promising sphere of Westmount, and after seducing Florentine, he rejects her in the ruthless understanding that he can move on more quickly without her and all she represents.

More important for my purposes than the bald facts of the plot are the terms in which Roy presents this tawdry drama. All the characters in the novel spend much of their time walking the city streets, either in the restless movements of the unemployed or in the purposeful search for new lodgings. The relationship between Jean or Florentine and the streets they walk is sharply contrasted, however. Jean knows this urban world for what it is—"les ruelles sombre [et les] impasses obscures" (*B d'O*, 189) ("dark, narrow streets [and] obscurity between houses" *TF*, 212). He knows that spring in this city is a "saison de pauvres illusions" (*B d'O*, 188) ("season of thin illusions" *TF*, 211), and he is determined not to wander like so many in this limbo. Quite simply, Jean Lévesque is in control of this world, and it is a control he gains at the sacrifice of his heart, of his gentler nature and, as Roy implies, of his humanity. On the night of his decision to abandon Florentine, we see Jean discarding the last elements of this humanity, "son ancienne et sterile pitié" (*B d'O*, 191) ("his old and sterile pity" *TF*, 214), as he determines to become like the mechanical amoral city he goes forth to conquer:

Tout lui était devenu odieux dans ce quartier, et plus encore que le souvenir d'une jeune fille délaissée la pensée que pendant une soirée entière il avait été occupé au fond à se justifier. Comme s'il avait à se justifier! Au delà de son depart, il voyait déjà ce que les êtres ambitieux d'une grande ville, à l'affut d'un hasard propice, aperçoivent tout d'abord dans la fuite: un terrain neuf à exploiter. (*B d'O*, 190–91)

(The whole place had become hateful to him. Not just the memory of a jilted girl, but worse: the thought that he had spent the whole evening justifying himself. What did he have to justify? Already, beyond his departure he could glimpse what the ambitious ones in a big city see in their onward flight: new lands to conquer!) (*TF*, 214)

Florentine, however, is always lost, confused, or frightened by the streets of St. Henri. As Jean realizes, she is like her name: "Florentine . . . Florentine Lacasse . . . 'moitié peuple, moitié chanson, moitié printemps, moitié misère. . . . Ces petites filles-là . . . doivent être ainsi; elles vont, viennent et courent, aveuglées, à leur perte'" (*B d'O*, 26–27). ("'Florentine . . . Florentine Lacasse . . . half song, half squalor, half springtime, half misery . . .' Those girls are like that, I suppose, he thought. They run this way and that like blind things, to their own ruin." *TF*, 27) In order to control the city, one must become like it by denying one's own springtime, one's connections with the organic, physical world and with one's own nature. This Jean, the male, can do at a price, but the pregnant Florentine cannot. Despite her relative good fortune in finally marrying the gentle Emmanuel Létourneau before he leaves for the war, Florentine will most likely become like her mother, a prisoner of this alien, urban wilderness, ruined by her own vulnerability as much as by Jean Lévesque.

That Florentine is ruined in the largest sense seems clear in the final scenes of the book. By accepting Emmanuel's love under false pretenses, she has acquiesced in the destruction of her own humanity. Gabrielle Roy holds out little hope for human beings trapped in the urban chains of their own devising. Emmanuel's parting view of St. Henri is of

un arbre, dans un fond de cour, qui poussait ses branches tordues entre les fils électriques et un réseau de cordes à linge. Ses feuilles dures et ratatinées semblaient à demimortes de fatigue avant même de s'être pleinement ouvertes. (*B d'O*, 345)

(a tree in a backyard, its branches tortured among electric wires and clotheslines, its leaves dry and shrivelled before they were fully out. *TF*, 383)

Like the tree, a crucial image in the urban/rural codes of the text, Florentine and by extension human nature, are blighted in the springtime of life by the imposition and encroachment of the unnatural urban world.

Most of Margaret Laurence's Canadian fiction is set in or against the small prairie town of Manawaka as either the immediate or remembered place of essential human values and communal heritage. Only one of these novels, *The Fire-Dwellers*, is set in a big city, and the title alone suggests the central metaphor of the book: the city, here Vancouver, is a hell; its inhabitants are the damned. Laurence's articulation of urban/rural codes shares much with Roy, but she differs in the greater specificity of her metaphors, and in the narrative techniques employed to suggest both the intensity of the destructive modern world and the contrast between city and country.

The Fire-Dwellers is presented entirely from the point of view of its middle-aged heroine and mother of four, Stacey MacAindra (formerly Stacey Cameron of Manawaka), either through first person voice, limited third, or interior monologue. The result is a strong and immediate sense of what it means to live in a modern city bombarded by constant news of death and destruction, surrounded by lonely, hostile people, by concrete and by car accidents, and cut off from your own inner nature as well as from the earth. It is the violent, purposeless life of fire-dwellers, those who live in constant fear for themselves and their children, alienated not only from their families but also from themselves. One night, with husband and children asleep, Stacey looks from the window at the city lights, the lights that "flash and shift like the prairie northern lights in the winter sky, here captured and bound."[13] She envisions the city in apocalyptic terms of legions and "skeletal horsemen" and then wonders desperately: "No other facet to the city-face? There must be. There has to be" (*FD*, 90). She cannot, however, balance this vision of destruction with a convincing, positive image of the city.

This description of the city—set in italics to emphasize its terrifying position *within* Stacey's imagination—is reinforced by related narrative techniques. For example, the screaming voice of the radio or the images on the television, which is called the "EVER OPEN EYE," are set in bold face capitals in order to stress Stacey's sensation of being surrounded and bombarded with violence. Punctuating a conversation with her sons is her awareness of its persistence:

POLICE TURN HOSES ONTO RIOTING NEGROES IN A CITY'S STREETS CLOSEUP OF A BOY'S FACE ANGER PAIN RAW THE WATER BLAST HITS HIM WITH THE FORCE OF WHIPS HE CRIES OUT AND CRUMPLES. (*FD*, 243)

Although they impinge less stridently, even the newspapers remind her that this "place is a prison" and "there is nowhere to go but here" (*FD*, 258–59). Stacey's increasing hysteria and self-alienation climaxes in an italicized nightmare in which she stumbles through a forest carrying her severed head (*FD*, 124).[14] Shortly after this she will act out the symbolism of the dream by escaping from the city to the British Columbia shore of saltwater, evergreens, and mountains, where she will try to heal her wounds sufficiently to keep functioning.

Two elements of the narrative provide a crucial contrast to the fiery prison of the city-self. One is this flight into nature and a brief affair with a younger man living in a cabin near the beach. Despite the comfort Stacey derives from these moments, the sense of well-being resulting from spontaneous communication with another human being, she realizes that complete withdrawal is impossible. This knowledge leaves her with only one alternate route to psychic wholeness, her memories. At isolated points Stacey's recollections interrupt the narrative in an indented passage offset visually on the page. These happy memories are invariably of herself or of the family by a lake surrounded by trees and berry bushes. But just as the escape into nature is a temporary thing, a gesture, so these memories of "the green world" are slim defenses against the facts of her urban existence—or, more accurately, they are little more than the murmurings of a remembered natural self within a vulnerable being who is controlled and dominated by dehumanizing forces. At the most, Stacey will endure by shoring up the fragments of herself against complete ruin. As the final lines of the book make clear, the future of this self, city, or world, is precarious: "She feels the city receding as she slides into sleep. Will it return tomorrow?"

In many ways, Laurence offers a more optimistic vision in the last book of the Manawaka cycle, *The Diviners*. There the heroine, Morag Gunn, has rejected existence in four cities—Winnipeg, Toronto, Vancouver, and London, England. Although Laurence by no means glosses over the ironies and inconsistencies of living a country life in a modern technological society—indeed, Morag wryly mocks her efforts at pioneer life in her imaginary conversations with the indomitable Canadian pioneer Catherine Parr Trail—she places her heroine in the congenial, almost magic, surroundings of a farmstead beyond a small village. While Morag may ironically call her rustic home "Beulah Land," her log house and neglected acres fronted by the river are nevertheless her home. The first novel she writes there is called *Shadow of Eden*; the second is *The Diviners* itself, and the creative springs within her are released by the landscape she inhabits. The profound contrast between *The Fire-Dwellers* and *The Diviners*, inherent as it is in the titles of each work, extends beyond superficial questions of setting or even image because it arises from the increased foregrounding of urban/rural codes within the Manawaka cycle.[15] In the city, one is consumed by spiritual fires that are denied meaningful expression or else one simply extinguishes those fires, thereby submitting to the dehumanizing forces symbolized by the city; one accepts an urban consciousness. In the country, one is able to live creatively as part of the flow of time and nature. Neither is easy; ease or simplicity is not Laurence's ambition. But the latter existence, informed by a rural consciousness, is better because natural and therefore more human.

The articulation of semantic codes expressing urban/rural polarities which we have seen in terms largely of background and setting in Roy or setting and metaphor for self in Laurence are defined with a new clarity, energy, and self-consciousness in the work of Margaret Atwood. Atwood's vision and poetics rest in her concept of "violent duality" and "duplicity," but this essential duality can, of course, be approached in a number of different ways—perceptual, aesthetic, ethical, or thematic.[16] Because of the coherence of her vision, of the system informing her work, attention to one aspect of a text necessitates an awareness of others; therefore, it is useful to think of urban/rural polarities in terms of the following codes for "City" and "Land" which together describe the world of objective reality, as well as generating metaphors for the self:

WORLD

City	Land
civilization	nature
European culture	North American culture
eye of reason ("Cyclops")	eye of senses ("wolves' eyes")
straight lines	curved space
vertical	horizontal
external (surfaces)	internal (interiors)
superimposition	subversive resistance
stasis	growth
head	body
male	female

SELF

These configurations occur in several of her novels, most notably in the dehumanizing, mechanical technocracy of Toronto in *The Edible Woman* (1969) or in the narrator's need, in *Surfacing* (1972), to leave this alien world and return to nature in order to rediscover herself. In *Life Before Man* (1979), Atwood employs a comparison between the green swamps of the dinosaurs and the gray aridity of contemporary Toronto in order to expose the sterility of urban lives. Many of Atwood's poems also focus upon this basic polarity. Thus, the "City Planners . . . each in his own private blizzard / . . . sketch / transitory lines rigid as wooden borders" while the insane pioneer in "Progressive Insanities of a Pioneer," like "The Planters" in *The Journals of Susanna Moodie*, imposes himself upon the land "with shovels" refusing to accept its "ordered absence."[17] Perhaps more frightening is the image of the self in "A Fortification" as armored, with body a metal space suit, "barriered from leaves and blood," which

> catch[es] sight of the other creature,
> the one that has real skin, real hair,
> vanishing down to the line of cells
> back to the lost forest of being vulnerable. (*AC*, 16)

This daily subjection of the self to the mechanics of civilization echoes Frye's words quoted above—that "man's real humanity [is] a part of the nature that he continually violates."

But the codes which I have outlined are most dramatically realized in Atwood's superb *Journals of Susanna Moodie*. Journal I opens with Moodie's arrival in Canada from England complete with European eyes, manners, and "incongruous pink" shawl. She immediately realizes, however, that she is "a word / in a foreign language," and despite her increasing terror, this initial understanding sets her apart from the men who "deny the ground they stand on."[18] Piece by piece she discards her false perceptions and expectations, and adopts the language and consciousness of this land until, like an ark, the animals arrive to inhabit her. When she leaves the wilderness for the city, it is with profound regret:

> There was something they almost taught me
> I came away not having learned. (*JSM*, 27)

In the second Journal she remembers the wilderness. "The Bush Garden" haunts her dreams until, in the poem "The Double Voice," she recognizes and accepts what Atwood describes as "the inescapable doubleness of her own vision" (*JSM*, 63). Journal III brings Mrs. Moodie, like her historical model, through illness and old age to death. It is in the last four poems, after her death, that we hear most decisively from Moodie. In "Thoughts from Underground" and "Alternate Thoughts from Underground," she offers a devastating summary of our civilization of "highway billboards" and "glib superstructures," and prays for our destruction:

> O topple this glass pride, fireless
> riveted babylon, prays
> through subsoil
> to my wooden fossil God. (*JSM*, 57)

Atwood's collage, the last of the six prepared for the *Journals*, faces "Alternate Thoughts from Underground" and serves as

Atwood's sixth collage from *The Journals of Susanna Moodie,* p. 56.
Courtesy of Margaret Atwood.

symbol, both in composition and contrasting images, of her protest.

The final poem, "A Bus Along St. Clair: December," gives us Moodie in present-day Toronto. Significantly, she has "turned herself inside out, and has become the spirit of the land she once hated" (*JSM*, 64). This is Mrs. Moodie at her peak of mythic force as she comes, not only to make us see the city as "an unexplored / wilderness of wires," but to destroy it. As land, nature, curved space, inside turned out, above all as woman, she mocks the city, that male dream of monuments, concrete slabs, silver paradise built with a bulldozer, imposed upon the land:

> it shows how little they know
> about vanishing: I have
> my ways of getting through. (*JSM*, 60)

Here Margaret Atwood has made explicit the urban/rural codes underlying her work and that of Roy and Laurence, and in the process she has reversed the usual sexual stereotype of the city as female, whether virgin, harlot, or mother. When she returns to these codes (from a slightly different perspective) in "Marrying the Hangman," from *Two-Headed Poems*, the speaker emphasizes this sexual polarity:

> He said: foot, boot, order, city, fist, roads, time,
> knife.
>
> She said: water, night, willow, rope hair, earth belly,
> cave, meat, shroud, open, blood.[19]

Where Florentine in *Bonheur d'Occasion* submits to her destruction in an environment manipulated by the male, and Stacey in *The Fire-Dwellers* acknowledges that she can neither escape nor control the dehumanizing violence of her urban existence nor reclaim those natural aspects of herself which are violated and diminished by her daily life, Atwood resurrects Mrs. Moodie in direct challenge to the masculine imposition of abstract pattern and technology. Although it would be simplistic to reduce rural/ urban polarity to a question of sexual stereotypes—the codes outlined above make that clear—the land, traditionally viewed by men as female, is well championed in the person of Mrs. Moodie. It may be difficult to perceive the great white goddess, or even Demeter, in "the old woman / sitting across from you on the bus" (*JSM*, 61), but her message is unmistakable:

> It would take more than that to banish
> me: this is my kingdom still.
>
> Turn, look up
> through the gritty window: an unexplored
> wilderness of wires . . .
>
> Turn, look down:
> there is no city;
> this is the centre of a forest
>
> your place is empty. (*JSM*, 60–61)

In conclusion, it would seem that the strong and usually positive identification with nature voiced by many Canadian writers results in the absence, to date, of much major urban literature.[20] But while this tendency to write about small towns and country or natural environments is often remarked by readers, it is seldom queried. Perhaps in the case of male authors, such as F. P. Grove, Sinclair Ross, Robert Kroetsch, or Jack Hodgins, the choice of setting and the frequent identification of nature with woman are unremarkable, but the comparable, and very positive, identification by female authors—especially by one as aware of feminist concerns as is Atwood—is noteworthy. From Simone de Beauvoir on, feminists have criticized the tendency in Western culture to limit and define woman by equating her with nature; too often, they argue, the woman/nature equation becomes a patriarchal trap excluding women from a full and active role in cultural endeavor.[21] There is, however, a profound emotional ambivalence toward nature apparent in Canadian literature that leads writers to both fear and value the power and/or vulnerability of the nonurban world. Moreover, for many Canadian writers, including the three under discussion, this ambivalence is not narrowly moral because the better, more human qualities are seen as "a part of the nature" which man, especially the male, exploits, violates, and destroys. By identifying woman with nature so emphatically, Roy, Laurence, and Atwood should be seen as reclaiming the potential of that equation, as reasserting the values of nature through the rural code, as refusing to depict their links with nature as merely biological or patriarchal traps.

In their quest for the peaceable kingdom these writers reject the dominance of urban over rural codes. In doing so they demonstrate their belief in the necessity for rediscovering "the lost forest of being vulnerable" and in the consequent possibility for a natural and fully human rebirth. Theirs is not a simplistic vision of a withdrawal into nature, but a plea for a fresh understanding of a ravished and misunderstood human landscape. The quest for the peaceable kingdom, as it gradually emerges in the works of Roy, Laurence, and Atwood, is a quest for a holistic vision of man-within-environment which transforms the opposed urban/rural codes into a new system of dynamic interrelatedness.²² But the first step must be the recognition, rehabilitation, and renewed appreciation of what we have lost, a task that female writers, by the very fact of their culturally determined position, may be best fitted to undertake.

NOTES

1. Northrop Frye, *The Bush Garden: Essays on the Canadian Imagination* (Toronto: Anansi, 1971), 239.
2. Robert Kroetsch, "The Canadian Writer and the American Literary Tradition," *English Quarterly* 4 (Summer 1971), 46. Canada's finest early modern painters, such as Tom Thomson, A. Y. Jackson, Lawren Harris, and Emily Carr, are primarily landscape painters. In fact, one of the distinctive features of Canadian art in general is its preoccupation with the immense, silent, and rugged northern landscape.
3. Raymond Williams points out that satire of corrupt city life, assuming the innocence of rural existence, goes back at least as far as Juvenal. See *The Country and the City* (London: Chatto and Windus, 1973), 47.
4. The term "code" is used here to describe an aspect of the system of signification created through linguistic patterns, images, settings, characters, and so on, which structures the meaning of a single text or of a group of texts.
5. Jung discusses the role of the city as woman at some length in *Symbols of Transformation* (Princeton, N.J.: Princeton Univ. Press, 1956), 207–18.
6. In the case of American fiction, I suspect that the negative feminization of the city is part of the larger pattern of solitary male flight from the restrictions of civilization that characterizes novels from Cooper and Twain to Kesey, Dickey, West, and Pynchon. In Jungian terms, this pattern represents a flight from the mother, with associated fears of

incest and death, to the so-called virgin land which appears to offer fresh opportunities for male conquest, without involving more complex, ambiguous relationships.

7. Work in the area of the city as portrayed in fiction by women (for example, the 1979 MLA session, "Cities of Sisterhood") would suggest that whether or not the city is perceived as specifically male, it is seen as hostile, degrading, and destructive for women, a place in which the female is powerless and abused. A consequent turning away from the city to the land is a potentially regressive and self-defeating posture, however, because it implies a rejection of the human culture and civilization in urban centers. In none of the three authors examined here is such a simplistic rejection endorsed; furthermore, for Laurence and Atwood, at least, the articulation of urban/rural codes, in addition to embodying a set of matched opposites, implies a necessary dialectic, an acceptance and balancing of polarities. In an unpublished paper delivered to the session on women and the city at the 1980 NWSA Conference, Lorraine McMullen, of the University of Ottawa, described the response to the city in several works by Canadian women and came to the conclusion that "nature begins to appear in fiction as a source of life for the urban woman."

8. Frye, 246.

9. Ibid.

10. Donald Cameron, ed. *Conversations with Canadian Novelists*, (Toronto: Macmillan, 1973), 131.

11. *Alexandre Chenevert* is the story of a bank clerk, beseiged by news of worldwide disaster and surrounded by the chrome prison of Montreal, who is dying of cancer. He leaves the city for a brief rest in the country at Lac Vert, only to learn that he is too much an alien to stay there or change his ways. Return to the green peace of paradise is an illusion for urban man.

12. *Bonheur d'Occasion* (Montreal: Editions Beauchemin, 1966), 28. The novel was first published in 1945, but all references are to this edition and are cited hereafter as *B d'O* in the text. English translations are from *The Tin Flute*, trans. Alan Brown (Toronto: McClelland and Stewart, 1980) cited as *TF*, followed by the page number.

13. *The Fire-Dwellers* (Toronto: McLelland and Stewart, 1973), 89. The novel was first published in 1969, but all references are to this edition and are cited hereafter as *FD* in the text.

14. In an earlier dream, Stacey is only allowed to rescue one of her children from the fire and go "away from the crackling smoke, back to the green world" (*FD*, 29).

15. A discussion of urban/rural codes in Laurence's fiction could easily be extended to include her organization of characters throughout the Manawaka cycle. For example, in "Pride and the Puritan Passion," *Études Canadiennes* 11 (1981), 55–61, Linda Hutcheon discusses the opposition of culture and nature in *The Stone Angel* as it is revealed through the values of the Curries and Shipleys and through Hagar's realization that her suffering is a direct result of her strong Currie rejection of nature. In

The Diviners, the same opposition is expressed through a more complex character paradigm with Jules Tonnerre, Morag's Métis lover representing the rural code.

Although it is largely irrelevant to this study, it is of interest to note Laurence's recent remark that "Natural imagery comes easily to me whereas urban imagery does not, largely because I am a small town person, not a city person. I really don't feel at ease in cities at all." *Études Canadiennes*, 22.

16. I discuss this point at length in *Violent Duality: A Study of Margaret Atwood* (Montréal: Véhicule, 1980), and "Margaret Atwood and the Poetics of Duplicity," in *The Achievement of Margaret Atwood*, eds. C. N. and A. E. Davidson (Toronto: Anansi, 1980).

17. "The City Planners" appears in *The Circle Game* (Toronto: Anansi, 1966), 27, and "Progressive Insanities of a Pioneer" in *The Animals in That Country* (Toronto: Oxford Univ. Press, 1968), 36, cited hereafter as *AC*. "Cyclops" and "Comic Books vs. History" from *Procedures for Underground* (Toronto: Oxford Univ. Press, 1970), 42 and 48, many poems in *Power Politics* (Toronto: Anansi, 1972), and "Note from an Italian Postcard Factory" and "Marrying the Hangman" from *Two-Headed Poems* (Toronto: Oxford Univ. Press, 1978), 43–44 and 48–51, also deal with these polarities.

18. *The Journals of Susanna Moodie* (Toronto: Oxford Univ. Press, 1970), 11, and 16; hereafter cited as *JSM* in the text. In *Savage Fields: An Essay in Literature and Cosmology* (Toronto: Anansi, 1977), Dennis Lee develops a fascinating model, which he calls "savage fields," in order to examine the efforts by certain Canadian writers to explore destructive dualisms; Lee considers *The Journals of Susanna Moodie* as literature of the savage field. See, in particular, his discussion on pp. 3–12, 47–60, and 116–17. Although Lee's phenomenological and structuralist argument is too complex to summarize here, it is worthwhile to note that Canadian critics, philosophers, and historians, as well as artists, seem peculiarly attracted by the effort to describe and overcome dualities. I would like to thank Margaret Atwood for granting permission to reproduce the Moodie collage, which appears on page 203.

19. *Two-Headed Poems*, 51.

20. There are, of course, exceptions to this, such as the novels of Hugh MacLennan and Mordecai Richler set in Montreal or those of Hugh Garner and Morley Callaghan set in Toronto. The claim to major importance by any of these writers, however, is at least debatable. Recent work by Hugh Hood and Dennis Lee, among others, suggests that Canadian writers are continuing to grapple with the city as setting or subject.

21. For discussion of Atwood's work in the light of this feminist concern, see Carol P. Christ, "Margaret Atwood: The Surfacing of Women's Spiritual Quest and Vision," *Signs* 2, no. 2 (Winter 1976), 316–30; Judith Plaskow's response to Christ in the same issue of *Signs*; Gloria Onley, "Power Politics in Bluebeard's Castle," *Canadian Literature* 60 (Spring 1974), 21–42; Roberta Rubenstein, "*Surfacing*: Margaret Atwood's Journey to the Interior," *Modern Fiction Studies* 22, no. 3 (Au-

tumn 1976), 387–99; Barbara Hill Rigney, *Madness and Sexual Politics in the Feminist Novel* (Madison: Univ. of Wisconsin Press, 1978); and Atwood's essay "Canadian Monsters: Some Aspects of the Supernatural in Canadian Fiction," in *The Canadian Imagination*, ed. David Staines (Cambridge, Mass.: Harvard Univ. Press, 1977), 97–122, in which Atwood argues that the Canadian hero's rediscovery of himself "involves an entry into the forest."

22. In her review essay, "Breaking through Patriarchal Nets to the Peaceable Kingdom," *West Coast Review* 8, no. 3 (Jan. 1974), 43–50, Gloria Onley argues convincingly for a growing trend in Canadian literature and art away from "dualism [which] is a pathogenic defense mechanism evolved by culture-bound man; for mind is immanent in the ecosystem it beholds."

SIDNEY H. BREMER

Willa Cather's Lost Chicago Sisters

MOST AMERICAN LITERARY CRITICS can tick off some half-dozen novels from the first phase of the "Chicago literary renaissance": Theodore Dreiser's *Sister Carrie* (1900) at the top of the lists, then *The Jungle* (1906) by Upton Sinclair and *The Pit* (1903) by Frank Norris, probably Robert Herrick's *Memoirs of an American Citizen* (1905) and Dreiser's *The Titan* (1914), and, maybe, *The Song of the Lark* (1914) by Willa Cather. Indeed Cather's novel does belong to these ranks in quality. But it doesn't quite fit in kind. The problem is not that much of the novel takes place outside Chicago; that is true of *Sister Carrie*, too. And Cather's heroine is, like Dreiser's, a newcomer who remains an outsider to Chicago and treats the city as raw material for her ambition. But unlike Carrie Meeber, Thea Kronberg never frees herself from ties to family and friends, and her art probes beneath materialistic artifice to root itself in organic forms from rural and urban sources alike. Along with novels written by turn-of-the-century Chicago women whose names are unfamiliar to us now, *The Song of the Lark* dissents from the fragmented, artificial, alienating image of the city in *Sister Carrie* and the other men's novels. In the Chicago women's novels, as in their lives, the city is informed by communal concerns, interfused with organic nature, and enmeshed in familial continuities. And although Cather's own trek from midwestern small town to eastern city included a much briefer stopover in Chicago than did Dreiser's, she was more a literary sister than he to the women who lived and wrote some fine, forgotten novels there.

The best-known Chicago novels, those written by men, crested a popular wave of fictional Chicago-watching that began to break at the time of the 1893 Chicago World's Fair. In remarkably similar ways and for over two decades, mostly male novelists from across the nation elaborated Chicago as America's "ultimate metropolis" and a "portentous" symbol for the future.[1] In their many Chicago novels, the individual—usually a lone newcomer—discovers the city already in full swing and still expanding. Their inflated rhetoric presents Chicago as a social "inferno" where "the high and the low are met together" in opposing camps of wealth and poverty; as an antinatural "magnet" of railroads and skyscrapers that fling a "blasphemy against nature"; as an economic "pit" where even the most rugged individuals turn out to be "cogs" in a run-away machine.[2] Denying any hope for community, their Chicago threatens to overwhelm everyone who must confront it alone, while their novels strain to keep the city at bay and to comprehend it in symbolic terms. Theirs is an outsider's vision of the economic city.

Theirs is also a familiar image that fits our dominant cultural paradigm of the city as a battlefield—a new New World for American Adams to conquer (at best), an asphalt jungle (at worst), and a "problem" for "outside experts" (in any case). Backed by such cultural currency, men's Chicago novels have totally eclipsed the less sharply defined, more continuous and experiential vision of Chicago in novels by women. It therefore bears saying that the women's novels are no less worthy of our attention then the men's, on either aesthetic or historical grounds. They range in quality—as do the men's—from excellent to merely curious. *The Song of the Lark* and Edith Wyatt's *True Love* (1903) are no less excellent than the best-known standards. Clara Laughlin's *"Just Folks"* (1910) and Elia Peattie's *The Precipice* (1914) are no less good and interesting than Herrick's pre-*Memoirs* novels and the Chicago novels of Henry Blake Fuller. Clara Burnham's *Sweet Clover* (1894) and Alice Gerstenberg's *Unquenched Fire* (1912) are no less historically noteworthy than Hamlin Garland's otherwise unremarkable *Rose of Dutcher's Coolly* (1895) or *The Money Captain* (1898) by Will Payne. Collectively and profoundly, the women's novels interpret important dimensions of urban experience no less than do the men's. They are now lost to us not because they are less valuable, but because they do not jibe with our dominant cultural understandings.

What are we to make, for instance, of the Chicago of drifting clouds and domesticated lawns, of uncles and cousins and extended family relationships that Edith Wyatt introduces in *True Love*? Like the Puritans' prospective ideal of "a city on a hill," this Chicago positively complements and fulfills nature instead of "blaspheming" against it. And unlike Dreiser's "Waif amid Forces," Wyatt's Chicagoans maintain their family relationships. Even a newcomer to Chicago finds herself en famille there, with her city cousins, aunt, and uncle. Even for her, "the sights of Chicago" figure less as an object for individual study than as a setting for social interaction, an organic context for living.[3] Consistently, *True Love* and its sister novels articulate a vision based in experiential continuities and communal affairs. The only problem is that these novels look so un-urban to our socialized eyes that we are hard pressed to accept their insights.

Specifically, women's Chicago novels present the city as part of a life experience that is continuous, embedded in natural forces and in communal ties and conflicts. For example, Burnham's *Sweet Clover* appeals not to distant observations, but to the participant's intimate knowledge of Chicago's lived-in qualities. This Chicago extends backward in time and outward in space, fulfilling pioneer aspirations in its gradual evolution from a "country village" to a World's Fair metropolis.[4] It is not a new reality cut off from the past or the countryside. Moreover, Chicago novels by women usually embrace nature as a powerful, complex presence within the city, whereas the men's novels tend to idealize nature and to present it as apart from the city. And when *The Song of the Lark* recognizes the vigorous and sordid "congestion of life" in stormy Chicago as the very essence of "the city itself," that organic image includes human crowds as well as stormy weather.[5]

Indeed the organic fabric of human life epitomizes "the city itself" in women's novels, which enmesh their characters in familial networks. If anything, their fictional Chicagoans suffer from too little, rather than too much, individualism. It is the closely knit "patterns of my home life and city" that Alice Gerstenberg's fictional alter ego must rupture in order to pursue her New York acting career in *Unquenched Fire*.[6] But she comes to regret her loss deeply. For the most part, the main characters in Chicago women's novels enact the communalism they learn to value, staying in Chicago and developing careers that support the city's familial patterns. Thus the main character in Laughlin's "*Just Folks*," a probation officer, discovers old family ties in the mixed neighborhood where she works, strengthens them through her work, and finally embraces them by making her married home there. And the novel's dramatic action turns on conflicts between competing social ethics—parochial loyalty to a primary group, on the one hand, and a reciprocal give-and-take among diverse groups, on the other—which several characters learn to negotiate along with Beth. Not one alienated individual's economic struggle against the city, but an entire urban society's struggle for civic mutuality is at issue in most Chicago women's novels.[7]

Edith Wyatt's *True Love: A Comedy of the Affections* best exemplifies the Chicago women's vision, because its special achievement is a structure fully appropriate to that vision. *True Love* makes collective family units its primary "characters" and simultaneously its embodiment of Chicago. On the one hand, the democratic Marsh family represents Wyatt's urban ideal, a social order that embraces the city's continuities. The Marshes are linked to Chicago's rural environs by the downstate family of Mr. Marsh's brother and to the city's past by Mrs. Marsh's aging father, his sister, and an old Civil War comrade who apparently lives with them. Mr. and Mrs. Marsh's four children complete the three-generational range of this extended family. They live in the grandfather's unpretentious home, where they welcome visitors to "the kindliest intercourse" and lively group activities. On the other hand, their elitist family friends the Hubbards—widowed Madame mother, her two sons, and her maiden cousin—have an elaborately decorated, "sepulchral" mansion. In this "penal spot" visitors put their sophistication to the test by exchanging calling cards and stiff formalities.[8]

These two city families anchor the novel's primary tensions, between participatory democracy and elitism as ethics for society. And the conflict extends beyond city limits, tying Chicago to its rural surroundings by involving country families, too. There the two social ethics are mixed—in the narrowly nuclear family of Mr. Marsh's sociable brother and sister-in-law and their snobbish daughter Inez, and the loose "family" of democratic Dick Colton, his becoming-snobbish sister Fanny, their Polish-

American aunt, and their ethnically diverse friends. This last, figurative family congregates in the lobby and dining room of a small-town hotel that Dick runs—as "free [a] place for everyone" to be "at ease and content" as the Chicago Marshes' home, and just as pointedly unlike the Hubbard house with its "little cold, bare reception-room."[9]

All together, *True Love*'s various families demonstrate the social characters and styles of democracy and elitism, as well as the conflicts between them—most dramatically in several interlocking romances. The romances themselves are a mix-and-match set. Within the democratic camp, city-woman Emily Marsh finds her appropriate mate in country-man Dick Colton. These two young people discover the expansive possibilities of a love that evolves through everyday interactions, unobsessed by display or sentiment. Within the elitist camp, by contrast, Emily's country cousin Inez is matched up with urbane Norman Hubbard, just long enough for their elaborate gestures of "true love" to expose the selfishness from which they proceed and the boredom toward which they tend. Between the two camps, finally, Fred Hubbard and Fanny Colton prove to be star-crossed lovers indeed. They mix and mismatch "strenuous" Norman Hubbard's "unpretentious" younger brother with "commonplace" Dick Colton's "exclusive" younger sister.[10] They marry outside either camp, on the run toward isolation together, then a violent separation when Fred commits suicide.

In structure as in theme, *True Love* is an insider's story, concerned primarily with a network of ongoing relationships on their own overlapping terms. It is "like one's own story in not being certain of the relative importance of its different persons and events," William Dean Howells remarked in a national review, which placed *True Love* at the forefront of "the Chicago School of Fiction." Howells went on to praise Wyatt for departing from the literary convention of larger-than-life romance by emphasizing daily, familial contexts: "Strangely enough, the lovers and self-lovers have families about them. . . . [The families] are not treated as mere pieces of mechanism for transacting the lovers' passion."[11] Indeed no single individual emerges as the central character in Wyatt's *True Love*—distinguishing it from other Chicago novels and marking an important breakthrough in novelistic convention generally. Even more fully than Howells's own 1890 novel, *A Hazard of New Fortunes*, *True Love* develops a successful collective form.[12]

As a highly original work and an epitome of the Chicago women's vision, *True Love* is certainly comparable in quality to the best of its contemporaries. But it is unlike men's standard Chicago novels in its disappearance from our literary canon—and in the kind of urban tradition it develops. In *True Love*, as in Chicago women's novels generally, the city is linked to the country in a society that centers in families, both biological and figurative. It is caught up in conflicting social ethics, the one fittingly organic, open, and democratic, the other artificially closed and elitist. Its individual members are characterized in terms of those families and social ethics. And social collectivities, not the machinery of economic systems pitted against alienated individuals, define the city.

The contrast between the Chicago women's novels epitomized by *True Love* and the nationally dominant men's novels directs our attention to the impact of residency and mobility on urban perspectives. Long-time residents like the women and newcomers like the men do see a city differently. In this case, however, the difference between inside and outside perspectives belongs to a more comprehensive pattern of sex-role expectations. That gender gap profoundly divided Victorian America's middle classes, to which the Chicago novelists typically belonged or successfully aspired. Women were *encouraged as women* to "stay at home" in fact and to express themselves as residents in fiction. On the other hand, men who were similarly "stuck" very long in Chicago—as were native Chicagoan Henry B. Fuller and transplanted Robert Herrick—*disappointed a masculine expectation* of independence, and they often avoided the posture of residential membership in their fiction; indeed these two men pioneered the economic and objectifying imagery that visiting men later played out. Moreover, women's urban experiences and perspectives generally differed from men's in ways that went well beyond the issue of residency and mobility. After all, Cather echoed the Chicago women's perception of their city as continuous, organic, and communal, even though she remained an outsider to its residential life.

Living and working in Chicago when it became a "literary

center,"[13] Cather's lost Chicago sisters shared a set of urban experiences that were significantly shaped by their feminine status. Besides remaining in the same city (unlike Cather), they had active roles (like Cather) in the male-dominated newspaper world, as well as in Chicago's female-dominated network of settlement houses and women's clubs, Little Theatre and Little Magazine enterprises. And in these endeavors, Chicago's women novelists joined hands with the likes of reformer Jane Addams, club woman Bertha Honoré (Mrs. Potter) Palmer, theatrical director Anna Morgan, and poet-editor Harriet Monroe. They contributed to their city in more diverse and more frequently collaborative ways than did their male compatriots. As their novels suggest, they stretched and re-created their "woman's sphere" in Chicago far beyond the limits of the public recognition they have received.

Most of Chicago's women writers were born in Chicago or, like Wyatt, moved there as young children. This meant that the primary emotions of childhood experience, more than the abstract concepts that people learn only slowly, formed the bedrock for their understanding of the city. They became acquainted with Chicago in its particularities, in the textures of daily experience radiating out, step by step, from their family homes. Middle-class home life provided a great deal of physical and social stability for them—in marked contrast, for instance, to Dreiser's experience of moving in and out of Chicago and living at five different city addresses with various family members before he set out on his own, eventually to other cities. Even as adults, Edith Wyatt, Clara Burnham, Clara Laughlin, and Alice Gerstenberg maintained their Chicago residency as a continuing fact, not just on paper. They lived in the same city, some in the same houses, as their parents. And although Elia Peattie followed her husband's career to Omaha just after their marriage and later moved on with him to New York, for nearly thirty years between they raised their children in her parents' old house in Chicago.

In addition to such factual circumstances, Chicago was home to its literary women in a special, metaphorical sense. As women they were expected to identify "home"—with all its personal and cultural connotations—as the center of their lives. "Home" was then, as it is today, the primary cultural metaphor for a woman's sphere of activities. And Chicago meant "home" to its women in

[216]

this sense. Even traveling women who identified strongly with Chicago as a home base tended to describe it in familial terms; eastern poet Amy Lowell called Chicago "my adopted city" during the height of her association there with Monroe's *Poetry Magazine*, which she dubbed "my mother." As an epitome of a woman's place, home was not coterminous with a physical house, as cultural critic Elizabeth Janeway has explained; and its particular embodiment differed for every individual woman.[14] But for turn-of-the-century Chicago women in general, the family home was central, implicated in civic and cultural, as well as personal and domestic activities. Alice Gerstenberg's unpublished autobiography typifies their experience. It focuses on her companionship with her mother, as together they joined the supposedly leisured "wives, sisters and daughters" who "whirled out of their houses to their clubs and committee meetings to manage benefits, or to start new goals" in the early 1900s. Her descriptions of these mother-daughter adventures regularly proceed from and return to their family house, where she details the entrance hall and reception room as well-kept settings for sociable comings and goings.[15] For Gerstenberg and other Chicago women, the family house was a domestic microcosm for—not a bulwark against—the city itself.

Chicago's home-based literary women were, however, hardly isolated from moneymaking, current political affairs, or public leadership. Wyatt worked as a teacher, wrote feature stories and essays "for which I have always had some demand [and payment] from publishers,"[16] became deeply involved in Progressive reform politics, and was recognized as a *Poetry Magazine* leader in a newspaper cartoon. Clara Laughlin edited a Chicago journal, turned out advice columns for *Good Housekeeping*, wrote popular novels and over twenty travel books, then ran Clara Laughlin Travel Services. Elia Peattie scrambled to make a living as the first "girl reporter" for the *Chicago Tribune* and later profited from her position as that newspaper's literary critic by contracting to write local histories and coffee-table anthologies, in addition to her short stories and novels and plays. Other literary women also worked as paid writers, not amateur contributors, for Chicago newspapers: Harriet and Lucy Monroe as art critics, later Margery Currey (who would be remembered as Floyd Dell's gracious consort) as a society editor, and still later poet Eunice

Tietjens as a war correspondent. Women regularly participated in the working world of journalism, with its pipeline to current events, although the all-male exclusivity of Chicago's Press Club and Whitechapel Club promoted a common impression that women had no part in the heyday of Chicago newspapers, and it is true that newspapers were established as a men's business in which women were usually relegated to the new arts and society sections.

Thus Chicago's clubs and settlement houses were hardly the only arenas of public affairs for women. But one cannot underestimate their special importance as centers of female leadership for women who lived and wrote in Chicago. The turn of the century marked the national height of the women's club movement, while settlement houses, often headed by women, stood at the forefront of American social reform. In Chicago their combined leadership formed an interlocking directorate that spearheaded the city's involvement in women's suffrage and social welfare. The clubs gained seriousness from association with reform, and the settlements gained prestige and financial support from association with high society. Writers were seldom their primary leaders, but these groups offered them collegial contacts with women who were then recognized movers and shakers. And because the clubs and settlements often couched their strong political thrust in literary study, they also provided professional literary women with a public forum that was associated with traditional sources of feminine "home rule."

In particular, most of Chicago's women writers were teachers or visitors or residents at Hull House at one time or another, and Peattie even quoted Addams's concept of the "civic family" as a central element in *The Precipice*, her fictional anatomy of social roles for Chicago women.[17] As a nationally celebrated writer as well as an activist, Jane Addams offered corroboration for the novelists' vision of the city as a base of human action, not an alien system. And the cooperative spirit of the settlement rank and file gave that common vision experiential reality in their lives.

That collaborative spirit also permeated Chicago's Little Theatre movement, which rivaled journalism in its importance to the city's emergence as a national "literary center" before World War I. The most public of arts, noncommercial drama was the province of women, too—despite doubts about the propriety of ladies becoming professional actresses. In her autobiography *My Chicago*, Anna Morgan presented her directorial leadership and dramatic coaching as an expression of the city, "worthy of record" because it involved "the earliest efforts in Chicago to produce . . . The Little Theatre."[18] Other Little Theatre pioneers included the Hull-House Players and poet-playwright Mary Aldis, at whose Lake Forest playhouse Monroe and Gerstenberg also had their plays produced. And when Maurice Browne later founded the famous, albeit short-lived Chicago Little Theatre in 1912, its producer was his Chicago-born wife, Ellen Van Volkenburg Browne, and her mother was its business manager. It was mostly the fruits of women's ideas and energies that Susan Glaspell and George Cramm Cook brought to the Provincetown Players from their early days in Chicago—where Glaspell, as a matter of fact, wrote a melodramatic Chicago novel in the women's mode, *The Glory of the Conquered* (1909).

Simultaneously a collaborative form of arts production and a public form of arts consumption, the Little Theatre movement expressed an urban aesthetic that women found especially compelling. Several of the city's literary women mentioned childhood ambitions to become actresses; in fact, Wyatt, Monroe, Peattie, Laughlin, and Gerstenberg all acted in theatricals at some time or another, in addition to writing plays and pageants for amateur groups and a few modern dramas to fill local playbills that otherwise ranged from classic Greek to modern Shaw. Specifically, an impetus toward making the private public, toward giving public voice to their persons, seemed to compel many Chicago literary women toward the stage.

A similar impetus also proved especially important in their poetry, which can be the most intimate literary genre. Most of the Chicago women who wrote novels also wrote poems as well as plays, and they regularly linked their poetry to the public medium of drama. A poet like Harriet Monroe saw her plays as "dramatic poetry."[19] Conversely, Mary Aldis wrote her best poems as dramatic monologues; and the public textures of choral speech and song infuse the poetic chants that several women wrote. While Vachel Lindsay was popularizing "primitive" chants in *Congo Songs* (1914), his female colleagues were developing chants as public songs of urban unity. Thus Wyatt chants her sense of sisterhood with Harriet Monroe in "City Whistles" (1916), a harbor song:

[219]

> Now the morning winds are rising. Now the morning
>   whistles cry.
> Fast their crescent voices dim the paling star.
> Through the misted city mainland, wide their questing
>   summons fly
> Many-toned—'O mortal, tell me who you are!'
> Down the midland, down the morning, fresh their sweeping
>   voices buoy:
> 'Siren ship! Silver ship! Sister ship! Ahoy! Sister
>   ship ahoy! Ship ahoy!'[20]

The streetmarchers' chant in a protest poem, "The Song of the Women" (1915) by Chicago's Florence Kiper Frank, a Jewish-American, is similarly typical in its collective urban voice:

> This is the song of the women, sung to the marching feet,
> Mothers and daughters of mothers, out in the crowded
>   street,
> Yea, and the mothers of mothers, white with the passing
>   years—
> This is the chant of the women, and wise is he who hears.[21]

In poetry as in drama, Chicago's women emphasize the participatory speech, rather than objectifying description, that characterizes their novelistic style, too. And in all three media, they affirm public forms of self-expression.

The motivating force of this collective affirmation is exemplified by Harriet Monroe's career as a poet and as founding editor of *Poetry Magazine*. One of the many women whose early ambition was to be an actress, Monroe fought hard to get the commission to write the "Columbian Ode" for the World's Fair. As a result, she proudly claimed one of the official "seats provided for the five hundred artists of the Fair" on Dedication Day in 1892. And when her Ode was sung, she received a bouquet "'from the ladies of Chicago'"—as the publicly recognized representative of poetry and of Chicago women. The Fair's chief architect, Daniel Burnham, got the point: "No other woman has ever been so honored, in the way you care for, in our country and time."[22]

Monroe valued public recognition for the "feminine" muse of poetry as for herself, for the human embodied in the feminine. As she explained twenty years later, in her promotional circulars for *Poetry* and in the magazine's first issue, she was determined not to have poetry "left to herself" while other arts gained public stature. Monroe also concurred in a belief articulated by Walt Whitman—in the motto she chose for the *Poetry* cover: "To have great poets / there must be great audiences, too." Affirming the artist's reciprocal relationship to society, her *Poetry* supported Chicago's women novelists in their emphasis on public speech, as well as their residential sense of the artist's civic responsibility. It is no surprise that many of them had their poetic works published and reviewed in *Poetry*—or in Margaret Anderson's more bohemian, but also local *Little Review*. Such public presentation was crucial for them as women participating in Chicago's cultural development.

In all their urban activities and creations, they sought to blaze new trails for women—beyond the increasingly nuclear private family, into public and collegial realms. But when they left their "shelters" in search of "kingdoms"—to use Monroe's terms, they tried to take the home strengths of familiarity and hospitality with them. Thus Monroe wrote of the *Poetry* offices, "I had never been the actual mistress of any home which had sheltered me, but this little kingdom was mine, and I rather enjoyed dispensing its fleeting hospitalities."[23] Theirs was a search for urban contexts of community that would unite their professional and familial strengths. That search informed the novels they wrote, the public arts they performed, the magazines they edited, and the clubs they joined in Chicago. But it finally ran up against the limits of their public recognition.

To one artists' club in particular nearly all of Chicago's literary women belonged. The Little Room extended into the professional arts the idea of gathering people across lines of specialization, which women's clubs and settlements had developed. It also brought men and women together as friends and colleagues, in marked contrast to most of the city's sex-divided social clubs and professional organizations. In 1898 the Little Room began meeting weekly in Chicago's new Fine Arts Building, where artists' studios, publishing houses, small theaters, and—significantly—women's clubs and political groups were housed together right downtown. Lucy Monroe suggested that they name themselves after a short story about a room in a family home, a "little room" that was visible only to the imaginative eye. And it was widely understood that the author of that story, Chicagoan Madeline Yale Wynne, embodied in her own person the Little Room's multimedia mix and commitment to hospitality. A painter, muralist, metalworker, writer, violinist, and embroiderer, Wynne was an "all-round artist," said Harriet Monroe, a woman who "passed no art without a salutation," said Peattie, and "a great encourager of others," said Morgan.[24]

By 1903 the Little Room was a going concern that included Chicago novelists Clara Burnham, Henry Blake Fuller, Hamlin Garland, Robert Herrick, Clara Laughlin, Will Payne, Elia Peattie, and Edith Wyatt, diverse other artists such as director Anna Morgan, newspaper columnist George Ade, sculptor Lorado Taft, dancer Lou Wall Moore, poet William Vaughn Moody, and cartoonist John T. McCutcheon, as well as Jane Addams, Daniel Burnham, the Monroe sisters, and other activists in civic culture. The Little Roomers' weekly conversations spawned collaborative work in the arts, including the annual Twelfth-Night theatricals that Anna Morgan directed for the group itself. Regularly the women of the Little Room—in their dual capacities as hostesses and artists—managed these "entertainments." And their leadership was recognized in the informal network among male and female members, which was maintained by correspondence when someone was out of town. The Little Room's give-and-take ethos, moreover, expressed the women's communal vision and may have justified one Chicagoan's claim then that "nowhere . . . is there an artistic colony so untainted by jealousy as is that of Chicago."[25] The women, for a time, had found a way to enjoy full collegiality with men and to share the home spirit with their colleagues.

But when the Little Room began to formalize its organization in 1902, a split developed between the unofficial (feminine) and official (masculine) workings of the club. Although women continued to head the "entertainment" committee and one woman joined each "class" of three elected to the Little Room's board of directors, men became the officers who called meetings and kept the money and records. Then a 1906 decision to include spouses as associate members laced the Little Room with literal family ties, confusing the status of the professional women who were attempting an extension of familylike dynamics beyond the private home.

As the Little Room was thus domesticated under the official leadership of men, a more bohemian colony of artists was also taking shape in some old World's Fair apartments that had been converted to studios out near the University. In this other setting, such literary artists as Susan Glaspell, Margery Currey, Sherwood Anderson, Floyd Dell, Eunice Tietjens, Vachel Lindsay, and Margaret Anderson actively rejected domestic conventions for sexual freedoms. Unfortunately, however, the notoriety of their sexual affairs obscured the value of the women's—although not the men's—literary achievements, in a classic case of the double standard. For the bohemians no less than for the more socially involved artists from whom they were now split off, the delicate balance between family spirit and artistic commitment was upset. And Chicago's literary women fell out from a vital cultural center, one way or the other.

Into the breach stepped Hamlin Garland, trying to establish a professional organization that would associate writers like himself with the city's public leadership—"'a real club like the Players'" in New York. And that meant a men's club. Working with a "Complete list of men" from the Little Room's membership roster in 1907, Garland sent out invitations: his new club would be a "widening of the scope of the Little Room," he wrote prospective members, because it would include "distinguished men of science . . . and other professions."[26] But it would exclude women altogether. For the most part, Chicago's literary men welcomed his suggestion, and Garland's crew soon installed themselves atop a Loop skyscraper where they met to lunch "with the boys" and to lionize visiting dignitaries. Their club was appropriately dubbed the Cliff Dwellers after the 1893 Fuller novel that had established Chicago's economic image for the nation, although Fuller was a social leader in the Little Room and one of the few men who refused to join Garland's club. Those who did join also continued their participation in the Little Room, but it took a back seat in their collegial affections, along with its women. Garland's autobiography records a few occasions when he himself went directly from the Cliff Dwellers Club to the Little Room— taking particular pleasure, for instance, in meeting local-colorist Alice French there: she greeted him "with the directness of a man, professing an abiding interest in all that I am doing," he wrote. Of course, Garland's sense of French's adulation, which he took for "directness," made her seem "companionable, a literary comrade" to be valued—but specifically "in a way few women achieve."[27] So when Chicago's "truly professional" women "sent emissaries to ask the officers of the Cliff Dwellers

Club, if the men would be willing to accept their female confrères,
. . . the reply was, 'No!'" In her unpublished autobiography,
Alice Gerstenberg goes on to tell how the women then "launched
out on their own" and, with novelist Clara Laughlin in the lead,
founded the Cordon Club. The name "meant, shall we say, something like many ribbons, or badges of honor, roped together"—a
fitting emblem for the women's vision of community, in contrast
to the skyscraping imagery of the Cliff Dwellers.[28] Not until 1914
would the division between the men and the women be healed,
when the long-established Writers Guild of men invited women
to a dinner to found a new Society of Midland Authors. All the
women on the Society's organizational committee were Little
Roomers, and both Clara Laughlin and Alice Gerstenberg eventually succeeded to the presidency of the new organization. But it
lacked the multimedia range and the informality that had been
hallmarks of the Little Room, where women's special strengths
and vision had shone.

Perhaps because they were minimized as literary hostesses to
their more established male colleagues during the Cliff Dwellers
years, it was then that the women produced most of their
Chicago novels, brought the Little Theatre movement to its peak,
got *Poetry Magazine* and *The Little Review* underway, and became
active Progressives and suffragists. They did not, however, sur-
pass in their novels the aesthetic success that Wyatt had achieved
with *True Love* in 1903, and they never fully recouped the professional recognition that the Cliff Dwellers had denied them.
Sculptor Lorado Taft, for instance, rudely challenged Anna Morgan's right to initiate a memorial book for Henry Blake Fuller in
1929—although she and Fuller had been extremely close friends,
as well as equal partners in catalyzing the Little Room's collegial
community. "Why the hurry? . . . Do you expect to sell it as a
Christmas book?" Taft asked offensively, and then went on: "I
had supposed that [such a book] would be the work of Fuller's
closest literary companions, men like [Hobart Chatfield-Taylor]
and [Hamlin] Garland. . . . Next Sunday Mr. Garland [who was
also Taft's brother-in-law] will be here and we can have a consul-
tation." Taft was hardly alone in dismissing collegial friendship as
unprofessional unless it was based on specialization and masculine hegemony. Ever since, Chicago's literary women as a
group have been remembered only as hostesses. Individually
each has been forgotten or viewed with wrenching condescen-

sion—Harriet Monroe being misrepresented, for example, as a "school mistress" who was herself "educated" by her achievements.[29] It is this context that explains the loss of the Chicago women's novelistic vision of urban experience.

In their novels and other literary works, as in their lives, Chicago's women emphasized the experiential continuities and involvements that are part of living in a single community from childhood on. Their communal vision reflected, as well, upon the collective activity of the Chicago women's clubs and settlement houses in which they shared. Their Little Theatre plays and newspaper stories also expressed—even more directly than their novels—their participation in the two major public art forms that established Chicago as a national "literary center" during this period. And in their own professional circles they developed broadly based artists' associations, such as the Little Room, and consciously pursued "collaboration" as a mode of artistic creation.[30] Surely such communal activities are important aspects of urban experience, intimately involved in the concentration of diverse groups and institutions that defines a city.

But these are aspects of urban experience that most of the men who wrote standard Chicago novels did not share. And the outsider's vision of the economic city in their novels reflects upon the experiences and expectations peculiar to their sex. For the most part these men were mobile and independent. As newcomers to Chicago they involved themselves in the city's strictly professional associations, such as the newspaper guild. And as men they were expected to be more interested in professional power than in social relationships. As men they probably experienced the city itself as inhibiting the mythic masculinity of frontiersmen, while their female counterparts found that the complex ties of feminine domesticity bound them in city and country alike, although the city offered to open up some new extensions of women's "home." Whereas the men were challenged to confront and to overcome their environment, dealing with society and nature and technology all as objects to be controlled, their female colleagues were constantly reminded of their embeddedness in the life processes of society and nature.

As a result, the men's Chicago novels tend to objectify the city as a national concern, while the women's novels deal more intimately with organic, regional textures. The Chicago women's novels convey what one of today's leading novelists has called "a very strong sense of place, not in terms of the country or the state, but in terms of the details, the feeling, the mood of the community, of the town." African-American Toni Morrison elaborates her point in ways that clearly link her experience to that of white women writers in Chicago seventy years ago: "I think some of it is just a woman's strong sense of being in a room, a place, or a house. Sometimes my relationship to things in a house would be a little different from, say, my brother's or my father's or my sons'. I clean them and I move them and I do very intimate things 'in place': I am sort of rooted in it, so that writing about being in a room looking out, or being in a world looking out, or living in a small definite place, is probably very common among most women anyway."[31]

Such an insider's perspective needs a regional, inclusive context of social familiarity to sustain its importance. But the turn of the century marked the simultaneous ascendancy of nationalism and specialization in American life, particularly in cities. The Little Room's eclipse by the Cliff Dwellers, by a New York model of "real" professional power, belongs to that development. As the profession of literature was increasingly delineated by national stature and genre specialization, more informal and multimedia styles of cultural leadership could easily fall through the cracks—particularly when those styles were exercised by women. The status and authority even of women with major achievements to their credit—such as Anna Morgan, Edith Wyatt, Clara Laughlin, and Harriet Monroe—were left open to question when the home spirit they sought to develop was denied broader social significance. So it was that native son Henry Blake Fuller, whose Chicago novel *With the Procession* (1895) adumbrated the women's vision and whose own life experience involved many lasting friendships with local literary women, confirmed the rising masculinist standard: "The creative impulse is masculine and so are all the forces that organize and propel," he wrote in the *Chicago Evening Post* during the time that men were assuming official leadership of the Little Room and that women's experiment in familial colleagueship was losing ground. "Feminine talent may deftly refine and perfect what already exists, but plausible simulations of the real thing" belong to man, who "sees more of life in general than woman can hope to see."[32] In other words, the status of women's cultural leadership, of their literary interpretations, and of their social experience are one and the same, all subject to trivialization from a perspective that identifies "the real thing" with an objectifying, masculine version of "life in general."

Or, as literary critic Nancy K. Miller has recently put the situation, "the maxims that pass for the truth of human experience, and the encoding of that experience in literature, are organizations, when they are not fantasies, of the dominant culture." And that dominant culture is masculine. Thus our generalizations about urban experience, no less than the literary constructions that correspond to them, are "in fact based on the masculine population" even when "stated sweepingly to cover the entire society," as historian David Potter proposed of all our "social generalizations" in his now-famous thesis.[33] The failure of the Chicago women's communal vision to gain ongoing recognition in either life or letters demonstrates the power of that masculine bias in our culture. We can know the full cost of that failure—and our loss—only when we attend to the metaphorical power of their vision and the historical vitality of the urban enterprise— the city of sisterhood—that it interprets for us.

NOTES

The research for this essay was supported by a grant from the American Philosophical Society, by released time from the University of Wisconsin-Green Bay Research Council, and by the energetic assistance of the staff of the Newberry Library in Chicago, in particular. In addition to published sources, the essay draws on materials found in the Newberry Special Collections, the Regenstein Library Special Collections at the Univ. of Chicago, the *Chicago Tribune* archives, and the Chicago Historical Society.

1. Henry B. Fuller, *The Cliff Dwellers* (New York: Harper, 1893), 242; Hamlin Garland, *Rose of Dutcher's Coolly* (1895; New York: Macmillan, 1899), 156.
2. Robert Herrick, *The Web of Life* (New York: Grosset & Dunlap, 1900), 77; *Cliff Dwellers*, 3; Theodore Dreiser, *Sister Carrie*, ed. Claude Simpson, Riverside pb. ed. (Boston: Houghton Mifflin, 1959), 16; Herrick, *The Gospel of Freedom* (New York: Macmillan, 1898), 104; Frank Norris, *The Pit* (New York: Collier, 1903); Upton Sinclair, *The Jungle*, Signet pb. ed. (New York: New American Library, 1960), 82.
3. Edith F. Wyatt, *True Love* (New York: McClure, Phillips, 1903), 3–5; cf. *Sister Carrie*, 16–18.

4. Clara Burnham, *Sweet Clover* (Boston: Houghton Mifflin, 1894), 32.

5. Willa Cather, *The Song of the Lark* (Boston: Houghton Mifflin, 1915), 200.

6. Alice Gerstenberg to W. David Sievers, 22 July 1955 (Alice Gerstenberg Mss., Newberry Library, Chicago).

7. The contrasting patterns here summarized for Chicago novels by men and women, as well as their implications for urban studies, are more fully explicated in my essay "Lost Continuities: Alternative Urban Visions in Chicago Novels, 1890–1915," *Soundings* 64 (Spring 1981), 29–51. I also discussed some of these materials in "Chicago in Fiction, Masculine Hegemony, and the Literary Canon," a paper presented at the MLA convention, Houston, 27 Dec. 1980.

8. *True Love*, 29, 177; Wyatt contrasts the two homes architecturally, too (10, 47).

9. Ibid., 215, 130, 177.

10. Ibid., 7, 96, 106, 269.

11. William D. Howells, "Certain of the Chicago School of Fiction," *North American Review* 176 (1903), 736.

12. Among the few available models, the publishing house associates in Howells's *A Hazard of New Fortunes* are a competitive grouping, not a communal group, and the novel centers on one person whose individual fortunes delimit the plot. The skyscraper inhabitants in Fuller's *The Cliff Dwellers* follow that pattern, although Fuller's George Ogden is almost as fully immersed in the group as is Wyatt's most prominent figure, Emily Marsh. A later attempt at a collective structure is made at the end of *The Jungle* by Sinclair, but that novel begins with a clearly delineated central character, and his merging into the proletariat at the end seems more propagandistic than structurally successful. It is possible that the genre of the novel itself, rooted as it is in a bourgeois heritage that stresses individualism, strains against collective forms.

13. Hugh Dalziel Duncan, *The Rise of Chicago as a Literary Center from 1885 to 1920* (Totowa, N.J.: Bedminster, 1964), exemplifies the common view of Chicago's ascendancy as being centered in an all-male newspaper world.

14. Lowell 1914–16 correspondence qtd. in Harriet Monroe, *A Poet's Life* (New York: Macmillan, 1938), 400; Elizabeth Janeway, *Man's World, Woman's Place*, Delta pb. ed. (New York: Dell, 1971), esp. pp. 11–26.

15. Gerstenberg, "Come Back with Me," unpublished [1962] ms., 130, 209, 95–99 (Gerstenberg Papers, Chicago Historical Society).

16. Wyatt to William Dean Howells, n.d., qtd. in Rudolf and Clara Kirk, eds., "Homage to William Dean Howells," unpublished ms., 22 (Wyatt Papers, Newberry Library, Chicago).

17. Addams qtd. in Elia Peattie, *The Precipice* (Boston: Houghton Mifflin, 1914), 182.

18. Anna Morgan, *My Chicago* (Chicago: R. F. Seymour, 1918), 44.

19. Monroe, *Poet's Life*, 175.

20. Wyatt, "City Whistles," in *The Wind in the Corn* (New York:

Appleton, 1917), 109–11, dedicated to Monroe and originally published in *Poetry* 9 (Dec. 1916), 114–15.

21. Florence Kiper Frank, "The Song of the Women," in *The Jew to Jesus and Other Poems* (New York: Mitchell Kennerley, 1915), 8–10.

22. *Poet's Life*, 46, 116–38; Daniel H. Burnham to Harriet Monroe, 22 Dec. 1892 (Monroe Personal Papers, Univ. of Chicago).

23. Monroe, "The Motive of the Magazine," *Poetry*, (Oct. 1912), 26–28; Monroe, *Poet's Life*, 317.

24. Monroe, *Poet's Life*, 197; dedication of Elia Peattie, *The Edge of Things* (Chicago: Revell, 1903), frontispiece; *My Chicago*, 153.

25. Hobart C. Chatfield-Taylor, Foreword, *My Chicago*.

26. Hamlin Garland, *Companions on the Trail* (New York: Macmillan, 1931), 336; Little Room Papers, passim., including undated [1908] invitation, signed by Hamlin Garland, Chairman, Attic Club [Cliff Dwellers] Provisional Committee (Little Room Papers, Newberry Library, Chicago).

27. Garland, *Companions on the Trail*, 460; cf. 320–38, 368–75.

28. Gerstenberg, "Come Back with Me," 262–63.

29. Lorado Taft to Anna Morgan, 20 Oct. 1929 (Anna Morgan Miscellaneous Papers, Chicago Historical Society); Bernard Duffey, *The Chicago Renaissance in American Letters* (East Lansing: Michigan State Univ. Press, 1956), 183, 66.

30. Gerstenberg to Kate Jordan, 18 Feb. 1916: "I do very much believe in collaboration, do you?" (Gerstenberg Mss., Newberry Library, Chicago).

31. "'Intimate Things in Place'—A Conversation with Toni Morrison," 19 May 1976 interview with Robert Stepto, rpt. in Dexter Fisher ed., *The Third Woman* (Boston: Houghton Mifflin, 1979), 167–68.

32. Fuller, "Our 'Young Lady Novelist'" and "'Lady Rose's Daughter' Displays Mrs. Ward's Genius in Maturity," clippings dated 1 June 1901 and 28 Feb. 1903 (Henry Blake Fuller Papers, Newberry Library, Chicago).

33. Nancy K. Miller, "Emphasis Added: Plots and Plausibilities in Women's Fiction," *PMLA* 96 (Jan. 1981), 46; David M. Potter, "American Women and the American Character," *Stetson Univ. Bull.* 62 (Jan. 1962), rpt. in *The Character of Americans*, rev. ed., ed. Michael McGiffert (Homewood, Ill.: Dorsey, 1970), 318–19.

CAROLYN MITCHELL

"A Laying on of Hands": Transcending the City in Ntozake Shange's *for colored girls who have considered suicide | when the rainbow is enuf*

NTOZAKE SHANGE'S CHOREOPOEM, *for colored girls who have considered suicide | when the rainbow is enuf*, presents the paradox of the modern American city as a place where black women experience the trauma of urban life, yet find the strength to transcend the pain.[1] The women depicted by Shange become physically and spiritually whole, thus free, through the psychic/ psychological healing power that resides in the ancient, fundamentally religious act called "the laying on of hands." The believer "knows" that touch can heal if the one who touches is empowered by God; thus, touching stabilizes a person physically while freeing the troubled soul to soar spiritually.

Shange uses the physically and morally desolate cityscape as a backdrop before which to reveal her spiritual vision of female strength and survival. In this respect, therefore, *colored girls* differs from the legion of literary works that depict the lives of urban Afro-Americans.[2] She neither denies nor romanticizes urban black experiences: the choreopoem graphically describes the complex ways in which the rape victim is further victimized by the "authorities"; it reveals the loneliness and guilt of the woman who decides to have an abortion; it details the betrayal women continue to experience in their relationships with men.[3]

While none of these problems is uniquely urban, they are exacerbated by the human estrangements that characterize city life. But Ntozake Shange does have a larger vision. One might think of this vision in terms of two concentric circles, with the outer circle temporarily more powerful than the other. The geographical and psychological "settings" represent one circle; the other is a fragile circle promising transcendence. The external circle is clearly discernible from the beginning; the internal is revealed slowly, growing in strength and intensity until *it* is the dominant one at the end. The second circle, at first a figurative one, becomes a visible, magic enclosure of women who, in joining hands, bless and heal one another while naming their own empowering female god.

Though the presence of the women in the cities cited by Shange may be a matter of exigency, the question of how to find and maintain hope in the face of despair is a crucial one. In spite of the dichotomies established between country and city and though much is made of the romance of country life, humankind has relentlessly gravitated to biblical, literary, and historical cities, the problems and pitfalls notwithstanding. To substitute the word "metropolis" for "city" sheds some light on what seems to be the primal search of all people for a centered, balanced existence. This partial explanation is valid because cities are geographically contained or "centered" entities, as opposed to the random "layout" of the country. Thus, two important ideas surface immediately from the notion of the city as a "contained entity." Paul Tillich, the theologian, offers both: the city as a "centralizing and inclusive place" and the city as a place that accepts both the "strange and the familiar."[4]

First, Tillich, in discussing the "centralizing and inclusive" nature of the city which, he says "influences the character of *man's* (emphasis mine) spiritual creativity," suggests that

we may take our point of departure from the Greek word *metropolis*, signifying the mother or central city. Everything that exists has the power to be only insofar as it is centered. This is especially true of human personalities and social groups. The power of being, often called vitality, increases in proportion to the degree of diversity which is united at a center. Therefore, man has more power of being than any animal, and a spiritual man has greater vitality than a man with an underdeveloped spirituality. . . .

In applying this ontology of the metropolis to the spiritual life of man, we find that the big city has two functions. It serves in a centralizing capacity and also in an including capacity, and each is dependent upon the other.[5]

According to Tillich, a "metropolis . . . is a center city. It is likewise an including city. It includes everything of which it is the center, and encompasses diversity and freedom of individual creativity and competition."[6]

Tillich uses the word "mother" to identify the genesis of the city, but the city he describes, paradoxically, is masculine.[7] It is an idealized, romanticized, theoretical place where men interact, where ideas flow, where creativity flourishes, and where competition works for the good of all. This vision of the city is one which supports equality of aspiration, mobility of action, and freedom of community that women, in fact, have never known. Tillich and Shange are diametrically opposed to one another in their interpretations of the city; I shall discuss later the ways in which Tillich's idealized city is transformed by Ntozake Shange into a more realistic image. Her poem, "i usedta live in the world," is the psychological turning point in the play and is most indicative of her different view.[8]

"i usedta live in the world" is set in Harlem, the black city within New York City, which figures in Afro-American literature as "Mecca," "the City of Refuge," and in current vernacular as the "Big Apple."[9] However, Harlem has not lived up to its promise; thus it is no surprise that one of the most powerful poems in *for colored girls* is located there.

The woman in blue compares the vastness of her former life in the "world" to life in Harlem where her "universe is now six blocks."

> i usedta live in the world
> then i moved to HARLEM
> & my universe is now six blocks
>
> when i walked in the pacific
> i imagined waters ancient from accra/ tunis
> cleansin me/ feedin me
> now my ankles are coated in grey filth
> from the puddle neath the hydrant
>
> my oceans were life
> what waters i have here sit stagnant
> circlin ol men's bodies
> shit & broken lil whiskey bottles
> left to make me bleed. (28)

She juxtaposes the memory of wading in the Pacific and being washed and nurtured to the filthy water running in the city gutter. The "oceans" were life to her, which suggests the religious reading of the ocean as "Source" or God.[10] In contrast, the city water, instead of cleansing, holds suspended whiskey bottles whose jagged edges threaten her life. The stagnant water also symbolically holds suspended the bodies of old men—the winos, the "flotsam and jetsam" of city humanity. These men and the water circling them form part of the gross external circle mentioned above. They are the reasons why the spiritual self/circle is such a fragile entity, for it is impossible at this point to deal with this self in the face of the threat to basic survival; the broken bottles in the hands of these men are potential murder weapons.

The poem continues, revealing "a tunnel with a train// i can ride anywhere// remaining a stranger" (29). The image of the tunnel/ train simultaneously suggests two meanings: the momentary enclosure necessary to arrive at a "larger" destiny/destination and the ultimate enclosure of estrangement which is the life of the stranger in the city. The city subways do reach destinations and one can "ride" them "anywhere," but, in fact, the lady in blue "rides" the subway and finds herself trapped by a twelve-year-old boy who makes sexual advances. She responds,

> NO MAN YA CANT GO WIT ME/ I DONT EVEN
> KNOW YOU/ NO/ I DONT WANNA KISS YOU/
> YOU AINT BUT 12 YRS OLD/ NO MAN/ PLEASE
> PLEASE PLEASE LEAVE ME ALONE/ TOMORROW/ YEAH/ (29)

Her hysterical response and the extorted promise of a meeting tomorrow capture the fear women in the city have for their lives. Granted that the boy may not be a fully grown sexual being, but he most likely possesses a gun or a knife, clearly approved extensions of male sexuality and power. The ambiguous words, "NO/ PLEASE/ I CAN'T USE IT," suggest that this neophyte of a man, having been temporarily stalled, attempts to give or sell some trinket to the woman. This offer further belittles and objectifies the woman, who mourns the loss of her freedom metaphorically rendered in her "imagined waters." Commenting on her current life, she says, "i come in at dusk// stay close to the curb," clearly common-sense tactics for survival in the city.

The twelve-year-old on the subway becomes an urban

"everyman" whose violence is contained by the "tunnel" image
now suggested in the "straight up brick walls" of the city tenements. The "young man fulla his power" emerges in relief
against the limp, powerless "women hangin outta windows//like
ol silk stockings." The lady in blue continues:[11]

> wdnt be good
> not good at all
> to meet a tall short black brown young man fulla his power
> in the dark
> in my universe of six blocks
> straight up brick walls
> women hangin outta windows
> like ol silk stockings. (29)

The helter-skelter, impersonally violent life in Harlem is compared to a more gentle existence when:

> I usedta live in the world
> really be in the world
> free & sweet talkin
> good morning & thank-you & nice day. (30)

The poem concludes, and the woman, no longer trusting, courte-
ous, outgoing, reveals that her six-block universe is a cruel, hopeless, inhuman dead end, a closed tunnel ending the promise of
freedom in the city. Life in Harlem is a cruel hoax:

> i cant be nice to nobody
> nice is such a rip-off
> reglar beauty & a smile in the street
> is just a set-up
>
> i usedta be in the world
> a woman in the world
> i hadda right to the world
> then i moved to harlem
> for the set-up
> a universe
> six blocks of cruelty
> piled up on itself
> a tunnel
> closin (30–31)

The city described by Shange offers none of the characteristics
idealized by Tillich. Rather than encompass diversity, it reflects
the fear of racial and sexual diversity. "Individual creativity" is

perverted into desperate schemes for survival. "Competition" becomes the "dog-eat-dog" syndrome, rather than the mythologized earn-and-share, secular spirituality of the marketplace. Few can discover a spiritual center in this environment. For Shange, the city must be demystified and demythologized so that the price of human survival there can be truly estimated. The paradox is that the women embody the essence of the *metropolis*, even though they (as black women) are doubly absent from the "defining" language.

Paul Tillich's second point is that the metropolis supports both the strange and the familiar:

> The anti-provincial experience furnished by the metropolis is typified by encounters with that which is strange. Meeting the strange can have two consequences. It can produce hate against the strange, and usually against the stranger, because its existence threatens the self-certainty of the familiar. Or it can afford the courage to question the familiar. In the metropolis, it is impossible to remove the strange and the stranger, because every neighbor is mostly a stranger. Thus the second alternative of questioning the familiar ordinarily prevails. . . .
> Since the strange leads to questions and undermines familiar tradition, it serves to elevate reason to ultimate significance. If all traditions are questionable, nothing but reason is left as the way to new spiritual content. There lies the connection between the metropolis and critical rationality—between the metropolis and the intelligentsia as a social group. The importance of the encounter with the strange for all forms of the spiritual life cannot be overestimated.[12]

For Tillich, the "strange" and the "familiar" are separate forces that collide with one another, providing the change necessary for a dynamic spiritual life. For Ntozake Shange, the strange and the familiar are the double face of a single entity colliding with itself and with its societal counterpart. The strange/stranger is housed within the individual self *and* in the neighbor next door; the "familiar" has an unrecognizable "face." The orderly process by which "the strange leads to questions and undermines familiar tradition" and finally elevates "reason to ultimate significance" is absent, for, as Shange shows, the path to spiritual transcendence for the urban dispossessed is a decidedly irrational one.

The family is the traditional, familiar entity which provides the sanctuary from which the strange is questioned. Contrary to form, Shange's "family" revealed in "a nite with beau willie brown," shows how the strange and the familiar coexist as one. For example, violence is at once "strange" and "familiar," as are the ignorance, poverty, and promiscuity that preclude any possibility of Willie and his "wife," Crystal, belonging to Tillich's "intelligentsia." Willie and Crystal are the "underside," the "sewer" side of the metropolis.

"a nite with beau willie brown" is set geographically in the prototypical ghetto (Harlem is suggested to me) and psychologically in Vietnam, whereas "i usedta live in the world" is split between the geographical Harlem and a psychological place on the Pacific Ocean. The mounting tension in the play as a whole climaxes in "beau willie" because there are no pleasant mythic memories (as in the "imagined waters" of the Pacific); there are only the nightmare memories of Vietnam. Vietnam, in this context, clearly embodies the strange and the familiar simultaneously: a strange place and people, but familiar violence. The madness at the core of America is reflected in the Vietnam experience and in the fact that Beau Willie is "shell-shocked" long before he reaches Vietnam. He is a young version of the old men in "i usedta live in the world." They are static, trapped in stagnant water, and Willie is like Fred Daniels in Richard Wright's short story, "The Man Who Lived Underground," who is almost swept away by the torrent of sewer water into which he has dropped while running from the police.[13] One knows instinctively that Willie will not live long enough to grow static, for the aftermath of Vietnam finds him speeding to destruction. Beau Willie is the perennial stranger in American life for whom the familiar only provides additional trauma.

Tillich's familiar seems obvious in the family structure represented by Willie, Crystal, and their children Naomi Kenya and Kwame Beau Willie Brown. But Shange creates a monster in Beau Willie. He is hardly the comfortable image of the next-door-neighbor-as-stranger. Willie is ruined by the war experience, which is clearly the last in a series of psychological events that have crippled him. He is the dominant figure in the poem, but he is bound to his woman Crystal. He is a dope addict; he is paranoid. The lady in red speaks for him:

> there was no air/ the sheets made ripples under his
> body like crumpled paper napkins in a summer park/ & lil
> specks of somethin from tween his toes or the biscuits
> from the day before ran in the sweat that tucked the sheet
> into his limbs like he was an ol frozen bundle of chicken/
> & he'd get up to make coffee, drink wine, drink water/ he

wished one of his friends who knew where he waz wd come by
with some blow or some shit/ anythin/ there was no air/
he'd see the spotlights in the alleyways downstairs movin
in the air/ cross his wall over his face/ & get under the
covers & wait for an all clear or till he cd hear traffic
again/ (43–44)

The words "there was no air" suggest that Willie's external and
internal environment are closing in on him. Both are hostile elements because he is shell-shocked from his war experience and
reacts to his urban world as if he were still under fire, as he clearly
is. He is obsessed with Crystal who has been

his girl since she waz thirteen/ when he caught her
on the stairway/

he came home crazy as hell/ he tried to get veterans benefits
to go to school & they kept right on puttin him in
remedial classes/ he cdnt read wortha damn/ so beau
cused the teachers of holdin him back & got himself
a gypsy cab to drive/ but his cab kept breakin
down/ & the cops was always messin with him/ plus not
getting much bread/

& crystal went & got pregnant again/ beau most beat
her to death when she tol him/ (44)

Like Richard Wright's Fred Daniels, Willie is harassed by the
police. His attempt to make a living driving a cab backfires. He
has no money. As I mentioned above, he is the perennial
stranger; his city is the cruel, demeaning world of social ignorance, illiteracy, promiscuity, and unemployment.

Beau Willie's madness increases as the poem progresses. His
"war" is complicated and Crystal is the object of his anger and
hostility because her ambivalence about marrying him calls his
manhood into question. For Beau, Crystal is clearly crazy because

                          . . . he just wanted
to marry her/ that's what/ he wanted to marry her/ &
have a family/ but the bitch was crazy/ beau willie
waz sittin in this hotel in his drawers drinkin
coffee & wine in the heat of the day spillin shit all
over hisself/ laughin/ bout how he was gonna get crystal
to take him back/ & let him be a man in the house/ & she
wdnt even have to go to work no more/ he got dressed
all up in his ivory shirt & checkered pants to go see

crystal & get this mess all cleared up/
he knocked on the door to crystal's rooms/ & she
didn't answer/ he beat on the door & crystal & naomi
started cryin/ beau gotta shoutin again how he wanted
to marry her/ & waz she always gonna be a whore/ or
did she wanna a husband/ (46)

The poem comes to a monstrous end as Beau breaks down the door and pleads with Crystal for another chance, coaxing her to let him hold the children. Using them as hostages and holding them out of the fifth story window, Beau extorts the promise of marriage from Crystal. He urges her to "say to alla the neighbors// you gonna marry me/" (48), but she is too stunned to speak above a whisper:[14]

> i stood by beau in the window/ with naomi reachin
> for me/ kwame screaming mommy mommy from the fifth
> story/ but i cd only whisper/ & he dropped em (48)

Though Willie is the focus of the poem, the story is, in fact, Crystal's story. Shange uses the portrait of male violence to comment on the ways in which women are robbed of life. Willie's monstrous act strips Crystal of her identity as a woman and a mother. Just as Willie is an extension of the twelve-year-old boy, she is truly the sister of the woman who tells her story in "i usedta live in the world." She is also the symbolic sister of all the women who speak in and identify with the play. The extremity of her life mirrors the worst that can happen to a woman's dreams and aspirations. Through Crystal's story Shange reveals the inner circle mentioned above. Having broken down the city and its female inhabitants to their most elemental level, and, having re-defined the conventional interpretations of the strange and the familiar offered by Tillich, Shange re-creates a picture more faithful to the irrational forces that have traditionally shaped female lives and female spirituality.

The name Crystal is interesting, for Willie is truly addicted to her as if she were indeed heroin. He cannot live with or without her and what should be the sanctuary of a love relationship instead "inspires" him to brutality. On the other hand, Crystal's name suggests the clarity and purity of the vision of the city of God:

Then he showed me the river of the water of life, sparkling like crystal, flowing from the throne of God and of the Lamb down the middle of the city's streets.[15]

To understand the dual role that Crystal plays is to understand the quantum leap from "a nite with beau willie brown" to the last poem, "a layin on of hands," for her reality is grounded both in the gross world of Willie and the ghetto and in the spiritual vision of the women she represents. Her tragedy insures the transcendence of the women for her tears are like the waters of the biblical river.

The fragile inner circle that represents the spiritual is first apparent in the title and is alluded to throughout the choreopoem. The promise of transition from despair to hope is revealed in the words of lady in brown, "& this is for colored girls who have considered suicide// but moved to the ends of their own rainbows" (3). The first "community" mentioned in the play is one composed of "colored girls who have considered suicide." Suicide, whether physical, psychological, or spiritual, is a dominant factor in modern life; therefore, it is significant that this is the point around which the "new" community is rebuilt, for gathering together to deny suicide is a life-affirming, spiritual act. Shange says, "One day I was driving home after a class, and I saw a huge rainbow over Oakland. I realized that women could survive if we decide that we have as much right and as much purpose for being here as the air and mountains do."[16] Preparation for the "layin on of hands" and the discovery of God at the end of the play begins here. Women should have the freedom to live and must claim it. The rainbow suggests the mythic covenant between God and Noah, symbolizing hope and life; it foreshadows the end when the declaration, "i found god in myself," explains why the "rainbow is enuf."

To claim the right "to be" is to confront antilife forces. This self-affirmation is the first step toward spiritual affirmation. The rainbow represents the promise of a whole life, and Shange reveals her unique vision, for she draws a new covenant when she alters the gender of God, finding "her" in self, and declaring love for "her." This "mother" god will certainly heal her battered daughters. For this reason, too, Crystal's loss of her children is significant; the rules of patriarchy which allow mother and children to be held hostage must be rewritten.[17]

The sisterhood revealed at the conclusion of the play is foreshadowed in several poems about stunted male/female relationships. The poem, "pyramid," discusses the competitiveness of dating in which women are pitted against one another— primarily because men are in short supply. The man in

"pyramid" "plays the field," thereby compromising the friendships of three women, but the poem ends on a positive note as the
women console one another:

> she held her head on her lap
> the laps of her sisters soakin up tears
> each understandin how much love stood between them
> how much love between them
> love between them
> love like sisters (33)

Here the women affirm the power of touch ("she held her head
on her lap") and the power of sisterly love. The ambiguous use of
the pronoun "her" in the first line addresses the merger of the
individual woman into collective "woman," whose psyche
cannot be divided by competition.

The lady in orange turns her love song into a "requiem" for her
old self because she can no longer avoid her own face; she needs
to "die" to be "reborn" into spiritual life and to claim her own
identity:

> so this is a requium for myself/ cuz i
> have died in a real way/ not wid aqua coffins & du-wop cadillacs/
> i used to joke abt when i waz messin round/ but a real dead
> lovin is here for you now/ cuz i dont know anymore/ how
> to avoid my own face wet with my tears/ cuz i had convinced
> myself colored girls had no right to sorrow/ & i lived
> & loved that way & kept sorrow on the curb/ allegedly
> for you/ but i did it for myself/
> i cdnt stand it
> i cdnt stand being sorry & colored at the same time
> it's so redundant in the modern world (34)

In "no more love poems #3," the lady in blue deals with the
accusation that black women are too emotional:

> we deal wit emotion too much
> so why dont we go on ahead & be white then/
> . . . .
> i'll find a way to make myself
> come witout you/ no fingers or other objects just thot
> which isnt spiritual evolution cuz its empty & godliness
> is plenty ripe & fertile/ (35)

The definition of godliness as "plenty ripe & fertile" is a crucial
turning point in female consciousness. Shange here addresses

the central contradiction in Tillich's identification of the *metropolis* as "mother or central city," but defining its primary function as the repository of reason, when reason is the one attribute women are accused of lacking. The fecundity of women's emotions with their life-giving and life-sustaining properties is juxtaposed to "thot (thought)// which isn't spiritual evolution cuz its empty." The words "plenty ripe & fertile" echo at the end of the play, for the bonding of the women suggests the female fertility cults of old.

In "no more love poems #4," the lady in yellow makes the essential link between worldly and spiritual love:

> but bein alive & bein a woman & bein colored is a metaphysical
> dilemma/ i havent conquered yet/ do you see the point
> my spirit is too ancient to understand the separation of
> soul & gender/ my love is too delicate to have thrown
> back on my face (36)

At the end of these poems, the ladies celebrate the beauty and energy of their love, lifting it above romantic trivialization. To disavow the "separation of// soul & gender" prefigures the female god, both as human woman claiming her place and as "god the mother." Of the many lines the women sing to describe the significance of their love, the most telling is chanted by the lady in purple: "my love is too sanctified to have thrown back on my face" (36), which places absolute value on human love and prefigures the sanctified holy love implicit in the laying on of hands.

Crystal, then, is the woman whose specific tragedy is an adumbration of all female tragedy. She is the victim who is overwhelmed, at least momentarily, by the fury of the madman. Through Crystal, each woman discovers the hope in herself, with "all the gods comin into me// laying me open to myself" (49). Each woman now understands what the lady in red means when she says "i waz missin somethin" (49). The lady in blue declares that what is missing is "not a man" (50). And the lady in purple is clear that it is neither her mother, nor motherhood that is missing:

> not my mama/ holdin me tight/ sayin
> i'm always gonna be her girl
> not a layin on of bosom & womb
> a layin on of hands
> the holiness of myself released (50)

The lady in red considers suicide:

> I sat up one night walkin a boardin house
> screaming/ cryin/ the ghost of another woman
> who waz missin what i was missin
> i wanted to jump outta my bones
> & be done wit myself
> leave me alone
> & go on in the wind
> it was too much (50)

She is split into two beings, but this confrontation with self (strange and the familiar) is the point at which healing and renewal begins:

> i fell into a numbness
> til the only tree i cd see
> took me up in her branches
> held me in the breeze
> made me dawn dew
> that chill at daybreak
> the sun wrapped me up swingin rose light everywhere
> the sky laid over me like a million men
> i waz cold/ i waz burnin up/ a child
> & endlessly weavin garments for the moon
> wit my tears (50)

The concrete landscape of the city with its occasional tree—unremarkable, lone, bare, struggling for survival in an environment indifferent or hostile to it—unfolds here. The lady in red "fell into a numbness" that, paradoxically, is relieved through the life-giving properties of the tree. Adrienne Rich suggests that the tree "is a female symbol," and is sacred.[18] Shange's tree is the sacred "mother," and her branches loving, cradling arms. The tree connects symbolically with Crystal as the final arbiter for the women, an idea that is enhanced by these words from Revelations, "On either side of the river stood a tree of life . . . , the leaves of the tree[s] serve for the healing of nations" (22:2).

The sun embraces the lady in red and "the sky laid over [her] like a million men." Shange alludes to the classical notion of the sky as male principle and the break with "earthly" men makes realignment with nature's balance possible. Through the images of hot and cold, she re-creates the fever associated with childhood, and prepares the way for rebirth. Female affinity and empathy with the moon are suggested in the image of one "endlessly weavin garments for the moon// with my tears." All the cosmic forces come together here as a unifying and healing whole.

The lines from the end of "no more love poems #4" provide a context for the discovery of God. The lady in yellow says:

> do you see the point
> my spirit is too ancient to understand the separation of
> soul & gender/ (36)

These lines suggest that body (gender) and soul cannot be separated; thus the woman knows wholeness. The final words of the lady in red contain the triumph of all the women, for she is finally and fully centered as she says, "i found god in myself/ & i loved her fiercely." The identification of God as female is one of the most problematic points in the play, for it redefines the image of God. But Shange truly understands what it means to be created in the image of God, for discovery of self is discovery of God. This is a declaration of freedom from a patriarchial god who supports the men from whom the women have split.

The poem, "a layin on of hands," suggests a specially formed community which has grown from the brokenness of life in the city. Crystal reminds me of Revelations, but the connection between her transcendence and that found in *colored girls* is that Shange's triumphant city is not the product of an apocalyptic vision, but is the result of new sight, for the physical metropolis remains unchanged. As Denise Levertov in her poem, "City Psalm," says,

> Nothing was changed, all was revealed otherwise;
> not that horror was not, not that the killings did not continue,
> not that I thought there was to be no more despair,
> but that as if transparent all disclosed
> an otherness that was blesséd, that was bliss.
> *I saw Paradise in the dust of the street.*[19]

Levertov's image of the "transparent all" echoes the moment of crystal purity, which is the moment of revelation that "disclosed / an otherness. " It is "in the dust of the street" that Shange's women suffer and grow in knowledge of the "strangeness of the familiar." It is their immersion in this paradoxical reality which forces them to confront themselves and which prepares them to have a dynamic spiritual vision. The women simply could not have been reborn had they not been cleansed and bound together by these unique experiences. They are not ghouls, children of horror, the joke, animals, or crazy people. They no longer need "somebody/anybody" to sing their song. They are no longer scattered half-notes.[20] But they differ radically from the idealized city beings hypothesized by Tillich. Through the life-enhancing hope of the rainbow, they form a covenant with a woman-God. They are "new" and now sing their own "righteous gospel." The laying on of hands is validated in the "holiness of myself released" (50). The women enter into a tightly wrought circle, symbolic of their spiritual vision and their earthly solidarity. This is the second, "inner" circle mentioned above, which is in tension throughout the play with the external circle. Here, the power and meaning of the inner circle are fully revealed. And the lady in brown dedicates the moment:

> this is for colored girls who have considered
> suicide/ but are movin to the ends of their own
> rainbows (51)

NOTES

1. Ntozake Shange, *for colored girls who have considered suicide/ when the rainbow is enuf* (New York: Macmillan, 1977). All citations are from this edition and are given in the text parenthetically. Shange does not use punctuation in a conventional way. Thus, the double slash (//) is used in my text to indicate the end of line of poetry since Shange uses the single (/) throughout the choreopoem as a poetic device.

The term "choreopoem" is used in my text as a synonym for the word "play." This is Shange's word and is found on the title page of her book. It reflects Shange's intent that the play be understood as a choral recitation of poems upon which limited dramatic form has been imposed.

2. The cities have been repositories of promise for blacks migrating from rural to urban America. They have sought economic and political freedom, psychological and cultural autonomy. During the first two decades of the twentieth-century southern black people, seeking to escape white violence and economic disaster, migrated to the North. The traditional myth of opportunity in the North was enhanced by national preparations for World War I and the hope for employment in the emerging defense industries. The promise of safety and a better economic life is usually seized upon by analysts as the sole interest of the emigrating black masses, but Alain Locke, editor of the anthology *The New Negro*

(New York: Atheneum, 1970), 6, suggests in the title essay that the black peasant was inspired by a newly emerging and more complex vision:

> The tide of Negro migration, northward and cityward, is not to be fully explained as a blind flood started by the demands of war industry coupled with the shutting off foreign migration, or by the pressure of poor crops coupled with increased social terrorism in certain sections of the South and Southwest. Neither labor demand, the boll-weevil nor the Ku Klux Klan is a basic factor, however contributory any or all of them may have been. The wash and rush of this human tide on the beach line of the northern city centers is to be explained primarily in terms of a new vision of opportunity, of social and economic freedom, of a spirit to seize, even in the face of an extortionate and heavy toll, a chance for the improvement of conditions. With each successive wave of it, the movement of the Negro becomes more and more a mass movement toward the larger and more democratic chance—in the Negro's case a deliberate flight not only from countryside to city, but from medieval America to modern.

These migration patterns continued until the 1970s, when many black people, inspired by the gains of the civil rights movement, retraced the steps of their ancestors back to the South. However, since the original migrations were to the North, life in northern cities is the focus of many 20th-century Afro-American writers. Authors such as James Weldon Johnson, Rudolph Fisher, Wallace Thurman, Jessie Fauset, to name a few early writers of the decade, and more modern, perhaps better-known writers such as Langston Hughes, Richard Wright, James Baldwin, Ann Petry, Ralph Ellison, Gwendolyn Brooks depict the Afro-American urban experience.

3. The first two poems mentioned here are "latent rapists' [sic] (12–16), "abortion cycle #1" (16–17). Most of the poems in *for colored girls* deal in some way with betrayal, but this is the specific theme of "no assistance" (10), and "somebody almost walked off wid alla my stuff" (39–41).

4. Paul J. Tillich, "The Metropolis: Centralizing and Inclusive," and "The Strange and the Familiar in the Metropolis," in *The Metropolis in Modern Life*, ed. Robert Moore Fisher (New York: Doubleday, 1955), 346–47. Shange identifies the "familiar" cities, but establishes the women as "strangers." For example, the characters in the play do not have "proper names," except in poems where she creates a story within a story; the women are "named" by the colors they wear, suggesting anonymity. They are placed *outside* the cities: the lady in red, "i'm outside baltimore"; the lady in blue, "i'm outside manhattan," etc.

5. Ibid., 346.

6. Ibid., 346–47.

7. Tillich's language is exclusively masculine. His central image is power; his primary example of power is the pope and the Roman Catholic Church.

8. The preceding poems interweave fascinating pictures of city

landscape with the emerging consciousness of the women as they grow from late adolescence in, for example, "graduation nite" (4–7), to adult complexity in the poem entitled "one" (24–28), in which a lonely urban woman takes a stranger home to bed, but must finally face the fact that the chance encounter is not satisfying and that she is lonelier than ever at its conclusion.

9. A mentor to many of the young black artists flocking to Harlem in the twenties, described it as "one of the most beautiful and healthful sections of the city." He ended his commentary on Harlem with the following words:

> I believe that the Negro's advantages and opportunities are greater in Harlem than in any other place in the country, and that Harlem will become the intellectual, the cultural, and the financial center for Negroes of the United States, and will exert a vital influence upon all Negro people.

James Weldon Johnson, "Harlem: The Culture Capital," in *The New Negro*, ed. Alain Locke (New York: Atheneum, 1970), 311. Johnson's words proved not to be prophetic. The promise of Harlem in the 1920s as a place where the urban dream of American blacks would come true failed and Harlem's prominence has eroded in the last two decades. It is interesting that Johnson's ideas are a secular echo of Tillich's and ironic that the diversity of the city described by Tillich is not fully realized as whites flee from areas into which black people move thereby compromising the vitality of place and creating ghettoes. Johnson's dream, therefore, cannot be realized because "the intellectual, the cultural, and the financial" are defined and controlled by white people, who remove these elements when they leave.

10. I am thinking, here, of the connection made by Jonathan Edwards, in his meditation number 77 on "Rivers" from *Images or Shadows of Divine Things*, "There is a wonderful analogy between what is seen in rivers, their gathering from innumerable small branches beginning at a great distance one from another in different regions . . . yet all gathering more and more together the nearer they come to their common end and ultimate issue, and all at length discharging themselves at one mouth into the same ocean. Here is livelily represented how all things tend to one, even to God, the boundless ocean" (*The Norton Anthology of American Literature*, I, ed. Gottesman, Holland, Kalstone, et al., [New York: Norton, 1979], 261).

11. In the stage directions, the other women silently enter here; their presence is a symbolic commentary on the universality of the problem.

12. Tillich, 347.

13. Richard Wright, "The Man Who Lived Underground," in *Black Voices*, ed. Abraham Chapman (New York: New American Library, 1968), 114–60. Shange's image of old men suspended in stagnant water is reminiscent of Wright's character who finds—literally and figuratively—all of life's potential amenities rotted or dead floating by in the sewer water. Just as I suggested that Willie and Crystal are the

"sewer" side of the metropolis, so Fred Daniels's world is that of the sewer, a metaphorical commentary on the quality of Afro-American life in the city.

14. The starkness of Beau Willie's infanticide has led critics to accuse Ntozake Shange of hating men. It is my opinion that she graphically, but compassionately, depicts the inhumanity of a system that in its racist, biased indifference to life, stunts a man's aspirations, makes him a murderer, and reduces him to insanity. His time in Vietnam is the most important factor to consider in his treatment of Crystal and the children. This point is endorsed by one of the most powerful dramatic productions of the postwar Vietnam veteran's life. This play is Emily Mann's *Still Life*, in which Mark, the veteran, in talking of his projection of violence, identifies his wife, Cheryl, as the war casualty.

15. Revelations 22:1, *New English Bible* (New York: Cambridge Univ. Press, 1971). Crystal's name also suggests the paradox of experience for the Afro-American mother that is captured in Langston Hughes's poem, "Mother to Son," in *Black Writers of America: A Comprehensive Anthology*, ed. Kinnamon and Barksdale (New York: Macmillan, 1972), 518.

Well, son, I'll tell you:
Life for me ain't been no crystal stair.
It's had tacks in it,
And splinters,
And boards torn up,
And places with no carpet on the floor—
Bare.
But all the time
I'se been a-climbin' on,
And reachin' landin's,
And turnin' corners,
And sometimes goin' in the dark
Where there ain't been no light.
So boy, don't you turn back.
Don't you set down on the steps
'Cause you finds it's kinder hard.
Don't you fall now—
For I'se still goin', honey,
I'se still climbin',
And life for me ain't been no crystal stair.

16. Carol P. Christ, *Diving Deep and Surfacing: Women Writers on Spiritual Quest* (Boston: Beacon, 1980), 99, as quoted from Ntozake Shange, *For Colored Girls Who Have Considered Suicide/When the Rainbow Is Enuf* (original Broadway cast recording) (New York: Buddha Records, 1976), jacket notes. One of the most sensitive, cogent, and pertinent discussions of the choreopoem appears in Carol Christ's essay, "'i found god in myself . . . & i loved her fiercely': Ntozake Shange." Christ's analysis of *for colored girls* stresses the processes of self-discovery, self-healing, and spiritual transcendence. In Christ's interpretation, the truth

of the "colored girls'" growth into personhood and faith overshadows
the bitter commentary and misinterpretation that characterize most criticism, which is that the play "trashes" black men, and reveals things
about black people that would be better left unsaid or certainly not said in
public. Christ, however, does not deal with the significance of the city in
the play.

17. The basis for my thoughts on patriarchy comes from Adrienne
Rich, "The Kingdom of the Fathers," in *Of Women Born: Motherhood as
Experience and Institution* (New York: Norton, 1976), 56–83.

18. Ibid., 100.

19. Denise Levertov, "City Psalm," *The Sorrow Dance* (New York:
New Directions, 1966), 72.

> The killings continue, each second
> pain and misfortune extend themselves
> in the genetic chain, injustice is done knowingly, and the air
> bears the dust of decayed hopes,
> yet breathing those fumes, walking the thronged
> pavements among crippled lives, jackhammers
> raging, a parking lot painfully agleam
> in the May sun, I have seen
> not behind but within, within the
> dull grief, blown grit, hideous
> concrete facades, another grief, a gleam
> as of dew, an abode of mercy,
> have heard not behind but within noise
> a humming that drifted into a quiet smile.
> Nothing was changed, all was revealed otherwise;
> not that horror was not, not that the killings did not continue,
> not that I thought there was to be no more despair,
> but that as if transparent all disclosed
> an otherness that was blessèd, that was bliss.
> *I saw Paradise in the dust of the street.*

20. The images in these three sentences are taken from the first
poem in *for colored girls* entitled, "dark phases" (1–2).

WENDY MARTIN

Another View of the "City Upon a Hill": The Prophetic Vision of Adrienne Rich

CITIES HAVE ALWAYS BEEN CENTRAL to Adrienne Rich's life and work. From the tradition-laden capitals of European civilization where she travelled as a student and apprentice poet to the New World centers of Cambridge, Boston, and New York City where she has lived most of her adult years and has developed her career and professional identity, urban life has provided opportunities for her personal, professional, and political growth. Her complex career has included many phases—she has been student, wife and mother, professor, nationally acclaimed poet, political activist of the sixties, and in the seventies lesbian feminist. In recent years, however, Rich has become alienated from cities and has envisioned Manhattan as a metaphor for economic exploitation and moral pollution; her poems reflect her increasing alienation from the racism, sexism, patriarchal capitalism which are expressed in the violence, pornography, economic oppression that she feels are characteristic of life in American cities.

In contrast to these urban problems is Adrienne Rich's prophetic vision of the community of women which for her embodies the ideals of the sanctity of individual existence, collective well-being, reverence for all forms of life. Rich's ideal of the city of sisterhood based on feminist/lesbian values is part of a larger American tradition of social revolution that began with the voyage of New England Puritans to the New World. Radical dissenters and nonconformists, these emigrants who composed the

Massachussets Bay Company created a philosophical and moral scaffolding for their religious and economic enterprise that has shaped social structure in the Northeast and in the United States ever since.[1] The "city upon a hill," as the Puritans described their vision of God's New World commonwealth, identified individual concerns with the needs of the community; spiritual and social goals were fused, and private and public values were aligned. The New World mission displaced the allegiance to European hierarchial aristocracy with the ideal of a covenanted community which served the needs of its members while conforming to God's divine plan.[2]

While the ideals of the community of women are based on feminist/lesbian values, the conceptual framework which brought it into being has its roots in early American history. Just as the Puritan "errand into the wilderness" was grounded in the conviction that the New World colony was a historic mission, so the feminist vision of cities of sisterhood is based on a belief that communities concerned with honoring and protecting life—a nurturing ethos—can help to reverse the destructive effects of patriarchal culture. As Adrienne Rich has observed,

I think we (women) have a mission to survive, ourselves, and to be whole people. I believe that this can save the world, but I don't believe that women have a mission to clean up after men's messes. I think we have to save the world by doing it for ourselves—for all women—I don't mean some narrow, restricted notion of what women are, only white women or only middle class women, or only Western women.[3]

This utopian community of sisters, like the commonwealth of saints, is a profoundly political phenomenon which results from an evolution in consciousness from acceptance of traditional values, or at least the effort to adjust to them, to questioning of these values, to rebellion and finally separation from the dominant culture to form a new social order. The new community, whether or not it exists in actuality, in turn has an effect on the perception of traditional political structures. In other words, by creating an alternate reality, the city of sisterhood, like the Puritan Commonwealth, gives a new shape to our national belief in the possibility of new beginnings.

In Adrienne Rich's early poetry, the city, especially the European city, represents centuries of civilization. But these urban landscapes encrusted with layers of culture—opera houses, museums, public squares, historical monuments—function as tableaux for the drama of universal concerns of war, passion, death, or they provide ornate settings for the poet's individual emotional development.

> To work and suffer is to be at home.
> All else is scenery: the Rathaus fountain,
> The skaters in the sunset on the lake
> At Salzburg, or, emerging after snow,
> The singular clear stars of Castellane.[4]

The Rathaus fountain, the lake at Salzburg, the stars of Castellane, the poet says, are merely backdrops for her intense feelings: personal emotions, not historic settings, give meaning to her life. These early poems are stylistically and structurally conventional; their predictable meters and polished images are as traditional as the poet's preoccupation with universal values.

In *Snapshots of a Daughter-in-Law: Poems 1954–1962*[5] the poet shifts her attention to her native land with its promise of progress and personal fulfillment. In this volume, Rich focuses more intensely on the literal circumstances of her life. For the first time, Rich writes about domestic experience from a female perspective. Here the domestic reality of the kitchen supersedes the city with its promise of the wider life—"the endless wing of possibility" ("To the Airport," *SDL*, 41). The structure of her poems becomes more experimental; her poetic line becomes longer and looser, and she begins to find her individual voice. The student who traveled freely in Europe is now a young wife and mother who must stay close to home. Because her own life has been narrowed by domestic necessity, the city loses its excitement.

> —Nothing is happening. —City,
> dumb as a pack of thumbed cards, you
> once had snap and glare
> and secret life; now, trembling
> under my five grey senses weight,
> you flatten
> onto the table.
>   (*SDL*, 49)

In this poem the city is a projection of the poet's feelings about herself. Here inner and outer realities converge as her subjective stasis, inertia, even deprivation affect her perception of a world that once hummed with vitality for her. There is a sense of youth deprived of opportunity to explore its potential.

The relationship of personal identity to urban space continues to be a central concern in *Necessities of Life: Poems 1962-1965* as Rich articulates her emerging awareness that individual experience cannot be arbitrarily separated from its public context—that physical place has a profound effect on the definition of self.[6]

> They're tearing down, tearing up
> this city, block by block.
> Rooms cut in half
> hang like flayed carcasses,
> their old roses in rags,
> famous streets have forgotten
> where they were going. Only
> a fact could be so dreamlike.
> They're tearing down the houses
> we met and lived in,
> soon our two bodies will be all
> left standing from that era.
> ("Like This Together," *NL*, 16)

Although the demolition of the buildings that literally contained the charged events of the poet's life destroys her tangible past, the sight of their shredded wallpaper paradoxically creates the nascent understanding that she cannot rely on external forms to validate her personal history. Ultimately this awareness enables Rich to live outside urban centers, but not until she has become painfully alienated from patriarchal culture and the cities, especially Manhattan, that embody its power.

Because of these frequent, arbitrary schisms that occur between private experience and public life in a culture devoted to mobility and profit, Rich begins to view the American city as a place of painful isolation, a place of diverse but separate realities and meaningless social relationships. Disappointment, disillusion, pessimism about the promise of American cities pervade this volume. In "Autumn Sequence" (1964), for example, city life is depicted as stale, devoid of texture and resonance. The impersonal dynamo that powers the transport of water to the sprawling metropolis eclipses the picturesque charm of the Rathaus fountain.

> Skin of wet leaves on asphalt.
> Charcoal slabs pitted with gold.
> The reason for cities comes clear.

There must be a place, there has come a time—
where so many nerves are fusing—
for a purely moral loneliness.

Beyond bloodsoaked lights of avenues,
is the crystal grit of flying snow,
in this water-drop bulging at the taphead,

forced by dynamos three hundred miles
from the wild duck's landing and the otter's dive,
for three seconds of quivering identity.

There must be a place. But the eyeball stiffens
as the night tightens and my hero passes out
with a film of stale gossip on his tongue.
    (NL, 36-37)

In this series of complex triplets, the yoking of opposites—
organic matter with inert pavement, clarity with grime, illumination with blood—undercuts the potential grandeur of the cityscape. Instead, Rich sees the urban center as an expression of a
massive displacement of emotional and physical energy, a
monomaniacal expression of a collective urge for mastery. But the
price is high: instead of nourishing social exchange, urban life
constricts human communication until authentic expression is
reduced to stale gossip.

For Rich, this schism between individual life and larger social
forms represents the cultural split between mind and body, nature and civilization, and finally oppressor and oppressed which
she feels is the basis of patriarchal order. "Spring Thunder"
(1965) expresses her growing disenchantment with the city as an
embodiment of this bifurcation:

Thunder is all it is, and yet
my street becomes a crack in the western hemisphere,
my house a fragile nest of grasses.

The radiotelescope flings its nets
at random; a child is crying,
not from hunger, not from pain,
more likely impotence. The generals are sweltering

in a room with a thousand eyes.
Red-hot lights flash off and on
inside air-conditioned skulls.
    (NL, 44)

Invasive technology emphasizes human vulnerability, and the demarcation between powerful and powerless is clearly drawn as the city is associated with technological nightmare and the oppression of the great mass of people by a few men who control the military-industrial establishment capable at any time of destroying life on earth.

The poems of *Leaflets: Poems 1965-1968*[7] express an increasing despair with masculine territoriality as manifested in the French civil strife, the Vietnam war, and Arab-Israeli conflicts which took place in the decade of the 1960s. Several poems in this volume explore the human cost of military conflict, and, in each of these poems, a city bears witness to the ravages of war. In "Jerusalem," the ancient site of countless battles, the city is filled with screaming sirens, blasted walls, spent shells, dead soldiers; in "Charleston in the 1860's," in which the details of the poem are derived from the diaries of Mary Boykin Chestnut, the odor of nitrate overpowers the evening breeze scented with pear, jasmine, violets; in "For a Russian Poet," a sympathy protest for Czechoslovakia in Moscow's Red Square suddenly becomes a scene of violence.

Part Three of *Leaflets*, "Gazals: Homage to Ghalib," consists of a series of poems of at least five couplets in which there is an improvisational interplay of associations and images. In these poems, based on an Urdu form, Rich uses the details of daily urban life to convey her political message: conversations in Central Park represent growing dissatisfaction with American political priorities, graffiti express the anger of disenfranchised people who pay the human price of arbitrary waste of resources, unequal division of power, and the exploitation of the mass of people through the collusion of powerful men. In these ghazals, Rich begins to depict cities as death-traps characterized by scenes of destruction, rape, and murder.

> If these are letters, they will have to be misread.
> If scribblings on a wall, they must tangle with all the others.
>
> Fuck reds   Black Power   Angel loves Rosita
> —and a transistor radio answers in Spanish: *Night must fall.*
> (*L.* 75)

Informal syntax, political slogans, vernacular expressions convey a sense of the fragmentation and dislocation of urban populations.

In the title poem of *The Will to Change: Poems 1968-1970*, [8] a Chinese restaurant, Yorkville, the Feast of San Gennaro, the A-train that "forages / under our bedroom" are correlatives of the poet's increasing alienation from Manhattan, which now seems to her a chaotic assemblage of fragmented, diseased lives of people who have been exploited and abandoned by patriarchal industrialists. The smoldering rage of the people occasionally ignites but is ineffectual. In this volume Rich reluctantly foregoes her belief in the possibility of change through political demonstration and mass action—the oppressive reality represented by the monolithic structure of the city seems too overwhelming to permit significant improvement in the conditions of the daily lives of its populace. Since she cannot save her culture, at least not immediately, she must save herself. Now it is not the city that is being demolished, but the poet herself who is tearing her own life from its context:

> 13.
> To put the prism in your pocket, the thin glass lens, the map
> of the inner city, the little book with gridded pages
> 14.
> To pull yourself up by your own roots; to eat the last meal
> in
> your old neighborhood.
> ("Shooting Script," WC, 67)

Replete with images of fragmentation and dissociation, this poem signals the poet's intention to explore new territory.

In *Diving into the Wreck: Poems 1971-1972* [9] the reality of urban waste and destruction rekindle the poet's rage. Part 10 of "The Phenomenology of Anger" (1972) conveys the poet's despair about contemporary urban life. Like Hart Crane in "The Bridge," Rich takes the subway as a terrifying descent into the bowels of Manhattan:

> 10. how we are burning up our lives
> testimony:
> > the subway
> > hurtling to Brooklyn
> > her head on her knees
> > asleep or drugged
>
> la vía del tren subterráneo
> es peligrosa
> (DW, 31)

The subway is a metaphor for the destructive trajectory of city life. The Spanish phrase that concludes the quotation literally says "the way of the underground train is dangerous." The pun on "way" underscores both literal and symbolic damage done by an increasingly depersonalized, mechanized society that leaves its citizens numbed by frustration and despair. Other poems in this volume, such as "The Stranger" (1972), depict this anger as sight "cleansing" and "visionary."

> Looking as I've looked before, straight down the heart
> of the street to the river
> walking the rivers of the avenues
> feeling the shudder of the caves beneath the asphalt
> watching the lights turn on in the towers
> walking as I've walked before
> like a man, like a woman, in the city
> my visionary anger cleansing my sight
> and the detailed perceptions of mercy
> flowering from that anger
> (*DW*, 19)

This rage liberates the poet from patriarchal civilization. Claiming for herself the power that has been assigned to men, Rich begins to define a vision of female collectivity that transcends patriarchal insistence on mastery, dominance, and territoriality.

Critics such as Burton Pike have argued that urban identity has been less cohesive—more "unstable and shifting"—in the past century.[10] But paradoxically, cities have permitted women to escape the constraints of rural and suburban life. For example, in the 1920s poets like H. D., Marianne Moore, Louise Bogan, and Edna St. Vincent Millay sought the relative freedom granted by urban anonymity, which permits social and cultural experimentation on a scale impossible in smaller communities. Using this autonomy, individual women developed new identities, and by the early 1970s, an urgent sense of female priorities was taking shape in the northeastern cities. "After Twenty Years" (1971) celebrates this emerging feminist community:

> It is strange to be so many women,
> eating and drinking at the same table,
> those who bathed their children in the same basin
> who kept their secrets from each other
> walked the floors of their lives in separate rooms
> and flow into history now as the women of their time

> living in the prime of life
> as in a city where nothing is forbidden
> and nothing permanent.
> (*DW*, 13)

Contrasting mutuality with separation, this poem suggests that these women are now a historical force. The anomie and flux of urban life, viewed negatively in Rich's previous work, are seen here as catalysts for positive change.

"The Fourth Month of the Landscape Architect," in *Poems: Selected and New, 1950-1974*,[11] suggests a need for a feminist alternative to the patriarchal city. Enumerating the ways that traditional social organization has crippled women, the poet demands the same freedom for American women that American men claim for themselves:

> A city waits at the back of my skull
> eating its heart out to be born:
> how design the first
> city of the moon? how shall I see it
> for all of us who are done
> with enclosed spaces, purdah, the salon, the sweatshop loft,
> the ingenuity of the cloister?
> (*PSN*, 225)

This is a profoundly political poem, in which Rich insists that there should be no division between male and female rights, between aesthetics and social action, or art and politics. Her artistic mission is to write words that transform our perceptions and thereby create possibility for a new world. For her, writing has revolutionary potential:

> The act of writing itself can bring out truths we didn't know we knew. The fact that it is written is going to have an effect on our consciousness—it changes consciousness . . . . Writing is a process of going from the conflicts and the strife of the unconscious into the sayable, into the actable.[12]

In *The Dream of a Common Language, Poems 1974-1977*,[13] "Twenty-one Love Poems" focus on the power and beauty of female erotic love against a background of urban pornography.

> Wherever in this city, screens flicker
> with pornography, with science-fiction vampires,
> victimized hirelings bending to the lash,

> we also have to walk . . . if simply as we walk
> through the rainsoaked garbage, the tabloid cruelties
> of our own neighborhoods
> (DCL, 25)

Lesbian love is seen as an antidote to misogyny. Rich now turns to nature and prehistory as a source of images for her alternate community. In "Mother-Right" she writes of the need to escape the man who believes "in what is his / the grass—the waters underneath—the air" and of women "making for the open" (DCL, 59). Seeking a new frontier where she can live according to her priorities, Rich examines the facts of women's daily lives in such poems as "Sibling Mysteries" and "Natural Resources." She focuses on the nurturing vision and reverence for life that has sustained them for centuries:

> I have cast my lot with those
> who age after age, perversely,
>
> With no extraordinary power,
> reconstruct the world.
> (DCL, "Natural Resources," 67)

In her prose volume, Of Woman Born,[14] Rich suggests that social structure be recast to honor the bond of mother and child. In other words, nurturance rather than territoriality would be the organizing principle of a new society. In the city of sisterhood, women would command their minds and bodies wielding female power that is transformative rather than dominating:

> We need to imagine a world in which every woman is the presiding genius of her own body. In such a world women will truly create new life, bringing forth not only children (if and as we choose) but the visions, and the thinking, necessary to sustain, console, and alter human existence—a new relationship to the universe. Sexuality, politics, intelligence, power, motherhood, work, community, intimacy will develop new meanings; thinking itself will be transformed.
> (DWB, 3)

Like the French feminist critics Julia Kristeva, Hélène Cixous, and Luce Irigaray, Rich insists that women need to think with their bodies and, if possible, to return to the preoedipal experience before the patriarchal grid imposed the bifurcation of mind and body, self and other.

In the poems of *A Wild Patience Has Taken Me This Far: Poems 1978-1981* [15] the truths of female lives are contrasted with distorted rendering of these lives in male art and history. Turning away from the city, Rich focuses her attention on the natural landscape in a variety of places ranging from California, New Mexico, Arizona, and Nebraska to Massachusetts. Bidding farewell to Manhattan in "The Images," she contrasts the experience of two women lovers who live and work together with the cruelty and violence of street life:

> the swell of cruelty and helplessness—
>   in one block between West End
>   and Riverside. In my dreams the Hudson
>   rules the night like a right-hand margin
>   drawn against the updraft
>   of burning life, the tongueless cries
>   of the city.
>   (*WP*, 3)

Many modern poets—Eliot, Frost, Crane for example—have viewed the city as dangerous or evil, and Rich shares their tradition. In addition, Rich describes the city as a monument to patriarchal culture; for her, the purple-tongued flower, an image taken from H. D.'s "The Master,"[16] is the metaphor for female erotic power that is not subject to pornographic distortion: "we are the thorn-leaf guarding the purple-tongued flower, each to each" (*WP*, 5). Rich describes the conflict of feminist and misogynist values as the "war of the images." She insists that women must *remember*, and so protect themselves from pornographic distortions, that dismember:

> I am remembered by you, remember you
>   even as we are dismembered
>   on the cinema screens, the white expensive walls
>   of collectors, the newsrags blowing the streets
>   (*WP*, "The Images," 5)

Describing her concerns at the time of writing this poem, Rich has said:

How do we exist when we have no accurate images of ourselves, or very few—this is what I was trying to write about in the poem "The Images." How do we exist, how do we create, when our existence is blotted out, is denied or distorted?[17]

In addition she has said that in this poem she was trying to write about the need for women to recognize their struggle for survival in a culture that denies the meaning of their experience:

We must stop experiencing our desire to survive as some kind of paranoia or man-hating. We are hated and feared, very profoundly—I don't mean by all, every individual man, but by the mindset of this masculine culture. And when we begin to recognize that, we begin to recognize the ways in which we identify with the hatred of women. This clarity of thought is terrible but also incredibly empowering.[18]

"The Images" marks a major turning point in Adrienne Rich's poetic career. Soon after it was written, she made a decision to leave Manhattan, a city that had been her primary ground for more than a decade. With her move to Montague, Massachusetts, not far from Amherst, her poetry has become more explictly concerned with the female principle as an antidote to patriarchy and the community of women which is affiliative rather than geographical.

Many of the poems in *A Wild Patience Has Taken Me This Far* are concerned with the elaboration of her vision of the city of sisterhood. In "For Julia in Nebraska," (1978-1981), Rich writes of the female community which is rooted in American history:

> but the matrices we weave
> web upon web, delicate rafters
> flung in audacity to the prairie skies
> nets of telepathy contrived
> to outlast the iron road
> laid out in blood across the land they called virgin—
> nets, strands, a braid of hair
> a grandmother's strong hands plaited
> straight down a grand-daughter's back
> (*AWP*, 16)

Such community is based on an intricate web of female relationships, not objectified in architectural plans of urban centers, institutional structures, or official historical records. Writing of the empathic female friendships that constitute a substratum of American life, Rich celebrates the power of these enduring networks.

With her departure from Manhattan, Rich writes increasingly of women in rural or pastoral settings. The countryside, whether it be in the American West or New England, seems to offer perspective on truths of female experience past and present. In each location, Rich finds traces of the female tradition and reconstructs the lives of forgotten American women from Massachusetts to New Mexico. Because the rural landscape promises the possibility of new beginnings, it is possible to imagine alternate communities. It is significant that radical feminists, like their Puritan ancestors, choose the countryside as the site of their new society.

This exodus from the established centers of power parallels the departure of Puritans from England to the Massachusetts Bay colonies in an effort to live according to their inner convictions. Like her American ancestors, Rich embarks on a spiritual journey away from those who oppose her deepest convictions toward a new world that she hopes will permit her freedom of self and spirit. This pattern of renewal, regeneration, reformation—of the possibility of beginning again—is a prominent characteristic of much American psychological and social life, and it is important to understand that Rich's effort to create a female community is part of this larger tradition. Like Puritanism, feminism is part of the larger pattern inherited from Protestantism in which reformation is a basic concept.[19]

Both Puritan reformation and feminist transformation are structurally similar: both envision the creation of a new world whether it be the city upon a hill or the community of women. The Puritan heart prepared to receive God's grace has its parallel in the feminist raised consciousness that extirpates male-identified values. Both Puritans and feminists accept struggle as an essential part of their lives as pilgrims or pioneers. Puritans were prepared to do battle against the forces of Satan. Similarly, in the "The Spirit of Place" Rich asks:

> Are we all in training for something we don't name?
> to exact reparation for things
> done long ago to us and to those who did not
>
> survive what was done to them   whom we ought to honor
> with grief   with fury   with action
> (*AWP*, 45)

This poem rings with militant conviction that echoes the determination of the first American pioneers who dedicated themselves to the community of saints, but the emphasis is on reparation instead of salvation, on survival instead of eternal life, on grief instead of guilt, on fury instead of fear, on action instead of introspection.

Although there is a dramatic contrast in the content of the feminist and Puritan vision, it is instructive to understand that there are striking parallels in form and that these shared patterns are an important part of American culture. For example, in defining the members of the community of women, Rich uses many of the formal and rhetorical devices of other separatist groups in the American past. Just as the Puritans invoked the examples of the visible saints as models of virtue, so Rich lists the names of the great suffragettes whose lives were dedicated to female emancipation:

> Matilda Joslyn Gage; Harriet Tubman;
> Ida B. Wells-Barnett; Maria Mitchell;
> Anna Howard Shaw; Sojourner Truth;
> Elizabeth Cady Stanton; Harriet Hosmer;
> Clara Burton; Harriet Beecher Stowe;
> Ida Husted Harper; Ernestine Rose
> ("Culture and Anarchy," *AWP*, 13)

Sustained by the belief that God's elect were destined to reform the New World, Puritans such as John Winthop, Edward Johnson, and Samuel Sewall called on the saints to bring light to the primeval forest of the New England colonies. Similarly, Rich urges feminists to dedicate themselves to "the transformation of society and of our relation to all life."[20] Elaborating her vision, Rich observes:

I simply believe that human society is capable of meeting the fundamental needs of all human beings, that we can give them a minimum standard of living; we can give them an education, we can create an environment which is more healthy to live in, and we can give people free medical care. We can provide these things for everybody in the society. We're not doing it, and I don't think there is any male system that is going to do that.[21]

In contrast to the Puritans' concern with the quality of life after death, feminists like Rich are committed to improving existence on Earth. In her view, male religious and social systems have had a negative effect on our civilization by emphasizing the importance of eternal life, power, and control. Urging that the city upon a hill open its gates to everyone regardless of sex, race, or class,

Adrienne Rich hopes that her vision of the community of women will be the beginning of a new chapter in American history.

NOTES

1. The influence of the Puritan errand into the wilderness has been the subject of many now classic studies of American culture in the past several decades. Some of the most influential of these studies are the following: Perry Miller, *Errand into the Wilderness* (Cambridge, Mass.: Harvard Univ. Press, 1956); Sacvan Bercovitch, *The Puritan Origins of the American Self* (New Haven: Yale Univ. Press, 1975), and *The American Jeremiad* (Madison: Univ. of Wisconsin Press, 1979); Larzer Ziff, *Puritanism in America: New Culture in a New World* (New York: Viking, 1973); Richard Slotkin, *Regeneration through Violence* (Middleton, Conn.: Wesleyan Univ. Press, 1973); Annette Kolodny, *The Lay of the Land* (Chapel Hill: Univ. of North Carolina Press, 1975); John Seelye, *Prophetic Waters: The River in Early American Life and Literature* (New York: Oxford Univ. Press, 1977).

2. For an excellent discussion of Puritan millennialism see Sacvan Bercovitch, "Rhetoric as Authority: Puritanism, the Bible, and the Myth of America," *Social Science Information*, 21, no. 1 (1982), 5-17.

3. Adrienne Rich, taped interview with the author.

4. Adrienne Rich, "The Tourist and the Town," *The Diamond Cutters* (New Haven: Yale Univ. Press, 1955), 4.

5. Adrienne Rich, *Snapshots of a Daughter-in-Law: Poems 1954-1962* (New York: Norton, 1963).

6. Adrienne Rich, *Necessities of Life: Poems 1962-1965* (New York: Norton, 1966).

7. Adrienne Rich, *Leaflets: Poems 1965-1968* (New York: Norton, 1969), 75.

8. Adrienne Rich, *The Will to Change: Poems 1968-1970* (New York: Norton, 1971.)

9. Adrienne Rich, *Diving into the Wreck: Poems 1971-1972* (New York: Norton, 1973).

10. Burton Pike, *The Image of the City in Modern Literature* (Princeton: Princeton Univ. Press., 1982).

11. Adrienne Rich, *Poems: Selected and New, 1950-1974* (New York: Norton, 1975).

12. Adrienne Rich, taped interview with author.

13. Adrienne Rich, *The Dream of a Common Language: Poems 1974-1977* (New York: Norton, 1978).

14. Adrienne Rich, *Of Woman Born* (New York: Norton, 1976).

15. Adrienne Rich, *A Wild Patience Has Taken Me This Far: Poems 1978-1981* (New York: Norton, 1981).

16. H. D., "The Master," has been reprinted in *Feminist Studies*, 7,

no. 3 (Fall 1981), 405-16. The lines from which Rich takes the image are "There is a purple flower / between her marble, her birch-tree white / thighs." For an analysis of this poem, see Rachel Blau DuPlessis and Susan Stanford Friedman, "'Woman Is Perfect': H. D.'s Debate with Freud," in the same volume of *Feminist Studies,* 415-30.

17. Adrienne Rich, taped interview with author. Also see Susan Griffin, *Pornography and Silence: Culture's Revenge against Nature* (New York: Harper and Row, 1982) for an elaborate feminist analysis of pornography.

18. Adrienne Rich, taped interview with author.

19. For a more extended discussion of this analysis, see Wendy Martin, *An American Triptych: Anne Bradstreet, Emily Dickinson, Adrienne Rich* (Chapel Hill: Univ. of North Carolina Press, 1984).

20. Adrienne Rich, "The Meaning of Our Love for Women," *Lies, Secrets, and Silences* (New York: Norton, 1979) 226.

21. Adrienne Rich, taped conversation with the author.

BLANCHE H. GELFANT

Sister to Faust: The City's "Hungry" Woman as Heroine

As Eugene Gant sets out for the "shining cities" of the North, in
Thomas Wolfe's novel *Of Time and the River*, his sister stands
beside him in Catawba's little railway station. Soon the paths of
brother and sister, once connected by family ties, will diverge,
never to reunite. The outbound train will take Eugene on a "road
to freedom," away from the "mournful" South to the North's
"golden cities"—ultimately to Boston, to Cambridge, and Harvard, where Eugene will discover the university's "enormous
library with its million books."[1] All of these books, which he tries
madly, obsessively, to read, prove incommensurate to his *hunger*,
a furious and relentless hunger—"literal, cruel and physical," he
calls it—and insatiable: a desire "to devour the earth and all the
things and people in it." Driven by this "ravening appetite,"
Eugene tries to "read everything that has ever been written about
human experience." He wants to "know it all, have all, be all."
Real life, no matter how crammed with experience, cannot satisfy
this epic craving; nor can realistic fiction, limited as it is to the
usual, contain the impossible fulfillment it demands. Eugene's
hyperbolic hunger, by ordinary standards egotistical if not simply mad, requires for its full expression literary forms that will
enlarge life: those of legend and myth. Not surprisingly, in the
first three books of *Of Time and the River*, Eugene's story is subtitled "The Legend of Man's Hunger in His Youth"; and Eugene
himself is called "Young Faustus." Later he is simply Faust.[2]
  After his father's death Young Faustus returns home briefly, to

hear of the hungers still unappeased in the sister he left behind. *"You're* the lucky one!" she told him at the railway station. *"You* got away! . . . to Boston—to Harvard." No one had imagined an equally "incredible escape" for her. No one had thought of buying her a ticket to "freedom" and including her in the city's "enchanted promise" by paying for her education. Unlovely and without charm, though enormously charged with life, she remains unenhanced by legend. If anything, legend diminishes her stature by emphasizing her deficiencies. For this frenzied Helen, a woman strikingly misnamed, lacks beauty. Her gaunt tormented face will inspire neither love nor poetry nor heroic strife: it will launch no ship.[3] Still, she has known supernal longings. Like her brother, she too has hungered for fame, has longed for adventure, voyages, cities, and the power of artistic expression. Recalling her "grand ambitions," Helen says wearily, "but that's all over now"—over for her, but not for Young Faustus, whose appetite she will try comically, lewdly, to keep aroused. Seeing her brother disconsolate, she promises him a huge dinner, enacting with sexually insinuating gestures a mock temptation scene meant to stir his ambition, lust, and gluttony. For in her frenetic monologue Helen shrewdly presents fame, women, and food as interchangeable male gratifications. Meanwhile she gratifies herself, appeasing her own hunger as she feeds her brother. By this act of displacement, she can merge martyrdom with seduction and sustenance. Ludicrous as she is, she pursues a purposeful strategy, comic and convoluted but effective in dramatizing herself as the eternal woman. In a typically feminine way she gives and demands love by offering a man *southern fried chicken, mashed potatoes, string beans, stewed corn, asparagus, steak, sliced tomatoes, deep dish apple pie and apple cobbler topped with cheese.*

Remarkable as she is as a literary character—with her tics and grimaces, her frenetic outbursts, her martyrdom—as a *woman,* Helen Gant represents a reality one wishes to repudiate. For we suspect that her persistent sacrifices to her family, always reviewed with resentment, disguise a debilitating fear of independence. Somehow she manages to tighten every constraint imposed upon her by her circumstances, her time, place, and sex; and yet she expresses, again and again, her passionate desire to be free. Crying for "peace and privacy," to be let *"alone* for five minutes," she abhors solitude and fears separation; unlike Eugene, she would never leave home because she has woven her own sense of identity about the members of the family she says she wants to escape. Perversely but to a purpose, she makes them dependent upon her, in this way avoiding a potentially dangerous pursuit of her own desires. Satisfying her hunger for life vicariously, she urges her brother to flight while she remains at home, constrained by a familiar domestic routine that precludes difficult choices. Her last words emphasize Eugene's freedom: "Now, it's up to you," she says. "Well, you do exactly as you please!" Doing as one pleases, she implies, is the man's prerogative. While Faustus wanders through the world, his sister must stay at home and cook.

I choose Helen Gant as a point of departure because I consider her a character we should know and, as Eugene did, leave behind. I want to argue that Faust has other sisters in American fiction radically different from Helen, women who share her hunger and her tremendous energy but transcend her fear. These women will dare to leave home, following a lonely and frightening "road to freedom" that leads them, as it did Eugene, to the library—"the citadel of the self," as one heroine called it. Once within this citadel, each woman reiterates the same belief: that her real self, repressed by life, will somehow be released by literature. Like the enchanted figure of fairytale, she keeps wishing for this release, feeling herself constrained by forces she cannot always name though she recognizes their effects in her unhappiness, her sense of inauthenticity, her stultification. Attracted to martyrdom and self-mockery, this heroine refuses the consolation they offer Helen; she lacks Helen's sense of farce but also her grotesqueness. She values maturity, but believes in the magic children love—a transforming magic that can vitalize sleeping beauty and turn her into a woman. Unlike the child, however, she refuses a fantasy of helplessness; she dismisses the prince from her dreams—and her life. She sets out alone to find for herself, within herself, the power of transformation. Like Faust, she believes that books will give her possession of power, and so she reads—compulsively, looking for ways to change her life. Seeing herself as an inchoate woman, or if formed, then somehow deformed, she wants to become a fully realized "person," someone she defines vaguely but succinctly as free.

She is an urban character. For reasons I shall discuss, the city evokes her desire for freedom and by its disorder—all the confusions of urban life usually considered devastating—promises her

[267]

fulfillment. A recurrent figure in fiction written by women about women, she appears also in other novels, classic and contemporary, where her features may be disguised or distorted or else so familiar that we seldom re-view their expressions. Because the underlying pattern of her life seems invariable, her impulse, purpose, and course of action the same, I consider her a generic heroine—one not yet subsumed by our usual stereotypes (or archetypes). As contemporary readers we should not overlook her presence, for she suggests to us the possibility of a woman's dignified survival, and in so doing, she points to a way out of the impasse reached by oppressed heroines who become self-starving, suicidal, or mad—heroines currently receiving much critical attention.[4] I call this generic figure a sister to Faust because she is embraced by the heroic aspects of his legend—his hunger for knowledge and autonomy (rather than his damnation)[5]— more closely than by any other, including those centered upon women. Like Athene, she represents intellect, but unlike the goddess, she is not born easily and full-grown. On the contrary, she labors long to become herself, undergoing a slow arduous birth. Though sometimes blamed for the troubles of the world she inhabits, she is not Pandora, a woman impelled idly by curiosity.[6] Like Eve, she reaches toward the tree of knowledge (and her metaphor also entails orality, eating), but her city, with its artifactuality and disorder, seems the very antithesis to Eve's garden. Nor is she simply a female version of Faust, for as a woman, she has modulated desire in ways inconceivable to him; and yet the family tie is as undeniable as that between Eugene and Helen Gant. Essentially, she is a sister—to the legendary brother whose hunger she shares, and to all the women in the cities of America whose drive for knowledge and freedom she personifies.

If she seems naive in her belief that literature can transform life, the books the heroine reads teach her sophistication, one of two lessons: that literature and life reveal the same secrets, literature inducting the reader into life's mysteries; or else that they are separate and irreconcilable, the truths of literature being in reality the fictions of life. As I shall point out, doubts may await the heroine (and the critic) at the end of her road to freedom, but she sets out—as perhaps all serious readers do—confident in the powers of literature. Standing in New York's great Public Library, one contemporary protagonist, a woman in her thirties, speaks for many others when she says: "If I were systematically to attack these volumes, one by one, reading from beginning to end, I could solve my life."[7] Her language clearly tells us that has found her life problematic, in need of *solving*, and that by *attacking* books, she has chosen to move to a solution actively, even aggressively. In another contemporary novel, an older woman continues to read on her deathbed as she has been reading all her mature life, methodically, compulsively, searching through a set of encyclopedia, book by book, for "labels" that would name "the point of life, and of having lived."[8] As still another modern heroine feels herself losing the point, she gives up reading great books, finding them "unbearable" because they made her "think . . . and . . . to think involves thinking about her own life."[9] Later, when she can face thinking, she resumes her education in Harvard's library, where we have already seen its million books linked to man's illimitable hunger.

I am proposing that in American novels women's hunger reveals itself in unexpected places and in unexpected ways. We are accustomed to seeing fictional heroines in a bedroom, hungering for love, but that they appear regularly in the library wanting knowledge we have conveniently overlooked. Reasons for "neglect," as we are realizing, are socially rooted, though they may manifest (or masquerade) themselves as purely literary matters pertaining to the canon. Since the canon excludes popular novels, and since many popular novels are written by women for women, the heroines who emerge in them, serious and instructive as they may be, fail to engage our critical attention. But in neglecting them, I believe we neglect also significant, perhaps crucial, aspects of women characters who appear in important contemporary novels (like *The Crying of Lot 49*) or in American classics (like *Sister Carrie*). For, the paradigmatic heroine of popular fiction outlines clearly a literary pattern that can help us understand complex and enigmatic characters whose meanings, however much they have been explicated, remain inexhaustible. Theodore Dreiser's Sister Carrie is a mystery still. She hungers, as we know, but not for a man's love, and not for anything we can clearly define. She dreams and desires, epitomizing finally an indeterminate and ineffable desire which can never be fulfilled. In the novel's two brilliant restaurant scenes, Carrie consumes food that increases her hunger, for as she eats she is reading a text whose theme is insatiability. Carrie learns to want "more" as she becomes a reader of the urban scene before her, glittering and yet ominous, pulsating with an energy to which she can respond only by wanting. Changing her name, her walk, her clothes, her expectations, she wants, like every hungry heroine, to be transformed. For her (as later for Oedipa Maas in *The Crying of Lot 49*), the city itself is a vast text, a coded system full of signs and significations whose meanings, once deciphered, would, she believes, change her life. So Carrie studies—she is always studying: the streets, the crowds, other women; the lines of a play; and finally, when last seen, a great book, Balzac's *Le Père Goriot*. How can we explain the novel's incongruous conclusion: that it ends with unintellectual Carrie, known not for her brains, nor even for her beauty, but for her expression of hunger, sitting alone, ruminating about life, and reading? I wish to suggest that more heroines read than we realize, to more serious purposes than we have noted, and more texts, real and symbolic, than we have analyzed.

While critics may have overlooked the hungry heroine, other characters find her provocative: she arouses them to sympathy or else to anger, and sometimes to violence. All see her potential for subversiveness. She refuses to stay where she "belongs," and by leaving home and abandoning men, she destabilizes the family. Though she will claim her acts are private, concerning only changes in her self, others perceive them as assaults upon society; and when she acts publicly, engaging in the radical politics of the sixties, for instance—as we see her doing in the *The Women's Room*—she may be killed, co-opted, ostracized, or driven to doubt her sanity. Indeed, if the hungry heroine could learn all she hungers to know—the secret of identity (pursued by great heroes like Oedipus Rex)—then she would achieve the ultimate "revelation" that such an oddly and aptly named heroine as Oedipa Maas seeks in Thomas Pynchon's *The Crying of Lot 49*. [10] To understand the end of life, its ultimate meaning, would make the generic heroine truly Faustian in her knowledge—and (unlike Faust) truly free. It would also transform a secular quest, with revolutionary implications for society, into a religious pilgrimage. In *The Crying of Lot 49*, a parodic novel with serious religious overtones, Oedipa journeys to a mysterious and ominous city that she tries to read in much the same way that Carrie reads Chicago: by deciphering meanings encoded in its surface streets and its labyrinthine underground. She wants to become so keenly "sensitized" that she will possess the "Word"; and though she seeks it in copies of a parodied Jacobean play, a corruptible text she discovers, and one that may be variant, illegible, or destroyed, she believes, like the paradigmatic hungry heroine, that when she reads the final Word she will become the executrix of her own will—an autonomous person. As we know, Oedipa ends in a locked room where she may find revelation or death. There she waits.

I am suggesting that complex and indeterminate novels about women in a city may be illuminated by the relatively simple explicit works in which I trace the configurations of the generic character I have been calling a "hungry heroine." The name is suggested to me by a book of stories I hope to see more widely read: Anzia Yezierska's tales of immigrant women in New York entitled *Hungry Hearts*. "I'm crazy to learn," Yezierska's nameless heroine cries in the final story: "I need school more than a starving man needs bread."[11] She is, in fact, a starving woman working for starvation wages in a clattering sweatshop she describes as "hell." Fantasies of escape transport her to "heaven"—"to the schools of America." Hungry heroines share this aberrant vision of heaven as a place replete with books. In *The Promised Land*, another immigrant, Mary Antin, finds libraries a "paradise" where "one could read and read, and learn and learn."[12] Even as a girl in Russia, she recalls, "I was so hungry for books that I went at them greedily." America intensifies this craving: here she falls upon books "as a glutton pounces on his meat after a period of enforced starvation." In the public library of Williamsburg, little Francie Nolan of *A Tree Grows in Brooklyn* follows an orderly plan to read "all the books in the world."[13] To her the shabby old library is a "beautiful" church: its books, sacred objects; its smells redolent of "burning incense at high mass." If Francie shows more control than Mary Antin, who pounces on her prey, she is no less hungry for "books . . . books . . . books" (original ellipses). On the fire escape where she sits and reads, she imagines herself high in a tree called in Brooklyn the "Tree of Heaven." There she could spend eternity with her bowl of candy and her books.

Such young heroines read with an avid hopefulness shared by older women, especially middle-class women who want to escape a daily boredom often indistinguishable from despair. Asked by her English professor to describe "an important experience" in her life, Ella Price, a suburban housewife, writes in *Ella Price's Journal:* "Nothing important has ever happened to me."[14] She has married the football player who was her high-school sweetheart, kept house in the suburbs of San Francisco, and brought up a pretty daughter. Now, at the age of thirty-five, she attends Bay Shore Junior Colleges, advised by her doctor to find "new interests" after she has suffered a desolating attack of panic because she "couldn't locate myself." She plods through novels with "female protagonists" who may help her find a self hidden behind the Barbie Doll face that conceals her real features. Typically, she goes to the library with a reading list in hand, directed there by her professor. Methodically, she searches through book after book for a way to release "something in me": the woman who feels. Unlike the fictional heroines she encounters, passionate women who "go after what they want," she has always hidden her feelings. Now books imagine for her a release of emotions she could not have imagined expressing herself. As she reads, a door begins to open:

the door of a closet where I'd hidden a lot of things that didn't seem to fit into my life, a closet stuffed so full that once I'd opened the door just a crack, I couldn't push it closed again, and things started tumbling out. . . .

I guess I'm afraid that if I let that stuff out it'll make a mess of my nice, neat little house. But it's too late now.   (63)

Ella Price discovers "freedom" only because no one, she thinks (mistakenly), has further plans for her. Since the plans for her "first lifetime," designed by "other people, or outside forces," have been fulfilled by marriage and motherhood, she can create a "second" life by releasing the "person" repressed until now. The books she reads in slow succession warn her against the woman she might become: someone invisible like Catherine Sloper in *Washington Square;* or trapped into a dull routine like Carol Kennicot in *Main Street;* or swept to passion and suicide like Emma in *Madame Bovary* and Anna in *Anna Karenina;* or independent but powerless like Anna of *The Golden Notebook;* or ambivalent like Candida. Each fictional heroine enacts a part of the entire process of transformation she is undergoing, teaching her to avoid helplessness, futile rebellion, and spurious freedom, and to develop strength though she is loved for her weakness by a hus-

band who says, "Lean on me, hon, I'll take care of you." Words
which have always seduced her as expressions of love now seem
to urge her into permanent helplessness. She sees her marriage
as a contract in which she agrees to be "sick and neurotic" to
please her husband. In *Androcles and the Lion,* she admires
Lavinia's "guts," and in *Antigone,* the transcendence of a woman
who refuses to be "trapped in sex." Such examples lead Ella
finally to abort the new life growing within her—the baby she
feels manipulated into conceiving—in order to give birth to her
self. Like all hungry heroines she wants to become a person born
of her own desires and needs, her own feelings: that is what she
means by autonomy. She ends with a simple assertion: *I feel.*
Then she stops, without a final period, so that her journey can
continue even though her journal has come to an end.

As an exemplary text, *Ella Price's Journal* shows clearly how the
hungry heroine can transform herself by transforming literature
into life. But while Ella demands of art its highest function, that of
shaping life, she reduces it to didacticism by turning each novel
she reads into a textbook. Meanwhile the novel in which she
appears, the novel she creates as she writes her journal, becomes
a series of explicit lessons. In a textbook, clarity is a virtue; and in
her journal, Ella pursues this virtue necessarily as she tries to
understand and revamp her self. But her personal needs conflict
with those of the work of art, which requires the complexities and
tensions that make the novels she reads "great." In comparison
with great novels—a comparison forced upon the reader by its
references—*Ella Price's Journal* lacks *literary* distinction: its didacticism seems banal, its colloquial language flat, and its characters
one-dimensional, figures in an allegory that Ella describes as her
life. Moreover—if more can be said in criticism without devastating a novel I consider interesting and instructive—Ella remains a
naive reader, unquestioning because she desperately needs the
answers she finds. Perhaps one should not expect from her the
sophistication (and cynicism) of a Ph.D. candidate studying literature at Harvard, from someone like Mira in *The Women's Room.*
Mira suspects that the great books she studies contain "lies"
because they stop short of the "real endings" life concocts.
"Suppose Antigone had lived," Mira thinks, jumping to a startling possibility unimaginable to Ella: "An Antigone who goes on
being Antigone year after year would be not only ludicrous but a
bore." Ella desperately needs Antigone to be as she has defined

her: "the hero in a story about loyalty and integrity and courage and freedom"; and if this definition is unexamined and simplified, still it motivates readers to act courageously. Perhaps courage will prove ineffectual in a society that punishes those who try to change it, but to submit to such pessimism at the beginning of the heroine's journey—as Mira submits at the end—means impassivity, hopelessness, and death. In *Ella Price's Journal*, as in other novels, the heroine not only avoids this fate: she achieves a positive goal. She becomes articulate. She expresses what she feels and she feels herself becoming an integrated whole person. For a woman who could not "locate" herself, this is not a negligible accomplishment.

I have already mentioned a recurrent character in whom the heroine sees her ideal person mirrored: the professor who complicates her life with longings for love. In Yezierska's story "Wings," when Shenah Pessah is with a young professor, she becomes ambiguously aroused, imagining her "person" in his as both an erotic and intellectual fulfillment. *Ella Price's Journal* describes going to bed with the professor as an obligatory initiation rite for a woman reentering college. But physical union, passionate (or disappointing) as it may be, involves a symbolic identification which once made allows the heroine to go on her way alone. Jane discards five farewell notes in *The Odd Woman* and could have written more, simply to tell her professor, "I decided to leave." Sometimes he is the one to leave, for once he initiates the heroine to the ritual of reading, arousing her desire for books—and life—he has fulfilled his function and can disappear. He may leave the heroine mystified, wanting more, as Carrie wants more from Ames. He may show her the difficulty (or impossibility) of ever reading correctly, as does Professor Emory Bortz, that strange unpredictable character who gives Oedipa an illegible text: "'I can't read this,' Oedipa said. 'Try,' said Bortz." The heroine's male mentor need not, of course, be an actual professor. As in *A Tree Grows in Brooklyn*, he may be a more advanced student than the heroine, or else a more sophisticated, intellectual interlocutor, someone who can teach even by his negative example. In *Brown Girl, Brownstones*, Clive says prophetically to eighteen-year-old Selina: "Look, how would you like to take lessons from me—so that when you're my age [twenty-nine] you won't be like me."[15] And she won't, for already she is "grabbing [at] life" as she gazes beyond his body to the books stacked on his

[274]

kitchen shelf. Like Francie in another part of Brooklyn, Selina spends her girlhood summers in the public library and dreams of going away to college.

Such dreams isolate the hungry heroine who pays a high "price" for the city's free education. As another of Yezierska's heroines says in the novel *Bread Givers:* "Knowledge was what I wanted more than anything in the world. . . . And now I had to pay the price. So this is what it cost. . . . No father. No lover. No family. No friend. . . . I must go on—alone."[16] Because she defies her father and her sister's husband, parasitical men who have ruined her sisters, Sara Smolensky becomes an outcast; but as she learns "to love being alone," she converts her isolation into freedom. Later she chooses solitude over marriage, refusing a wealthy lover who excites her with his passion while he remains unmoved by hers: "You're only books, books, books," he shouts, having already told her that "only dumbheads fool [with] . . . education and books and all that sort of nonsense." Like James Joyce's fabulous artist as a young man, the young heroine must fly by all the nets that would confine her: duty to parents, sexual passion, marriage. In some ways her flight is more perilous than his, since in giving up love, she loses her timeless identity as a woman, suffering a kind of death so that she can live her new life. Eventually, if she is lucky, a man may come along and love the self-created "person" she has become. Most novels end before he can appear.

In her total isolation, as she starves and freezes in her rented room, someone does visit Sara, coming as if by magic to bring her warmth and food—a feather quilt and pickled herring—and love: "selfless, dark, pleading love." Sara's mother, a poor oppressed immigrant woman, who represents above all the person Sara wants *not* to be, travels through the cold night, from New Jersey to East Side New York, to help her daughter. Lurking in the background of most heroines is a helping mother, usually a poor illiterate woman who struggles and schemes for the daughter whose hunger she herself may arouse. In the novel, mothers transcend the divisive differences in American life. Whether they are Chinese, black, or white, living in San Francisco, Harlem, or Brooklyn, working in laundries or factories, all share the dream of a better life for their daughters. In Louise Meriwether's novel of Harlem, *Daddy Was a Number Runner,* the mother says:

"You don't have to do no domestic work for nobody, Francie." We was in the kitchen fixing dinner. "You don't be no fool, you hear? You finish school and go on to college. Long as I live you don't have to scrub no white folks' floors or wash their filthy windows. What they think I'm spending my life on my knees for? So you can follow in my footsteps? You finish school and go on to college. Somebody in this family got to finish school. You hear what I say?"

"Yes, Mother, I hear."[17]

This little Francie growing up in Harlem might have been named after the heroine of *A Tree Grows in Brooklyn*, a girl who inherits the legacy of hunger from her illiterate Irish grandmother. When Francie Nolan was born, Grandmother Rommely had told her daughter Katie, a poor ignorant janitress, the "secret" of how to make "a different world" for her child:

The secret lies in the reading and the writing. . . . Every day you must read one page from some good book to your child. Every day . . . until the child learns to read. Then *she* must read every day. I know this is the secret.   (74)

Francie's "library" originates with Aunt Sissy's christening present, a twenty-five-cent "worn-out copy of Shakespeare" and a "swiped" Gideon Bible. Years later as Katie Nolan tries to save her children from the "filth and dirt" of Williamsburg streets, she rediscovers her mother's secret. Suddenly, she sees that the difference between vulgarity and fineness comes not from money, as she might have thought, but from educaton: "It was education that made the difference. . . . That's what Mary Rommely, her mother, had been telling her all those years. Only her mother did not have the one clear word: education!" (185).

Desire for an education may force the heroine into open conflict with her mother whose strength she finds inspiring but overwhelming. If she is to become her own self, she must escape a bindingly intimate relationship. In *Brown Girl, Brownstones,* Selina Boyce affirms her kinship with her mother as she leaves home: "You see I'm truly your child. Remember how you used to talk about how you left home . . . as a girl of eighteen and was your own woman? I used to love hearing that. And that is what I want. I want it!" Thousands of miles away from Brooklyn, in San Francisco's Chinatown, another daughter defies the mother she emulates:

"I'm smart, and I can win scholarships. I can get into colleges. . . . I know how to get A's. . . . I could be a scientist or a mathematician if I want. I can make a living and take care of myself. . . . I'm not going to be a slave or a wife. . . . I'm going to get scholarships, and I'm going away."[18]

To this ringing pronunciamento, with its traditionally male motif of "going away," the mother replies that she already "knows about college": "What makes you think you're the first one to think about college? . . . I went to medical school. . . . I don't see why you can't be a doctor like me." But though the heroine may be like someone else, and may consciously seek someone else to show her who she is, she must establish her difference from the women whose values she assumes. The mother who in China had been Doctor Brave Orchid, and honored "Lady Scholar," now sorts dirty clothes in a Chinatown laundry, but she bequeaths to her American-born daughter timeless stories that celebrate women's courage, intelligence, and will. These qualities inspire the heroine to imitate and also defy her mother and, by leaving her, to answer the question she had once asked: "Which would you rather be? A ghost who is constantly wanting to be fed? Or Nothing?" Ghost or modern woman warrior or both, the heroine knows she will never be nothing, for she has learned from her mother that work gives a woman an identity: "Don't worry about me starving [she says]. I won't starve. I know how to work." Like Brave Orchid, who left China to create a new life in a new land, the Dragon daughter of a Dragon mother must "go away."

Inevitably, the heroines of immigrant background evoke the perennial legend of America as a Golden Land. They see a new Canaan where "learning flows free like milk and honey." With this glowing if clichéd hyperbole, Shenah Pessah presents herself as a new Columbus in a story called, appropriately, "How I Discovered America."[19] Like Columbus, Shenah explores an unknown territory, a new world opening upon "visions upon visions" of freedom: "I saw before me free schools, free libraries, where I could learn and learn and keep on learning." Shenah sees these glorious possibilities in Manhattan's Lower East Side, a neighborhood scarred with poverty, struggle, violence, and waste. In the slums of great cities successive waves of immigrants have always renewed the dream of America. Even when the heroine is native-born, she emanates from an immigrant tradition, being spiritually and filially related to women like Brave Orchid, who braved the Pacific to reach San Francisco, and Irish Grandmother Rommely, who crossed the Atlantic to settle in Brooklyn.

In Brooklyn, Francie Nolan goes to the neighborhood library every day for years, and day after day the librarian fails to recognize her. To this indifferent woman, Francie is faceless and nameless, no one in particular. Before she leaves for college, Francie deliberately forces the librarian to look at her, disrupting an established impersonal routine by demanding recognition: "'I've been coming here since I was a little girl,' said Francie, 'and you never looked at me till now.'" The fretful librarian complains that "there are so many children," their sheer number evokes indifference, a buffering mask that protects city people. Urban density, the incessant pressure which shapes the social forms of city life, envelops Francie in anonymity. At once dangerous and liberating, anonymity annihilates her identity, but also it allows her to choose her own name. Like the novel's symbolic tree, which grows out of arid soil, Francie emerges from the dense crowd of anonymous city faces to insist upon recognition of her presence; and every aspect of city life commonly considered invidious seems to strengthen her desire that she be seen as her self. Desire as expressed in the physiological metaphor of hunger becomes elemental, synonymous with life itself. The hungry heroine believes that she can live passionately, even in the city's slums and skulking back streets; and that she will live as a person who is free. Freedom seems to her inherent in a fluid if disorganized urban society, one that by its disorder and indifference has released her from the roles assigned to women by history and myth. Inevitably, the city severs a traditional relationship between nature and women; the heroine no longer need act as earth-mother, the woman who, like Willa Cather's famous Ántonia,[20] satisfies herself by nurturing others. In a city throbbing with dreams and desires, the heroine learns to identify her own needs; and living among strangers, she has privacy in which to cultivate personal desires usually condemned by family and friends as "selfishness." Anonymity releases her from the traditional constraints of small-town life, from constant surveillance, gossip, and public censure, all outlined in *Main Street*, a novel that helped educate Ella Price. Enjoying physical and social

[278]

space in the city, the heroine moves about freely and experiences movement as freedom. For her, the territory ahead—the essence of freedom in male myths of the West—lies around the corner, a few streets away, in another neighborhood where nobody knows her and where she alone will say who she is. Like Sara Smolensky, she needs only enough courage to move a few blocks away. She may never escape the traps and confinement inherent in life itself, but she can escape a tyrannical father or a debilitating husband and their imprisoning definitions. Joe Price has defined a wife as a neurotic and helpless woman, and that is what he wants; and Mr. Smolensky has defined a daughter as submissive and self-effacing, a slave. The hungry heroine can reclaim herself from these definitions by renting a room of her own. Even if she wants to remain at home, home itself has become temporary in the city, family ties tenuous, traditions of family loyalty demolished as easily and irrevocably as the tenement destroyed overnight to make way for a new building. Excitement of the new, of a new self and a new life, can modulate the sense of loss and transform it into liberation. The hungry woman in the city shares with the immigrant a hope that displacement means opportunity.

Social indifference, considered the bane of city life, also liberates the heroine from constraints, particularly those that seem to her, perhaps mistakenly, inseparable from love. She wants a love that leaves her free and intact, a vision she may have learned from men. In the novels she has read, the hero flees from a devouring woman, an archetypal figure who projects his fear of engulfment. Similarly, the heroine runs from love that disguises possessive desire. She prefers solitude to loss of self, and in the city she can be alone without seeming eccentric, deficient, or a failure. Solitude does not mean isolation, a fate that has driven rural characters to desperation or madness. The heroine compares and differentiates herself from others in the city, strangers and friends, learning from them who she is. Asserting her own identity, choosing her own name, she resists the forces of urban anonymity and indifference, turning them into a test of her own will. Devastating as the city can be for any individual—its violence and destructiveness need no documentation—its illimitable possibilities excite passion.[21] The hungry heroine feels passionately alive, even to pain. Hunger of course is painful, but also elemental and driving. Unlike heroines who deny themselves as a way of denying their society, suffering silent women, the hungry heroine does not choose pain; she rejects masochism and madness as foils in a sexual power-play; she would never starve herself like the anorexic heroine, or make her own inanition and death a form of passive resistance. She starves because she is poor, but like Sara Smolensky, she will spend her last pennies for bread so that she can sustain herself and survive. She chooses action over passivity, pursuing knowledge as a direct access to power.

What knowledge can achieve for a woman may remain uncertain in the novel, for it ends often with the heroine's declaration of independence rather than with her tangible accomplishments. The Woman Warrior announces her plan to go as far away as China, where she hopes to discover her roots and the truth about the stories by which her mother has shaped her life. When she returns home, a self-created person, she will establish a new life so far only vaguely defined. In an earlier memoir of a Chinese-American girl growing up in San Francisco—Jade Snow Wong's (now highly criticized) *Fifth Chinese Daughter*²²—a less vehement but no less hungry heroine outlines more specific plans for a new life: having been transformed from an obedient Chinese daughter into an American woman, Jade Snow opens a shop which will support her while she writes. San Francisco is essential to her plans, as are all cities to the heroine seeking independence, for there, as the Woman Warrior said, "she can work." Sara Smolensky returns to the East Side to earn her living as a school teacher: "Home! Back to New York! [she cries,] Sara Smolensky, from Hester Street, changed into a person!" Like Cinderella, Sara celebrates her transformation with new clothes, a new home, and a new union—a "honeymoon with myself." Eventually, she does find a prince, in fact the principal of her school, who recognizes the affinity for which every hungry heroine longs—that she and a learned man "are of one blood." Having been recognized as a sister, she can become a wife.

While such transformations evoke a happy ending, they also define the limits of the hungry woman's imagination and of the social world in which it has been shaped. Young or old, immigrant or native-born, each woman suffers, struggles, and works, only to conform finally to a stereotype. As a school teacher, Sara becomes a surrogate mother: "My job was to teach—to feed hungry children." Guilt taints her happiness. Seeing the huddled peddlers on Hester Street, the impoverished anonymous crowd from which she has escaped, she finds happiness "hard to enjoy": "I felt like one sitting down to a meal while all the people around him were howling hungry." Altruism did not bother Faust, or Eugene Gant, that vortex of egotism; they feast while others hunger, and their unappeasable appetites have inspired poetry. In contrast, women who appease their hunger without guilt inspire childlike fantasies: they are allowed "the happy endings" they seek by the fairytale matrix of their story. As symbolic accounts of female development, fairytales describe the emergence of the self as a process of transformation:[23] Cinderella changes into a princess, needless to say, and the ugly duckling into a swan. An ugly duckling, the hungry heroine escapes tyrannical demands for physical beauty which must defeat a woman as her beauty fades. In Edith Wharton's novel *The House of Mirth*, Lily Bart sees her doom etched in the incipient lines of her face; but the heroine who values her intellect more than her complexion and her person more than her personality can survive without beauty. Reversing usual standards of judgment for women, she respects brains: "When I get to college," the modern Woman Warrior shouts, "it won't matter if I'm not charming. And it doesn't matter if a person is ugly; she can still do schoolwork." Doing schoolwork, as we have noted, may be a circuitous path back to motherhood. We have yet to see a portrait of the satisfied hungry woman who transcends either social stereotypes or fairytale transformations. Perhaps the most we can expect now is the portrait of a woman in process, her consciousness still emerging, her self in a state of becoming as she seeks the power to *be*. We have accepted inchoateness in our portraits of the developing male. *Of Time and the River* ends with Eugene still reaching toward his identity as an artist, and Joyce's great novel tells us who Stephen Dedalus aspires to be but does not show us unironically who he has become.

We know who Edith Wharton and Willa Cather became, to choose two of our most celebrated women writers, both "omnivorous" readers, the hungry heroines of real life. Writing of her emergence as an artist in *A Backward Glance*, Wharton recalls on page after page the endless number of books she "devoured."[24] When she was a child, "home" and "New York" were synonymous to her with "the kingdom of my father's library." Critics can of course trace achievement to neurotic sources, but I find the persistent imputations cast upon the origins of Wharton's art ungenerous and peculiar. That she wrote out of intense personal needs has become somehow a special criticism of her work—a criticism implicit in Edmund Wilson's influential essay called (ironically, I find) "Justice to Edith Wharton."[25] A recent biography uses Erik Erikson's theories of human development (now held suspect by many feminist critics) to interpret Wharton's "hunger," her driving creative force, as "a residue of infantile emotion."[26] If Wharton suffered from "the undispelled, unmitigated rage of the hungry and unsatisfied infant," so do we all. That is why we all recognize and respond to hunger as a metaphor for desire; and desire, Willa Cather insisted, is the elemental source of art. Like Edith Wharton, Cather read "omnivorously," hungrily, her biographer tells us.[27] Whatever her emotional problems, difficult to document because many of her personal papers have been destroyed, no psychobiography can make us doubt her luminous art, an achievement that makes us expect from American woman writers the great novels they have still to create.

I would like to end by demanding the novel I expect and want, one whose style and form are commensurate to the Faustian theme of a woman's healthy hunger, her desire for personal freedom. But great novels are not written because of a reader's demand, and great novelists, though nurtured by social and literary traditions, are not willed into being by an audience. Obviously, there has always been an audience responsive to heroes and heroines who express inordinate desire, aspiring like Faust to an ultimate freedom for which we contemporaries have only such vague sociological terms as *personal autonomy.* [28] The magnificent Fausts created by Goethe and Marlowe failed finally to define freedom any more clearly or to achieve it; and their inordinate desire damned them to hell. Nevertheless, they inspired the genius of poetry. The realistic novel as a genre not only avoids the heights of poetic language, but also, inherently, prohibits the portrayal of an autonomous person. For since the realistic novel predicates a society for its protagonist, it must inevitably show individual freedom to be circumscribed. How can one be free, autonomous, and still part of a society? This is the issue that Freud resolved pessimistically by stressing our inevitable discontents with civilization. Novels can remove a character from society and show freedom in isolation. As we know, the imaginative appeal of Robinson Crusoe persists to our time; we still respond with interest and delight when Crusoe appears in American fiction in the guise of modern man. But an autonomous woman living alone in the city, independent emotionally as well as economically, tests our disposition as readers, for she threatens our sense of an established order as much as she satisfies our sense of daring. She challenges the realistic novelist who wants to dramatize autonomy as an actual state of being within the constraining social world we recognize as our own. Nevertheless, we can discern the pattern that ideally her life would follow, and though any single heroine may not trace this pattern in its entirety, even when she deviates from it, she reveals its heroic intention and design.[29] Her *desire* for personal freedom places her clearly within the context of urban literature, for desire has always been the great energizing theme of the American city novel since the startling appearance in 1900 of Dreiser's *Sister Carrie*. For a woman, a writer or heroine, to express impelling desire (other than a desire for love) requires courage, for she must defy literary and social conventions. I commend the daring she shows when she avows sheer voracious hunger for knowledge, for power, for possession of her self. If this daring has not yet found its full scope, we can be encouraged by the signs we see. Recently, desire has begun to inspire American women novelists as a theme of their own. The beginnings may still be tentative, ending in abortion—or with abortion, as does *Ella Price's Journal*. Novels describing the hungry heroine may still be inchoate because they express an inchoate but emerging consciousness, establishing a precedent for heroines who are not passive, or self-starving, suicidal, or mad: rather, vigorously and healthily hungry. If some will say infantilely hungry, I look forward to growth and development and maturity. Then we might have a heroine who inspires the poetry commensurate to her Faustian aspirations. Meanwhile, with Oedipa Maas, one of my favorite heroines, I wait.

NOTES

1. Thomas Wolfe, *Of Time and the River* (New York: Scribner's, 1935), 89. Once in the library, Eugene read "insanely, by the hundreds, the thousands, the ten thousands . . . a ravening appetite in him demanded

that he read everything. . . . He pictured himself as tearing the entrails from a book as from a fowl" (91).

2. Eugene is also Orestes, Telemachus, Jason, Antaeus, Kronos— no dearth of myths for his aggrandizement.

3. In the last book of the novel, called "Faustus and Helen," Eugene is "impaled upon the knife of love" (911) as he meets the beautiful Helen of myth and male desire.

4. For a discussion of madwomen and anorexics as figures of rebellion, see Sandra M. Gilbert and Susan Gubar, *The Madwoman in the Attic* (New Haven: Yale Univ. Press, 1979). Also in an essay-review in the Fall 1979 edition (Number 8) of *University Publishing*, Professor Gilbert pursues the symbolic meaning of "anorexic renunciation" ("Hunger Pains," 1 and 11-12). Dr. Hilde Brucke in *The Golden Cage: The Enigma of Anorexia Nervosa* (Cambridge, Mass.: Harvard Univ. Press, 1978) describes anorexics as young people engaged in a "blind search for a sense of identity and selfhood": "they would rather starve than continue a life of accommodation" (x).

In her study of "female madness" in contemporary American fiction, Mary Allen declares herself dismayed, enraged, and frustrated at the depiction of women in the novels she discusses. *The Necessary Blankness: Women in Major American Fiction of the Sixties* (Chicago: Univ. of Illinois Press, 1976), 13. See particularly the chapter on Sylvia Plath's *The Bell Jar* in which Allen views the heroine's madness and attempted suicide as her "defiance." Describing Plath's heroine, Patricia Meyer Spacks has said: "In her view, psychosis is virtually a female necessity, leaving only a choice of madness" (*The Female Imagination* [New York: Knopf, 1975], 147).

A tradition of happy submission to woman's predetermined role also mitigates against the emergence of a hungry heroine. See Barbara Welter, "The Cult of True Womanhood," *American Quarterly* (1966) 18: 151-74.

We should note that from Puritan times on, women were warned of the dangerous effects of education; they could be driven mad not through repression but through too much learning. See Ann Stanford's essay "Images of Women in Early American Literature" in *What Manner of Woman: Essays on English and American Life and Literature* (New York: New York Univ. Press, 1977), ed. by Marlene Springer. The essay notes "the fate of Ann Hopkins" (recorded in John Winthrop's journal), who lost her wits by "giving herself wholly to reading and writing" (193). In an interesting early novel about college-educated women, the woman who earns a Ph.D. suffers a mental collapse: "I broke down, that's all. I can't stand anything now that takes thought" (172). A university professor pointed out earlier that there are "men and women—but women particularly . . . staggering under a mental load too heavy for them" (96). The novel's heroine has a bachelor's degree, a manageable load. See Elia W. Peattie, *The Precipice: A Novel* (Boston: Houghton Mifflin, 1914).

5. In her essay "The Female Faust," Ann Ronald discusses a damned heroine who sells herself to the "devil" for "love and security," giving up her *self*. See *Feminist Criticism: Essays on Theory, Prose, and*

The City's "Hungry" Woman as Heroine

Poetry, Cheryl L. Brown and Karen Olson, eds. (Metuchen, N.J.: Scarecrow Press, 1978), 212-21. As literary figures, the "female Faust" and the "sister to Faust" whom I describe are antithetical, each representing an aspect of the Faust myth, the former his damnation, the latter his aspirations and desire.

6. A recent "semantic" interpretation of Hesiod's account of Prometheus presents Pandora as a "gaster" or maw, "an insatiable belly devouring the *bios* or nourishment that men procure for themselves through their labour." As a "female belly," Pandora hungers for food and sex, thus representing voracity and lasciviousness, the "bitchiness" of women. See Jean-Pierre Vernant, *Myth and Society in Ancient Greece* (Atlantic Highlands, N.J.: Humanities Press, 1980), 178 ff.

Note a professor's fear of the woman "bitch" who devours books—and her professor-husband—as she studies for a Ph.D. Saul Bellow, *Herzog* (New York: Viking, 1964).

7. Gail Godwin, *The Odd Woman* (New York: Knopf, 1974).

8. Lisa Alther, *Kinflicks* (New York: Knopf, 1976).

9. Marilyn French, *The Women's Room* (New York: Simon & Schuster, 1977).

10. Thomas Pynchon, *The Crying of Lot 49* (Philadelphia: Lippincott, 1966).

11. Anzia Yezierska, *Hungry Hearts* (Boston: Houghton Mifflin, 1920).

12. Mary Antin, *The Promised Land* (Boston: Houghton Mifflin, 1912).

13. Betty Smith, *A Tree Grows in Brooklyn* (New York: Harper, 1943), 18-21.

14. Dorothy Bryant, *Ella Price's Journal* (New York: New American Library, 1972) 35.

15. Paule Marshall, *Brown Girl, Brownstones* (Madison, N.J.: Chatham Bookseller, 1959), 240.

16. Anzia Yezierska, *Bread Givers* (New York: Doubleday, Page, 1925), 208.

17. New York: Pyramid, 1971, 173. In this novel, mothers repeatedly urge their children, sons and daughters, to go to school.

18. Maxine Hong Kingston, *The Woman Warrior: Memoirs of a Girlhood Among Ghosts* (New York: Knopf, 1976), 201.

In Sylvia Plath's *The Bell Jar* (New York: Harper and Row, 1971), Esther Greenwood also earns A's in school, but her desire for education is factitious: "All my life I'd *told* myself studying and reading and writing and working like mad was what I wanted to do, and it actually *seemed* to be true" (34). When Esther feels herself "starving," it is not for books but for caviar and crabmeat, contaminated foods that poison her. She imagines heaven as "kitchens . . . stretching into infinity"; in them are avocado pears stuffed with crabmeat. In her study of "the female imagination," Professor Patricia Spacks notes that Esther's "madness, her suffering, are offered as metaphors of normalcy"; but in expressing herself through metaphors rather than action, Esther remains stereotypically passive, though she may believe herself rebellious. In New York, Esther sees none of the possibilities for freedom that the city offers the hungry heroine. Rather, she chooses to see only the debasement of women into objects of fashion and sex. Like Maria in Joan Didion's *Play It as It Lays*, she found(ed)—and created—a city that confirmed her nihilistic views of life. See the following footnote.

19. See *Hungry Hearts* (note 11). The multiple meanings of *found*— as an act of discovery, response, and creation (one founds a country)— apply to Shenah's quest for someone to understand the "vague, blind hunger for release that consumed" her. When her teacher understands, Shenah discovers America and also her own responsibility for creating, or founding, the land of freedom she seeks.

20. Willa Cather, *My Ántonia* (Boston: Houghton Mifflin, 1918, 1946). Note that Ántonia's father begs Jim Burden to teach Ántonia to read: "Te–e–ach, te–e–ach my Án–tonia" (p. 27), but Ántonia has no time for study.

21. For a discussion of the "benign" effects of urban disorder, particulrly the freedom it allows, see Richard Sennett, *The Uses of Disorder: Personal Identity and City Life* (New York: Knopf, 1970).

22. Jade Snow Wong, *Fifth Chinese Daughter* (New York: Harper, 1950).

23. Bruno Bettelheim, *The Uses of Enchantment: The Meaning and Importance of Fairy Tales* (New York: Knopf, 1976).

24. Edith Wharton, *A Backward Glance* (New York: Appleton-Century, 1934). See Chapter III *passim*. The phrase "the kingdom of my father's library" appears on 42.

25. Edmund Wilson, "Justice to Edith Wharton," *New Republic* (June 29, 1938) 95, 209-13.

26. Cynthia Griffin Wolff, *A Feast of Words* (New York: Oxford Univ. Press, 1977). Chapter 1, "A Portrait of the Artist as a Young Woman," describes Wharton's genesis as a writer in psychoanalytic terms. Ultimately, Wharton's art compensates for an "irradicable" " 'hunger for love' " that traces back to traumatic infantile emotions, "a sense of deprivation" felt as "coldness and hunger."

27. James Woodress, *Willa Cather: Her Life and Art* (New York: Western, 1970). See pp. 40-41 for a discussion of Cather's "huge, eclectic consumption of literary material."

Gertrude Stein read so widely and eclectically that like Eugene Gant she feared she would exhaust the library: "When she was young she had read so much, read from the Elizabethans to the moderns, that she was terribly uneasy lest some day she would be without anything to read. For years this fear haunted her but in one way or another although she always reads and reads she seems always to find more to read," *The Autobiography of Alice B. Toklas* (New York: Harcourt, Brace, 1933), 68.

In an interview in *Paris Review* (Winter-Spring 1963) 29: 87–114, Katherine Anne Porter described her early reading of Shakespeare, Dante, Homer, Ronsard, "the old French poets in translation," Montaigne, Voltaire, Jane Austen, Turgenev, Brontë, Henry James, Hardy, Dickens, Thackeray—all this (at least) by the time she was sixteen.

George Eliot and Virginia Woolf were famously "omnivorous"

readers. See Gordon Haight, *George Eliot: A Biography* (New York: Oxford Univ. Press, 1968), 23 and Chapter I, *passim;* and Virginia Woolf's voluminous reading notebooks. In *Three Guineas* (New York: Harcourt Brace, 1938), Woolf described woman's "desire for education" as "innate," that is, natural and inevitable, like hunger (36).

28. For a view of Goethe's Faust as a hero on "a quest for self-realization," the essential quest, however diminished, of the hungry heroine, see Hermann Wiegand, "Goethe's *Faust:* An Introduction" in *Faust: Backgrounds and Sources* (New York: Norton, 1976), tr. by Walter Arndt, ed. by Cyrus Hamplin, 446-72. Marlowe's Faust has been considered the incarnation of desire, but in a brilliant essay, Edgar A. Snow shows both desire and the self as problematic. Faustus doubts whether he has a self that exists prior to and wills desire, and whether he can ever create a self that would fulfill desire. The essay raises complex questions about consciousness, language, and being which help us understand, even if only by contrast, the dimensions of Faust's "sister." See "Doctor Faustus and the Ends of Desire" in *Two Renaissance Mythmakers: Christopher Marlowe and Ben Jonson* (Baltimore: Johns Hopkins Univ. Press, 1977), 70-110.

29. I want to suggest that we re-view our familiar books to discover in them tentative explorations of the possibility for female autonomy. Consider, for example, Jo in Louisa May Alcott's *Little Women* (1868). Jo "devoured" the books of Aunt March's library and browsed "voraciously" through Mr. Laurence's library; she insisted upon her individuality and dreamt of doing something "splendid" with her life; she leaves home, exercises her talent, achieves success—but somehow comes to capitulate to common wisdom: a woman does something "splendid" when she marries (preferably in poverty), bears children, and runs a school for boys.

We might also look again at Helen Bober in Bernard Malamud's *The Assistant* (New York: Farrar, Strauss, and Geroux, 1957). Helen longs for education, a college degree, a new life for herself, but gradually she projects her dreams upon the lover she meets night after night in the public library. She *feeds* him the books that have nourished her imagination, gradually losing her identity as a hungry heroine and falling into the convoluted reasoning of Helen Gant that allows her to appease her hunger by feeding a man.

SUSAN MERRILL SQUIER

Literature and the City:
A Checklist of Relevant Secondary Works

Works particularly useful:

Anderson, Stanford, ed. *On Streets.* Cambridge, Mass: MIT Press, 1978.

Beker, Miroslav. "London as a Principle of Structure in *Mrs. Dalloway. Modern Fiction Studies* 18 (Autumn 1972), 3, pp. 375-85.

Benjamin, Walter. "On Some Motifs in Baudelaire." *Illuminations,* ed. Hannah Arendt. New York: Schocken, 1969, 154-200.

Berg, Barbara. *The Remembered Gate: Origins of American Feminism, The Woman & The City 1800-1960.* New York: Oxford Univ. Press, 1978.

Berman, Marshall. *All That Is Solid Melts into Air.* New York: Simon & Schuster, 1982.

Bradbury, Malcolm. "The Cities of Modernism." *Modernism: 1890-1930,* eds. Malcolm Bradbury and James McFarlane. Harmondsworth, England: Penguin, 1976, 96-104.

———. "London 1890-1920." *Modernism: 1890-1930,* ed. Malcolm Bradbury and James McFarlane. Harmondsworth, England: Penguin, 1976, 172-90.

Bradbury, Malcolm, and James McFarlane, eds. *Modernism: 1890-1930.* Harmondsworth, England: Penguin, 1976.

Brewster, Dorothy. *Virginia Woolf's London.* New York: New York Univ. Press, 1960.

Byrd, Max. *London Transformed: Images of the City in the Eighteenth Century.* New Haven: Yale Univ. Press, 1978.

Chevalier, Louis. *Laboring Classes and Dangerous Classes in Paris during the First Half of the Nineteenth Century,* trans. Frank Jellinek. New York: Fertig, 1973.

Czarnowski, Thomas V. "The Street as a Communications Artifact." *On Streets,* ed. Stanford Anderson. Cambridge, Mass: MIT Press, 1978, 207-12.

Davidoff, Leonore. "Class and Gender in Victorian England: The Diaries of Arthur J. Munby and Hannah Cullwick." *Feminist Studies* 5 (Spring 1979), 1, pp. 87-141.

Dyos, H. J., and Michael Wolff, eds., *The Victorian City: Images and Realities*, 2 vols. London: Routledge & Kegan Paul, 1973.

Fanger, Donald. *Dostoevsky and Romantic Realism: A Study of Dostoevsky in Relation to Balzac, Dickens, and Gogol.* Cambridge, Mass.: Harvard Univ. Press, 1965.

Gelfant, Blanche Housman. *The American City Novel.* Norman: Univ. of Oklahoma Press, 1954.

Handlin, Oscar, and John Burchard, eds., *The Historian and the City.* Cambridge, Mass.: Harvard Univ. Press, 1963.

Hayden, Dolores. "Challenging the American Domestic Ideal." *Women in American Architure,* ed. S. Torre. New York: Whitney Library of Design, 1977, 22-39.

————. *A "Grand Domestic Revolution": Feminism, Socialism, and the American Home, 1870-1930.* Cambridge, Mass.: MIT Press, 1980.

Howe, Irving. "The City in Literature." *Commentary* 51 (May 1971), 60-68.

Jacobs, Jane. *The Death and Life of Great American Cities.* New York: Random House, 1961.

Levitas, Gloria. "Anthropology and Sociology of Streets." *On Streets,* ed. Stanford Anderson. Cambridge, Mass.: MIT Press, 1978, 225-40.

Levy, Diane Wolfe. "City Signs: Toward a Definition of Urban Literature." *Modern Fiction Studies,* 24 (Spring 1978), no. 1, pp. 65-74.

Lynch, Kevin. *The Image of the City.* Cambridge, Mass.: MIT Press, 1960.

Marcus, Jane. "Thinking Back through Our Mothers." *New Feminist Essays on Virginia Woolf,* ed. Jane Marcus. London: Macmillan, 1981, 1-30.

Mumford, Lewis. *The City in History.* New York: Harcourt, Brace, and World, 1961.

Potter, David M. "American Woman and the American Character." *Stetson University Bulletin* 62 (Jan. 1962); rpt. in *History and American Society: Essays of David M. Potter,* ed. Don E. Fehrenbacher. New York: Oxford Univ. Press, 1973, 278-303.

Raleigh, John H. "The Novel and the City: England and America in the Nineteenth Century." *Victorian Studies* 11 (1968), 291-328.

Rosaldo, Michelle Zimbalist. "Women, Culture, and Society: A Theoretical Overview." *Women, Culture, and Society,* ed. Michelle Zimbalist Rosaldo and Louise Lamphere. Stanford: Stanford Univ. Press, 1974, 17-43.

Schorske, Carl E. "The Idea of the City in European Thought: Voltaire to Spengler." *The Historian and the City,* ed. Oscar Handlin and John Burchard. Cambridge, Mass.: MIT Press, 1963, 95-114.

Sennett, Richard, ed., *Classic Essays on the Culture of Cities.* Englewood Cliffs, N.J.: Prentice-Hall, 1969.

————. *The Fall of Public Man.* New York: Knopf, 1974.

————. *The Uses of Disorder: Personal Identity and City Life.* New York: Knopf, 1970.

Simmel, Georg. "The Metropolis and Mental Life." *Classic Essays on the*

Susan Merrill Squier

Culture of Cities, ed. Richard Sennett. Englewood Cliffs, N.J.:
Prentice-Hall, 1969, 47-60.
Singleton, Mary Anne. *The City and the Veld*. Lewisburg, Pa.: Bucknell
Univ. Press, 1977.
Sizemore, Christine. " 'The Small Cardboard Box': A Symbol of the City
and of Winnie Verloc in Conrad's *The Secret Agent*." *Modern Fiction
Studies* 24 (Spring 1978), no. 1, pp. 23-39.
Spears, Monroe K. *Dionysus and the City: Modernism in Twentieth Cen-
tury Poetry*. New York: Oxford Univ. Press, 1970.
Squier, Susan Merrill, "The Politics of City Space in *The Years:* Street
Love, Pillar Boxes and Bridges." *New Feminist Essays on Virginia
Woolf*, ed. Jane Marcus. London: Macmillan, 1981, 216-37.
———. " 'A Track of Our Own': Typescript Drafts of *The Years*." *Moder-
nist Studies: Literature and Culture 1920-1940* 4 (complete), 218-31.
Stange, G. Robert. "The Victorian City and the Frightened Poets." *Victo-
rian Studies 11*, Supplement (Summer 1968), 627-40.
Tillich, Paul J. "The Metropolis in Modern Times: Spiritual Aspects."
The Metropolis in Modern Life, ed. Robert Moore Fisher. New York:
Doubleday, 1955, 346-48.
Vidler, Anthony. "Scenes of the Street: Transformations in Ideal and
Reality, 1750-1871." *On Streets*, ed. Stanford Anderson. Cambridge,
Mass.: MIT Press, 1978.
Weimer, David Rhoades. *The City as Metaphor*. New York: Random
House, 1966.
Welsh, Alexander. *The City of Dickens*. Oxford: Clarendon Press, 1971.
Williams, Raymond. *The Country and the City*. New York: Oxford Univ.
Press, 1973.

Additional relevant works:

Abrams, Charles. *The City Is the Frontier*. New York: Harper and Row,
1965.
Agulhon, Maurice. *Une Ville ouvrière au temps du socialisme utopique:
Toulon de 1815 a 1851*. Paris: Mouton, 1971.
Alexander, Sally. "Women's Work in Nineteenth-Century London: A
Study of the Years 1820-1850." *The Rights and Wrongs of Women*.
Harmondsworth: Penguin, 1977, 59-111.
Anderson, David D. "Chicago as Metaphor." *Great Lakes Review* 1
(Summer 1974), 3-15.
Bahr, E. "Kafka and the Prague Spring." *Mosaic* 3 (1970), no. 4, 15-29.
Baird, James R. "The Infernal City." *Ishmael: The Art of Melville in the
Contexts of International Primitivism*. New York: Harper Torchbooks,
1960.
Baker, Houston A., Jr. "The Environment as Enemy in a Black Autobiog-
raphy: *Manchild in the Promised Land*," *Phylon* 32 (1971), 53-59.
Barth, Gunther. *City People: The Rise of Modern City Culture in
Nineteenth Century America*. New York: Oxford Univ. Press, 1980.
Baver, Johann. *Kafka and Prague*, trans. P. S. Falla. New York: Praeger,
1971.

Blodgett, Harriett. "City of Other Worlds: The London Novels of Colin MacInnes." *Critique* 18 (1976), no. 1, 105-18.
Bremer, Sidney H. "Lost Continuities: Alternative Urban Visions in Chicago Novels, 1890-1915." *Soundings 64* (Spring 1981) 29-51.
Cannon, Jo Ann. "The Image of the City in the Novels of Italo Calvino." *Modern Fiction Studies* 24 (Spring 1978), 83-90.
Cobb, Richard. *Paris and Its Provinces 1792-1802.* London: Oxford Univ. Press, 1975.
Cohen, Sarah Blacker. "Saul Bellow's Chicago." *Modern Fiction Studies* 24 (Spring 1978), 139-46.
Coleman, B. I., ed. *The Idea of the City in Nineteenth-Century Britain.* London: Routledge & Kegan Paul, 1973.
Cornell, Kenneth. "Zola's City." *Yale French Studies* 32 (1964), 106-11.
Cota-Cardenas, Margarita. "The Chicana in the City as Seen in Her Literature." *Frontiers* 6 (Spring-Summer 1981), no. 1-2, pp. 13-18.
Daumard, Adeline. *Les Bourgeois de Paris au XIXe Siècle.* Paris: Flammarion, 1970.
Davidoff, Leonore. *The Best Circles: Society, Etiquette, and the Season.* London: Croom Helm, 1973.
Dupee, Frederick W. "Henry James and the Great Grey Babylon." *Partisan Review* 18 (1951), 183-90.
Duncan, Hugh Dalziel. *The Rise of Chicago as a Literary Center from 1885 to 1920.* Totowa, N.J.: Bedminster, 1964.
Ellul, Jacques. *The Meaning of the City,* trans. Dennis Pardee. Grand Rapids, Mich.: Eerdmans, 1970.
Ewen, Elizabeth. "City Lights: Immigrant Women and the Rise of the Movies." *Signs: Journal of Women in Culture and Society* 5 (Spring 1980), no. 3, pp. 545-66.
Festa-McCormick, Diana. *The City as a Catalyst.* Cranbury, N.J.: Associated Univ. Press, 1979.
Finel-Honigman, Irene. "Oran: Protagonist, Myth, and Allegory." *Modern Fiction Studies* 24 (Spring 1978), 75-81.
Fleishman, Avrom. "The Symbolic World of *The Secret Agent*." *ELH* 32 (1964), 196-219.
Fries, Marilyn S. "The City as Metaphor for the Human Condition: Alfred Döblin's *Berlin Alexanderplatz (1929)*." *Modern Fiction Studies* 24 (Spring 1978), 41-64.
Gamarnikow, Eva. "Introduction to the Special Issue on Women and the City." *International Journal of Urban and Regional Research* 2 (Oct. 1978), no. 3, pp. 390-403.
Gillis, John R. "Servants, Sexual Relations, and the Risks of Illegitimacy in London, 1801-1900." *Feminist Studies* 5 (Spring 1979), no. 1, pp. 142-73.
Grace, Sherrill E. *Violent Duality: A Study of Margaret Atwood.* Montreal: Vehicule Press, 1980.
Grinestier, Paul. *The Poet and the Machine,* trans. Martin B. Friedman. Chapel Hill: Univ. of North Carolina Press, 1961.
Gullason, Thomas A. "The Prophetic City in Stephen Crane's 1893 *Maggie*." *Modern Fiction Studies* 24 (Spring 1978), 129-37.

Gundin, James. "Megalotopia and the WASP Backlash: The Fiction of Mailer and Updike." *Centennial Review* 15 (1971), 38-52.

Gurko, Leo. "Edward Lewis Wallant as Urban Novelist." *Twentieth Century Literature* 20 (1974), no. 4, pp. 252-61.

————. "The Secret Agent: Conrad's Vision of Megalopolis." *Modern Fiction Studies* 4 (Winter 1958-59), 307-18.

Guzlowski, John, and Yvonne Shikany Eddy. "Studies of the Modern Novel and the City: A Selected Checklist." *Modern Fiction Studies* 24 (Spring 1978), no. 1, pp. 147-53.

Hayden, Dolores. "Catharine Beecher and the Politics of Housework." *Women in American Architecture*, ed. S. Torre. New York: Whitney Library of Design, 1977, 40-49.

————. "Melusina Fay Peirce and Cooperative Housekeeping." *International Journal of Urban and Regional Research* 2 (1978), 404-20.

————. *Seven American Utopias: The Architecture of Communitarian Socialism 1790-1975*. Cambridge, Mass.: MIT Press, 1976.

————. "Two Utopian Feminists and Their Campaigns for Kitchenless Houses." *Signs: Journal of Women in Culture and Society* 4 (Winter 1979), no. 2, pp. 274-90.

————. "What Would a Non-Sexist City Be Like? Speculations on Housing, Urban Design, and Human Work." *Signs: Journal of Women in Culture and Society. Special Issue, Women and the American City*, vol. 5 (Spring 1980), no. 3, S170-S187.

Howells, William D. "Certain of the Chicago School of Fiction." *North American Review* (1903), 176.

Hutchins, Patricia. *James Joyce's Dublin*. London: Grey Walls Press, 1950.

Jacobs, Jane. "Downtown Is for People." *The Exploding Metropolis*. Editors of *Fortune*. Garden City, N.Y.: Doubleday Anchor Books, 1958.

Jaye, Michael C., and Ann Chalmers Watts. *Literature and the Urban Experience: Essays on the City and Literature*. New Brunswick, N.J.: Rutgers Univ. Press, 1981.

Johnson, James Weldon. "Harlem: The Culture Capital." *The New Negro*, ed. Alain Locke. New York: Atheneum, 1970.

Jung, Carl G. *Symbols of Transformation*. Princeton, N.J.: Princeton Univ. Press, 1956.

Landa, Louis A. "London Observed: The Progress of a Simile." *PQ* 54 (Winter 1975), 275-88.

Lewald, A. Ernest. "An Introduction to the Literature on Buenos Aires and Its Inhabitants." *Modern Language Journal* 45 (1961), 161-64.

Lindsay, Jack. *The Monster City: Defoe's London 1688-1730*. New York: St. Martin's Press, 1978.

Lorenz, Paul. *Sapho 1900: Renée Vivien*. Paris: Julliard, 1977.

Marcus, Jane. "The Divine Rage to Be Didactic," Introduction, Elizabeth Robins, *The Convert* (1907). London: Women's Press, 1980.

Marx, Leo. "The Machine in the Garden." *New England Quarterly* 29 (1956), 27-42.

————. *The Machine in the Garden: Technology and the Pastoral Ideal in America*. New York: Oxford Univ. Press, 1964.

————. "Pastoral Ideals and City Troubles." *Journal of General Education* 20 (1969), 251-71.

McLean, Robert C. "*The Bostonians:* New England Pastoral." *Papers on Language and Literature* 7 (Fall 1971), 374-81.

Morgan, Anna. *My Chicago.* Chicago: Seymour, 1918.

Morris, R. A. "Classical Vision and the American City: Henry James's *The Bostonians.*" *New England Quarterly* 46 (1973), 543-57.

Mumford, Lewis. "Utopia: The City and the Machine." *Daedalus* 94 (1969), 271-92.

Murray, Jack. "Proust's Beloved Enemy." *Yale French Studies* 32 (1964), 112-17.

Murry, J. Middleton. *Coming to London,* ed. John Lehmann. London: Phoenix House, 1957.

Nichols, Prescott S. "Paris as Subjectivity in Sartre's *Roads to Freedom.*"*Modern Fiction Studies* 24 (Spring 1978), 3-21.

Parent-Duchâtelet, A.J.B. *De la prostitution dans la ville de Paris.* 2d ed., 2 vols. Paris: Bailliére, 1837.

Parssinen, T. H. "Bellamy, Morris, and the Image of the Industrial City in Victorian Social Criticism." *Midwest Quarterly* 14 (1973), 257-66.

Pearl, Cyril, *Dublin in Bloomtime: The City James Joyce Knew.* New York: Viking, 1969.

Pike, Burton. *The Image of the City in Modern Literature.* Princeton, N.J.: Princeton Univ. Press, 1982.

Podhoretz, Norman, "Gibbsville and New Leeds: The America of John O'Hara and Mary McCarthy." *Commentary* 21 (1956), 269-73.

Prescott, Joseph. "Local Allusions in Joyce's *Ulysses. PMLA* 68 (1953), 1223-28.

Reck, Rima Drell. "Mauriac's Inferno." *Yale French Studies* 32 (1964), 118-23.

Rose, Alan H. "Sin and the City: The Uses of Disorder in the Urban Novel." *Centennial Review* 16 (1972), 203-20.

Rosenberg, Carroll Smith. *Religion and the Rise of the American City: The New York City Mission Movement 1812-1870.* Ithaca, N.Y.: Cornell Univ. Press, 1971.

Rubenstein, Roberta. *The Novelistic Vision of Doris Lessing: Breaking the Forms of Consciousness.* Urbana: Univ. of Illinois Press, 1979.

Saegert, Susan. "Masculine Cities and Feminine Suburbs: Polarized Ideas, Contradictory Realities." *Signs: Journal of Women in Culture and Society,* vol. 5, Supplement (Spring 1980), no. 3, S96-S111.

Sherman, George W. "The Influence of London on *The Dynasts." PMLA* 63 (1948), 1017-28.

————. "The Wheel and the Beast: The Influence of London on Thomas Hardy." *Nineteenth Century Fiction* 4 (1949), 209-19.

Siegel, Adrienne. "When Cities Were Fun: The Image of the American City in Popular Books, 1840-1870." *Journal of Popular Culture* 9 (Winter 1975), 573-82.

Sprague, Claire. "Without Contraries Is No Progression: Lessing's *The Four-Gated City.*" *Modern Fiction Studies* 26 (Spring 1980), no. 1.

Stafford, William T., and Margaret Church, eds. *Modern Fiction Studies*

Special Issue: The Modern Novel and the City, vol. 24 (Spring 1978), no. 1.

Stimpson, Catharine R., ed. Signs: Journal of Women in Culture and Society Special Issue: Women and the American City, vol. 5 (Spring 1980), no. 3.

Szuberla, Guy A. "Dreiser at the World's Fair: The City without Limits." Modern Fiction Studies 23 (Autumn 1977), 369-79.

Taylor, William R. "Psyching Out the City: New York City and the Photographer," Essays in Honor of Oscar Handlin, ed. Richard Bushman. Boston: Little, Brown, 1979, pp. 245-89.

————. "New York et l'origine du skyline: la cité moderne comme forme et symbole." Urbi: Arts, Histoire, Ethnologie du Ville, vol. 3 (March 1980), 1-17.

Tavernier-Courbin, Jacqueline. "Towards the City: Howells' Characterization in A Modern Instance." Modern Fiction Studies 24 (Spring 1978), 111-27.

Thernstrom, Stephen, and Richard Sennett, eds. Nineteenth Century Cities: Essays in New Urban History. New Haven: Yale Univ. Press, 1969.

Tindall, William York. The Joyce Country. University Park: Pennsylvania State Univ. Press, 1960.

Titche, Leon L., Jr. "Döblin and Dos Passos: Aspects of the City Novel." Modern Fiction Studies 17 (Spring 1971), 125-35.

Trachtenberg, Alan. "Experiment in Another Country: Stephen Crane's City Sketches." Southern Review 10 (1974) no. 2, 265-85.

Trachtenberg, Alan, Peter Neill, and Peter C. Bunnell, ed. The City: The American Experience. New York: Oxford Univ. Press, 1971.

Tuan, Yi-Tu. Topophilia: A Study of Environmental Perception, Attitudes, and Values. Englewood Cliffs, N.J.: Prentice-Hall, 1974.

Tuttleton, James W. "Leisure, Wealth, and Luxury: Edith Wharton's Old New York." Midwest Quarterly 7 (1966), 337-52.

Warner, Sam B., Jr. The Private City. Philadelphia: Univ. of Pennsylvania Press, 1968.

Weber, Max. The City, ed. Don Martindale and Gertrude Neuwirth. New York: Free Press, 1958.

Wells, Walter. Tycoons and Tourists: A Regional Look at Hollywood Fiction of the 1930's. Carbondale: Southern Illinois Univ. Press, 1973.

Westbrook, Wayne W. "Louis Auchincloss' Vision of Wall Street." Critique 15 (1973), no. 2, pp. 57-66.

White, Morton, and Lucia White. The Intellectual Versus the City: From Thomas Jefferson to Frank Lloyd Wright. Cambridge, Mass.: Harvard Univ. Press, 1962.

Wirth-Nesher, Hana. "The Modern Jewish Novel and the City: Franz Kafka, Henry Roth, and Amos Oz." Modern Fiction Studies 24 (Spring 1978), no. 1, pp. 91-109.

Contributors

Sandra Dijkstra, an independent literary agent, is currently a visiting lecturer in the Department of Literature at the University of California, San Diego. She has taught in the areas of women's studies and literature and has published articles and reviews in *Feminist Studies, Women and Literature,* and the *French Review.*

Susan Rava is a lecturer in French at Washington University in St. Louis. She has published articles on Proust, Borges, and the narratee.

Elyse Blankley's essay in this volume is drawn from her doctoral dissertation entitled *"Daughters in Exile: Paris and the Expatriot Woman of Letters, 1900-1945."* She currently teaches at the University of California, Davis, and is working on a critical biography of Renée Vivien.

Nancy Paxton is currently teaching Victorian literature at Northern Arizona University and completing a book on George Eliot, Spencerian evolution, and motherhood.

Louise A. DeSalvo is an associate professor of English at Hunter College of the City University of New York. She is author of *Virginia Woolf's First Voyage: A Novel in the Making* (Totowa, N.J.: Rowman & Littlefield; London: Macmillan, 1980) and editor of *"Melymbrosia": An Early Version of "The Voyage Out."* She is presently co-editing Virginia Woolf's adolescent and young adult diaries as well as the letters of Vita Sackville-West to Virginia Woolf, which will be published in 1984 by William Morrow.

Susan Merrill Squier is an assistant professor of English at SUNY Stony Brook, where she teaches modern British literature, feminist criticism, and women's studies. She has published articles in *Twentieth Century*

Literature, Modernist Studies, Anima, and *New Feminist Essays on Virginia Woolf,* ed. Jane Marcus. (London: Macmillan, 1981). Her book, *Virginia Woolf and the Politics of City Space,* will be published in spring 1985 by the University of North Carolina Press.

Jane Marcus is an associate professor of English at the University of Texas at Austin. The recipient of a National Endowment for the Humanities Research Fellowship, 1977-1978, an ACLS fellowship, and a Newberry Library Fellowship, Marcus is the editor of *New Feminist Essays on Virginia Woolf* (London: Macmillan, 1981; rpt. Lincoln: Univ. of Nebraska Press, 1982) and of *The Young Rebecca West: 1911-1917* (New York: Viking, 1982).

Sydney Janet Kaplan is director of the Women Studies Program and associate professor of English at the University of Washington. She is the author of *Feminine Consciousness in the Modern British Novel* (1975). She is currently working on a critical study of Katherine Mansfield.

Christine W. Sizemore has taught English literature since 1978 at Spelman College, Atlanta. Before that, she taught for six years at Georgia State University, where she offered a course on "The Urban Vision." She has published numerous articles on both seventeenth-century prose and modern fiction.

Sherrill E. Grace is an associate professor of English at the University of British Columbia, where she teaches modern Canadian and American literature. She is the author of *Violent Duality: A Study of Margaret Atwood* (1980) and *The Voyage That Never Ends: Malcolm Lowry's Fiction* (1982). She has co-edited a collection of criticism on Atwood, *Margaret Atwood: Language, Text, and System* (1983), and is currently at work on a study of literary expressionism.

Sidney H. Bremer is an associate professor of Urban Studies at the University of Wisconsin-Green Bay, where she also teaches women's studies and literature. She is currently working on a book, provisionally titled *The Many Cities of American Literature,* for which she received an ACLS fellowship in 1980-1981.

Carolyn Mitchell is an assistant professor of English at the University of Santa Clara, where she teaches American, twentieth-century and Afro-American literature, and women's studies. She has published reviews and an article on the journey motif in Afro-American fiction.

Wendy Martin has taught American literature at Queens College since 1968. She is a specialist in early American literature and has published extensively on American women writers. Her articles and reviews have appeared in *Early American Literature, Eighteenth Century Studies, Studies in Romanticism, Signs, Wordsworth's Circle,* and *Ploughshares.* She has also published essays in *Woman in a Sexist Society* (Basic Books), *Shakespeare's Sisters* (Indiana University Press), and the Norton Critical Edition of *Adrienne Rich's Poetry*. Her monograph on the work of Adrienne Rich appeared in the Scribner's *American Writers Series*. She has also published *An American Sisterhood: Feminist Writings from the Colonial Times to the Present* (Harper and Row). She is founding editor of *Women's Studies: An Interdisciplinary Journal*, and her book on the lives and work of Anne Bradstreet, Emily Dickinson, and Adrienne Rich is forthcoming from the University of North Carolina Press (Chapel Hill) in 1984.

Blanche Gelfant teaches twentieth-century American literature at Dartmouth College. She has written a pioneer study of urban fiction, *The American City Novel*. Her essays have been widely published and deal with such major figures as William Faulkner, Virginia Woolf, John Dos Passos, Willa Cather, and Ernest Hemingway. She has published also on such contemporary women writers as Ann Beattie and Grace Paley. She has been the recipient of various awards, among them a National Endowment for the Humanities Fellowship and a Rockefeller Foundation Humanities Fellowship. She holds an endowed Chair at Dartmouth College as the Robert T. Maxwell Professor of Arts and Sciences.

Index

Women Writers and the City has been composed into type on the Variable Input Phototypesetter in ten point Palatino with two points of spacing between the lines by Computer Composition, Inc. The book was designed by Muriel Underwood and Frank O. Williams. Thomson-Shore, Inc., has printed the book by offset lithography on acid-free paper by S. D. Warren, and the book was bound by John H. Dekker & Sons.

THE UNIVERSITY OF TENNESSEE PRESS : KNOXVILLE